Your Child and Religion

Your Child and Religion

Johanna L. Klink

SCM PRESS LTD

Translated by R. A. Wilson from the Dutch
Kind en geloof (fourth impression, 1971),
published by Uitgeverij Ambo n.v., Bilthoven.

334 01837 4
First English edition published 1972
by SCM Press Ltd, 56 Bloomsbury Street, London
© SCM Press Ltd 1972
Printed in Great Britain by
Northumberland Press Limited, Gateshead

Contents

Your children are not your children.
They are the sons and daughters of Life's longing for itself.
They come through you, but not from you,
And though they are with you, yet they belong not to you.
You may give them your love, but not your thoughts,
For they have their own thoughts.
You may house their bodies, but not their souls,
For their souls dwell in the house of tomorrow, which you cannot
    visit, not even in your dreams.
You may strive to be like them, but seek not to make them like you.
For life goes not backwards, nor tarries with yesterday.
You are the bows from which your children as living arrows are
    sent forth.
The Archer sees the mark upon the path of the infinite, and He
    bends you with His might, so that His arrows may go swift and
    far.
Let your bending in the Archer's hand be for gladness;
For even as He loves the arrow that flies, so He loves also the bow
    that is stable.

Kahlil Gibran, The Prophet

Preface

Any book which goes through four impressions in a single year, as this book did in Holland, is clearly meeting a need of some kind. In our modern world, the best-sellers are often those books which meet the need to be entertained, but Dr Klink takes pains to point out that hers is not a work of this kind. 'The reader who is only looking for amusing stories about children who ask whether God lives on a cloud will be disappointed' (p. 2). Here, rather, is a compendium of experience from childhood and reflection upon childhood which, while not providing any easy answers – for there are none – provides the raw material which may help parents and teachers to form their own sympathetic understanding of the child's situation and to see why children ask the awkward questions that they do ask.

An indication of the somewhat unusual format of the book may be useful. The framework and the longer passages of discussion are, of course, by Dr Klink herself, but to make her points she resorts to a good deal of illustrative matter. Some consists in the remarks of parents and children, and these are quoted anonymously, with an indication of children's ages. Some of the material is readily accessible to English and American readers, and where this is the case, full source references to the original works (or English translations) are given in the text. Finally, coming as it does from a wider European setting, Dr Klink's book quotes from works in Dutch, German and French which have not been translated into English. Here, following the original Dutch edition of the present work, quotations are identified by the name of the author and the titles of the books are listed in the bibliography at the end of the book, but no detailed references are given.

1 Introduction

As I am not in a position to undertake the more difficult task, that of education itself, I shall try and carry out the lighter task, and describe it.
Jean-Jacques Rousseau

Children are born, one generation follows another, and so it goes on. Man still has faith in the future. Parents wonder: What can we give our children? Love, a home, a little bit of culture. But supposing you want to give your children not just your love, and worldly goods, but something that can give meaning to their lives, whatever may befall them. If only we could give our children faith!

It is easy to teach a child manners, even if he sometimes makes difficulties, to send him to school, to give him information about the world we live in. But to teach your children to believe is far from easy!

'We are so uncertain in our own faith. And even if we believe, can we make our faith real in our lives for our children to see? With children this is what matters so much.'

Consequently, religious education is something that most parents no longer take for granted. It now seems to have become a really pressing problem. Everything is so different from the past. There have been times when it could have been taken for granted. You took your children with you to church, you sent them to Sunday school, or they learnt at school to say the catechism, to make their confession and to receive communion. In the past it was almost a habit, something which touched daily life at every point.

But now people begin to wonder: What have we made of our own childhood experiences in this field? We cannot simply tell our children what we ourselves learned in the past – but what are we to tell them? What are we to pass on to our children and what will they make of it?

This book does not give an answer to all these questions. Its purpose is to reflect on these problems with its readers. About five hundred parents and teachers recalled their own childhood memories and described conversations with their children about God, about death, about why and what for. When several thousand remarks and questions from children were gathered together and set in order, they seemed to contain almost all the themes of Christian doctrine, from creation to the 'last things'. Some of them are put forward tentatively in this book as the beginning of a 'little theology for parents', or, if you will, a 'shorter catechism'. They are not given, however, in the form of question and answer but with more questions than answers.

Most of these remarks, as the reader will see, were taken down from children of about four or five years of age. This book is especially about the young child.

We could have given not only their age but also the denominational background of their family. It became evident, however, that the conversations parents had with their children had very much more in common than their denominational differences might have suggested. The difference between Roman Catholic and Protestant virtually disappeared.

Because all the letters came from church circles, it is only to be expected that this book should be directed particularly towards those who in one way or another are in contact with the Christian tradition. For those who have rejected this tradition, the book will still be too much along the old lines and will not go far enough. For those who have never been in contact with it, it will probably be based too much on fixed assumptions, for example that the Bible is the source from which our faith is inspired. The anecdotal nature of the book results from the quotations from letters and autobiographies. This should be a warning that it has no scholarly pretensions. The theme 'Your Child and Religion', however, is not the concern of theology alone, but also of psychology and educational theory. To make sure of treating the matter thoroughly, statements by specialists have been added to each chapter. This may also be of use to discussion groups of young parents and others concerned with the upbringing of children, so that the book may serve not only for private reading, but also as a working text.

The reader who is only looking for amusing stories about children who ask whether God lives on a cloud will be disappointed. The purpose of the book is to help you to gain a more profound understanding yourself, and in your attempt to explain these things to your own children.

A TIME OF CHANGE

Before, we had the answers; we may have had questions, but we found answers. Now that we no longer have any answers and there are only questions left, you begin to wonder: Will there ever be a time when one can get an answer – instead of more and more questions? Questions which, however, you cannot do without, which you actually want.
Michel van der Plas

I do not believe, however, that it is existentially possible to live continuously in a state of questioning. We are born for answers. As an interim period it may be possible, as the incubation period of a new certainty, but not as a permanent condition.
Godfried Bomans

Suppose we were to give our children nothing of our own faith, and their situation came to be one of complete barrenness, then we do not know whether they would come to ask the same questions which concern you as much as me.
Michel van der Plas

I cannot imagine that my daughter would never look down at the toes of her shoes and ask herself: Here I stand now, who am I and where am I going? And then I would feel guilty if I had never given her anything at all by way of an answer.
Godfried Bomans

But they keep asking me – each in their own way – about what I believe. They will not be put off with books in the bookcase. They want to hear it from me in simple words like yes and no.

It concerns what I believe about God. It is a question of whether I profess this belief, whether I have any doubts or inner reservations. I am expected to make the reasons clear, if there is anything that I believe.

I thought: You cannot leave children to fend for themselves. They are too small and too vulnerable to be cast into the chaos where I have landed. Wait till you know something that you can give them in life instead: a firm support in life, firm ground beneath their feet. There is so much that you have less of to give them than your father gave you.
Rogier van Aerde

The changes in our life do not consist of a single transition from a former age to a new one, in which you have to undergo a single change, like getting used to a new environment when you move house. The changes have become permanent, change is perpetual, you are always in the removal van. It is a life on wheels. It is an unsafe feeling, but there is more freedom.

If a person is certain in his own faith, things will be well with his children too. But this is the source of the great hesitation in religious education: we are no longer certain ourselves. You sometimes carry about the faith of years ago as an alien element, and have the feeling that one day it will have vanished. And this is disturbing, because it occupies such a central place in life.
L. Kuylman-Hoekendijk

Parents have a tendency to run away from questions which they have never answered for themselves. My children's questions have confronted me with my own immaturity and emptiness in knowledge and understanding.

If there is a strong bond with their mother, the children have a tendency to guess your thoughts and to talk about what concerns you.

But since the old secure idea of God has been so much put into the dock in recent years, I am oppressed by not really knowing exactly what it signifies, and even worse, by not knowing what explanations I have to give my children.

We find religious education difficult. The hardest thing, we find, is that you only want to pass on to your children what you are a hundred per cent in favour of yourself. But children do not understand our vague hints and want bold and concrete explanations. They ask for matter-of-fact information about God, heaven and death. How can I find the words in which to convey faith in sober and honest terms, which the children can understand? We have sometimes had the feeling that we have failed in this respect because we would rather do nothing than say something dishonest.

I was brought up in strict orthodoxy myself and have wanted to do differently with my own children. I have not succeeded. Can we parents do this without some guidance and teaching? The old-fashioned way (hell and damnation) has disappeared, but how do we set about it now? We do not know.
Parents

Anyone who sets out to bring children up gets no free stay of execution. Here and now, at every unprepared moment of his life, he has to answer the question: What is it for?
M. J. Langeveld

Some of the people who are bringing up children know that they are a different kind of person from their parents and that they can believe in a different way from their parents. They know that they must adjust themselves to their children, who belong to the present age and who are confronted with a different content and experience of faith from their own in their childhood and youth.

With other parents, being left more to themselves causes difficulties. They have little idea what to do with the freedom. Large scale improvisation does not come easily to them. This can lead to spasmodic attempts to carry on along the old lines, with a risk of short-circuiting.
M. W. Steenmeyer-van Rij

It is the particular problem of our generation of parents and teachers to know how to share with our children the depth and dimension of Christian experience in terms which do not distort it. But they themselves provide the clues if we will listen. As children they need help in 'working it out for themselves', below the conscious level, in their relationships with those they trust, so that later on they have the content of experience with which they may 'fill out the words' and the tradition they have inherited.
Ruth Robinson[1]

Every change can only begin with youth, with those who are not weighed down by prejudices and who do not think the thoughts of yesterday. The world has so changed that there is no longer any place for the thoughts of yesterday.
Max Tau

Not only Christian belief in God, but any concept of God at all can never again be taken for granted without further discussion. At the present day, the starting point and constant background of everything that is said about God is provided by a concealed or explicit atheism. Many of our contemporaries already take this for granted as readily as their forefathers took for granted their belief in God. And so far as Christians are genuinely in touch with contemporary ideas, they cannot remain unaffected. Even Christians are nowadays at a loss for words when anyone asks them about their experience of God. However full their

heart is, the words are no longer there.
Heinz Zahrnt[2]

The fact remains that for some obscure reason something has gone wrong between Man and God as in these days he is represented to Man. Hence the impression one gains from everything taking place around us is of an irresistible growth of atheism.
Teilhard de Chardin[3]

The Child

What would the world be like without children? We cannot imagine. There would certainly be less joy and less humanity. It would be a hard world, perhaps with no mercy in it.

It is remarkable that man, the most highly evolved creature on earth, begins life as the most helpless. He is much more dependent and helpless than an animal. He is born too soon. Looking at a newborn child, one can scarcely imagine that it will become a man who will one day manage a large firm. At such a moment it seems an absurd thought.

How long does it take to become a human being? Perhaps twenty years. But in nine months a child goes through an evolution which has taken millions of years, and then emerges into the civilization of the twentieth century. It is marvellous with what unbelievable speed – like lightning – a human child becomes familiar with the complicated world we live in.

A creature born of human beings does not become a human being in isolation from other humans. He does not even learn to speak without them. This is a particularly great responsibility for those through whom and amongst whom the child comes into the world. Parents share in this process of becoming human; in a manner of speaking, they live for a second time, when they see it happen and are involved in it. But in the meantime they have forgotten what it is to be a child. Adults can no longer feel and no longer think as children, and only a few vague memories have remained. They have a blind spot about it, they have grown out of it, and they no longer know what it is like.

This is not just because they can no longer recall it. An adult looks upon a child from a position of a certain superiority. An adult is a full human being; he has made it. Anyone who has not yet reached this stage does not count, and is not yet considered a fellow human being in the full sense. Children have not yet reached this stage, do not yet count and have nothing yet to contribute when it comes to the point. People can sometimes chat with each other without taking any account of the fact that there is a child in the room as well. It makes not the slightest difference to the conversation. The child is ignored.

It could be that we human beings prefer not to be reminded of the experiences of a time in our lives when we were defenceless and dependent. Or perhaps the resistance goes even deeper? A child makes an appeal to our bad conscience and to our attitude to God.

Here is someone just starting to be a human being, primitive, still capable of trust without suspicion, still without any real guilt and not embittered by the experience of life; a mirror to our own humanity.

Man was born into the world as a child. And as human beings we are never left to ourselves; the child comes between us.

Ellen Key called the twentieth century the century of the child. That was in 1906. The century had only just begun. Was she not right? How much is done for children at the present day! In the toyshop we find the adult world reproduced in miniature, even including the moon rockets. In pleasant modern infant schools, full of life and colour, children can build, paste and paint. And even in churches there are little chairs and sticky paper, cut-out and colouring materials for them to express themselves.

How children must have been neglected in previous centuries, when they were abandoned or sold to chimney sweeps, wandered half-naked about the streets, were beaten black and blue in dark, cold rooms by brutal schoolmasters, or, no more than a century ago, used in factories and mines as labourers.

Times have certainly changed!

It is even said that in the past the child really did not exist, or hardly existed at all; he was merely a smaller version of the adult. And in the past people lived differently from us. They did not live in the small protected family of father, mother and children, but in larger communities with numerous relations and many servants. In this world children jogged along as best they could and soon grew wise.

In the course of the centuries the child has slowly changed. He was 'discovered' in the time of Rousseau and since then, in the age of education which followed, has received a place of his own over and against adults, above all as the object of instruction and exhortation. Since then the child has grown further and further away from the adult; he has been given his own world, and special places and books are set aside for him.

Was the child really discovered in the age of the Enlightenment? We may say that in part he was. However, he was also excluded from the world of adults in a separate place of his own. This may be connected with the rise of well-defined cultural ideals of development, refinement, respectability and morality. There, in his place apart, the child became a kind of projection screen, in so far as he came to stand over against adults. The latter could now project on to the child their nostalgia for their own innocence and escape their own bad consciences by exaggerated admonitions. We have only to read the books written for children in previous centuries! In this way people could work off their own anxiety and guilt feelings on their children. And many adults were able to maintain their vast superiority only by belittling their children.

It is perhaps inaccurate to describe this only in the past tense.

The picture would, however, be too dark, if we did not also recognize that a great deal more respect was also paid to children in these centuries of education. More and more was done about education, schools were changed from places of custody and prisons into institutions which introduced the child to our culture. Children's books, children's masses and Sunday schools came into being.

It may be that in the present age this development is undergoing a change of direction. For we are beginning to notice that we have set children too much apart, and that the gap between them and the world of adults is growing constantly greater. The period of a person's life before this gap is bridged is growing constantly longer. The revolt of youth in recent years is in violent reaction against superior adults who are always laying the law down to children and belittling them. It is really a protest against the eighteenth and nineteenth centuries. The time has come when we must once again begin to look at children with other eyes as full human beings, who fulfil a unique function in the world of men.

In the church, too, the child must emerge from the separate children's corner and begin to take a full place in the believing community. Too much preaching has completely ignored children. They have not had any say in the matter.

Should children at the present day be allowed more 'participation'? Then, perhaps, it would once again be 'the century of the child', or better still, of the man of the future.

THE HISTORY OF THE CHILD

In antiquity a father had the right to sell or kill a child. A child was as completely without rights as an animal or a piece of furniture.

In the Middle Ages a child already had to work when he was four years old. A farmer would sooner get a veterinary surgeon to his sick cow than a doctor to his sick child.

At the beginning of the nineteenth century, in many European countries, small children of four to six were sold to chimney sweeps, who lowered the poor creatures down hot chimneys and drove them up again with goads or burning straw.
Ruth Dirx

Adults in the Middle Ages behaved more like children. They possessed a diminished sense of responsibility, living from hand to mouth, without taking much account of the past and the future.

The child does not appear on the scene until the fifteenth century, and the youth becomes an important figure in the second half of the eighteenth century.

Between the sixteenth and eighteenth centuries the change began; adults grew more adult and young people remained young longer.

Before the seventeenth century there was a society with no conflict between generations, in which the problem of respect for the comparatively few elders was not posed, a society in which a young person gradually came into his place. There is virtually no trace of the crises of puberty that are typical of the nineteenth and twentieth centuries. Young and old wore the same clothes, took part in the same games, sang the same songs, and worked at the same callings. The art of the fifteenth century still has no eye for the babyish features of small children. In poetry there is no respect shown for the child, unless to tell of what reappears in the grown man. There is no difference in terminology for adults and for children. The origin of the great importance placed on children, which is typical of the West, must be sought in part in the endeavours towards moral education made by church groups.

The more educational theory was directed towards the child, the more it took account of what was supposed to be the nature of the child, ... the more infantile it made the children and youths, and the greater the distance became from the adult world.
J. W. van Ussel

In the marriage books and household books of the sixteenth to
the eighteenth centuries, the duties of parents are largely confined
to discipline. The child's own will is of diabolical origin and has
to be broken.
Ruth Dirx

I had no free will in the slightest degree. I could not do what my
father had not commanded, though he gave me enough work to
do. I was only allowed to speak when he asked me something, and
I had to ask my father's permission for everything and rarely
received it.
Recollections of a worker, 1850

Columbus only discovered America, I discovered the child.
Victor Hugo

Rousseau was the first person who saw the child and therefore
stopped treating him as an adult. All manifestations of a right
approach to children are implicit in this discovery of Rousseau.
The publication of real children's books, the manufacture of
proper children's clothes, the building of playgrounds, and not
least the laying down of precise educational principles – all these
modern signs of the understanding of the child go back to him.

In the eighteenth century the process of separation between the
adult and the child began. The psychological process of puberty
came into being in that age.

Without either knowing or desiring it, the adult, by the particular form of his adulthood, keeps the child as long as possible
in a childlike or youthful condition, that is, in a condition of
immaturity.

Adults are 'mysterious' in the way they present themselves to
the child. The adult world is a different world, and the child
realizes this if parents approach him.
J. H. van den Berg

Civilization actually continues this original helplessness. The
more a person has to learn, the longer he remains helpless: much
longer in modern society than in a primitive community.
Hans M. M. Fortmann

SEPARATION

Anyone who wishes to see how the child's world is set apart, and
wants to see with his own eyes how the child is cut off from our

world and placed – lovingly – in a place of his own should go and look at the playgrounds in a city. They are marked off by hedges and fences, islands in the middle of the adult world, islands of relative safety in a deadly adulthood, islands of necessary exile.
J. H. van den Berg

The child is a cultural phenomenon of our own age, and kindergartens and children's nurseries an ultra-modern cultural reserve. There is no ordinary place for children in our society.
J. van Haaren

CAN THE CHILD BE HEARD?

With baptism a child is theoretically raised to the level of a person, but in people's general outlook a low opinion of everything that belongs to the existence of the child is too deeply rooted.
Ruth Dirx

Children should be seen and not heard.
Proverb

Educational theory represents one essential characteristic of humanity which adults do not like to be reminded of: weakness and helplessness which demand one's loyalty; to which one is bound because one has called it into life, or which at least has had no opportunity to ask for its existence. The child disturbs the adult and is of no moment. The child has only to be good and quiet and not be heard or seen; he is the woman's concern, and only through the wife, and only incidentally, is he worthy of the husband's attention.
M. J. Langeveld

In the world of adults he is only a child. He must wait until he is grown up to do anything which is worth while. In a certain sense he is a stranger, who is tolerated on condition that he keeps quiet.
Paul Osterrieth

Up to the present day the child has never been valued as a personality, as a member of society; he is only for the future, he is still becoming, and does not count until he has 'grown up'.
Maria Montessori

It seems that one is not a full human being until one has stopped being a child. People like to understand children by the standards of adults. The child is therefore reduced to a negative figure, one who has not yet grown up.
M. J. Langeveld

The child is not simply a reduced adult, a miniature adult. We must not look too soon in the child for the person he will later become.
René Voeltzel

THE UNIQUE PERIOD OF LIFE

Infancy is real life, not a preparation for life. It is ... actual experience in life. This makes life a real and growing thing, unfolding from the beginning.
Frances Wickes[1]

Childhood is in reality the door, which is open and leads to the most unexpected and marvellous manifestations of human nature, of which we perhaps suspect neither the riches nor the possibilities.
Paul Osterrieth

This emergence of the unique, which is more than waking or birth, this gift of being able to begin again, again and anew.
Martin Buber

If anyone were to ask me, When were you most yourself? Which of the different stages of life meant most to you? Which would you choose?, I should reply: the earliest years of childhood.
Carl Spitteler

Childhood is unique, and not just because of its value to a person as an adult.

The period of childhood is a very definite period in the history of a person's life, the only time when particular things can happen. It is a field where beautiful flowers and ripe fruit can grow, which can only grow on this field. Childhood is in contact with the divine mystery. We can overlook its original and distinctive nature if we regard it as only a sort of preparation. The morning of life is something more than the forenoon that precedes the great midday. The charming games of the earliest years of life have a significance which is more than that of simply a prelude

to the serious business of existence.
Karl Rahner

THE BELIEVER AS A CHILD

One can say that a person is a believer when in his deepest being
he becomes a child.

For a Christian there is no question of his having to give up
being a child; not only does he remain a child, but all his life is
the continuation of childhood, the constantly increasing fulfilment of it.
Karl Rahner

Christianity has always known with certainty how important it is
that man should begin as a child. A religion that every year gathers
us about the crib has to be aware of this.

The love of the heart has always known that because the
child is man's weak spot, he shall guide the world.
M. J. Langeveld

3   When Faith Begins

Is a young child yet capable of believing in God? There is no unanimous answer to this question.

'Ah,' people say, 'a child can be so innocently devout, so receptive to religious ceremonies, and little children ask endless questions about God. How dare people claim that a little child is not yet in a state to believe! The innocent trust of children actually puts us to shame.'

But others say: 'A child is so suggestible, so easily repeats what the grown-ups say, and is easy to influence and indoctrinate. After all, he still does not have any attitude to God which is his own and comes from himself. He still believes completely in his own parents, and therefore cannot make any real contact with the God of mankind who is someone other than his father and mother.'

In Christian tradition, faith is a communication with God, a trust in him who is above his creation, and an answer to what he has revealed to men.

Faith never comes about on its own. It must be aroused. Men are obviously the mediators in this process. You cannot give faith to another. But something can go out from us which arouses in someone else the possibility of believing, although some people seem to be more receptive to it than others.

When can faith begin in a human life? At about eight years old, when the child begins to break away from the very close links it has always had to its parents? At twelve years old, when childhood is left behind? Or not until the beginning of adulthood?

When does love begin in a human life? Can that be specified? Love, too, must be aroused, and grows unnoticed in the first contact between parents and child. You cannot say: 'At that time the child began to love us.' For from the very moment of birth the human link exists which slowly begins to dawn in the child. You cannot date the moment when the child first really responded to your love. For really it begins at the beginning.

In the same way, faith and everything that contributes to it can only begin at the beginning.

Naturally, the faith of an adult is different from that of a child. The same is true of love. The seed is not yet the plant, the stalk is not yet the flower, the flower is not yet the fruit; and yet the plant begins with the seed that falls on to the ground.

How unreal it sounds, then, when parents go to buy religious books for their children, who have reached a certain age, because they 'want to do something about it'. They have already 'got something started' long ago, without knowing it, because it begins at the beginning.

Since Sigmund Freud we have become familiar with the idea that the first years of life are of almost overwhelming importance for the whole of the rest of one's life. In these years the basic pattern of the personality is formed. The first eighteen months have even been called 'the foundation of the whole architecture of the personality', and above all of the emotions, and the first seven years have been recognized as the most important period in a person's life. Should not the most important period in life, during which the first experiences take place which are to influence our further development, also be the most important for the coming into being of faith? It is in any case the period of greatest sensitivity, in which a child is still helpless and receptive. Nor is it true that a little one first of all receives somewhat superficial impressions and later comes to appreciate the depth of life. It may even be that the person whose life is just beginning goes through depths of which we ourselves have lost all recollection.

It already begins at birth. The child comes out of the water into the air, out of the darkness into the light, and is released from total protection and begins to exist in an unknown separate space. This is his very first experience of life. A human being begins life in this world crying. And from that moment he continues to look for security, warmth and safety, probably for his whole life. One of the basic motives of human religion!

For adults, their children's first years seem an idyll, but for the person at the beginning of life it is perhaps anything but that. A little child has no more than a very tiny area in which it can exist: the safety and security which his parents give him. All around him is the great unknown. He cannot yet see anything as a whole and is at the mercy of the experiences of the moment, and can therefore experience fears against which adults have secured themselves. He experiences moments of hopeless desolation when all that sustains him threatens to disappear, but also spontaneous abandonment to the comforting protection of human beings.

So much happens through various crises which follow quickly upon one another; more happens than in many later years. There is the encounter with a second person, the father, with strangers, with another reality apart from one's own, which can even be threatening and dangerous. There is the crisis of independence in the second year of life, the discovery of the other sex, the emotional struggle round about the third year of life, when the basic pattern of human relationships is formed. In these first years of life the discovery takes place of the self and others, of man and woman, of friend and enemy, of the world with its good and evil, delight and dangers, and even of the riddle of existence: life and death.

There is perhaps no period of life which is so concerned with faith! The process of becoming a human being is deeply inter-woven with the coming into being of faith. It is these earliest and most basic experiences of life which form the emotional basis upon which faith can grow. In any case, they form the prelude to the history of a person's faith, and perhaps the theme of the fugue which is to be recapitulated throughout all the rest of his life.

For faith, too, consists of a birth, a breaking away from the bonds with which man is bound at first, a turning away from concentration on one's own self and a trusting self-commitment to the Other. That is why a distinction is made between religiosity and faith – a distinction which is not always made in the quotations which follow.

If one wanted to make a clear distinction between the two, one might call religiosity the desire directed towards oneself, the urge to return to the primitive union of the embryo and the magical hope for a God who will satisfy us and fulfil our desires.

Faith is to relinquish all this, and to turn towards reality, to give oneself up to God and to accept one's own responsibility.

A child is perhaps more intensely affected by what takes place deep down in man than many people in later years.

Is it just chance that immediately after the first three critical years of life there is an unusual interest in God, in the riddles of life and death?

A new crisis of life and faith takes place in the years of puberty, and then again at the beginning of adult life. But at this time, too, the same kind of event is taking place: a birth, a coming to one's self, and the encounter with and commitment to the Other, the God of men.

Who would dare to say that this process of 'coming to faith' only begins with the encounter with someone else who believes or with the church at a later period of life?

Anyone who attains to faith realizes that this is a process that has gone on throughout his whole life.

THINKING ABOUT LIFE

How do I know that I'm me?
Girl aged four

Mother, I don't think it's very nice that I was born and that perhaps I still have to live a long time.
Boy aged four

Why did God make men, why do they live?
Boy aged seven

I'll creep back into you, because I don't find life very nice.
Girl aged eight

You are really alone all the time, aren't you? – How do you mean? – Well, you were born alone, you feel pain alone and you die alone.
Boy aged eight

How thick is the air? Is it different from the ground? Does it hurt the ground where there are holes in it? Why are there shadows? Why are they crooked? Why do they go away? Where does the light come from? How does the clock know what time it is? When am I not a little boy but a big man? Why are you older when it is your birthday? What house did I live in before I was born? I couldn't see then because I was in my mother's tummy. I could see nothing and hear nothing when I was in my mother. What does my back look like? You can't see your own face, can you? How can you see? When you are blind, how can you not see? Don't you think it silly that people's blood lives inside them? Is there a pipe inside me? When I sleep I have dreams and I see things. How does that happen? My eyes are shut when I sleep, aren't they? How can I see everything in my dreams when my eyes are shut? A voice goes fast, doesn't it?
Boy aged four, quoted by Sophia Fahs

THE PROFUNDITY OF CHILDHOOD EXPERIENCES

Was I not alive when I was learning to look, to hear, to understand, to speak? ... Did I not then acquire so much and so rapidly that in all the rest of my life I have not acquired a one-hundredth part as much? From a five-year-old boy to me is only a step. From a new-born babe to a five-year-old boy there is an immense distance. Between an embryo and a new-born babe there is an enormous chasm, while between non-existence and an embryo there is not merely a chasm but incomprehensibility.
Leo Tolstoy[1]

Then one day at dinner my great-uncle William Middleton says, 'We should not make light of the troubles of children. They are worse than ours, because we can see the end of our trouble and they can never see any end,' and I feel grateful, for I know that I am very unhappy and have often said to myself, 'When you grow up, never talk as grown-up people do of the happiness of childhood.'
W. B. Yeats[2]

I must have been six or seven years old when I stood with my father on the schoolyard and saw a stork making its nest on our neighbour's roof. I begged my father to put a cartwheel on our roof, and then a stork would surely come and nest there. But he explained to me that this could not be done with a schoolhouse, that it belonged to the parish and went with the job. The knowledge that the house we lived in did not belong to us robbed me of some of my certainty and childlike happiness. For days I kept asking, until the grown-ups grew tired of it, whether this and that belonged to us, and whether we could take it with us if we went away. I have never forgotten that conversation.
Erika Hoffmann

When it rained, what misery, what wretchedness, what despair! Yes, real, abysmal, boundless despair.
  A child does not realize that events are transitory. He thinks that because it is now raining everywhere and continuously it will always rain.
  I know from my own experience that an iron fence round a house, a fleeting glance into a cellar, could give me serious dreams, full of meaning, the following night, and that any great novelty,

such as my first sight of flowing waters, would be followed by a
real storm of dreams.
Carl Spitteler

I have another image of the mind in its springtime, perhaps from
my second year of life.
   I am somewhere, I know not how, why or with whom, in the
country in the neighbourhood of Warsaw. In a plain too wide to
see across there stands, lonely and isolated, a wretched cottage,
and around it endless meadows and water, as though there had
been a flood. There is no child, and no adult with me, and no
animals, trees or meadows to be seen. Nor do I ever go into the
house. It is as though I am utterly alone in the world, a second
Noah in the flood, and the house is my ark.
Bogumil Goltz

I have a recollection of one Christmas time and the visit of Santa
Claus, when as a little child I was torn away from the profound
security of my mother's lap – she was telling me a story – into a
chilly, noisy loneliness. This caused me a great inward pain, which
no one else noticed, but which was so horrible that one could not
imagine a small child could feel so much.
   I believe that I suddenly became conscious of what happens to
us unconsciously in the moment of our birth, when we are pushed
out of warm security into the uproar and chaos of the day, out of
the restful world of our mother into the disturbing world of our
father. But one thing is certain: I have never suffered anything
worse than that experience.
Maria Waser, quoted by Erika Hoffmann

THE DISCOVERY OF THE SELF

I shall never forget the event, which I have never told anyone,
which I experienced at the birth of my self-consciousness, to which
I can give a time and place.
   One morning I was standing as a very young child, in the door-
way of the house, and looked to the left towards the woodpile,
when suddenly the inner vision 'I am' came down like lightning
from heaven and the light has remained ever since.
Jean Paul

It was not until later, after the second year, that I distinguished
myself as a person from the world, saw the difference between

myself and things outside me, and discovered myself as a 'self'. I was standing in the inner yard; I could still point to the place. I was astonished at this birth, or rather at this action.
Moritz Carrière

As clearly as in a painting hanging before me on the wall, I see myself on my fourth birthday. I am walking up to a triangle of light formed by the junction of three streets: rue Edmond Valentin, rue Sédillot and rue Dupont des Loges, where we lived, in a triangle of sunlight. Into this lake of light I was being pushed along, sucked up, and, while I rowed with my arms and legs I said to myself: I am four years old and I am Jacques.

Call it what you will: the birth of personality. I experienced no feeling of panic, but a glow of all-embracing joy had come over me, a flash of lightning from a cloudless sky.
Jacques Lusseyran

It must have been in that year or earlier that I discovered myself for the first time. In the big room in Oberesslingen there were two long narrow mirrors on the wall between two windows, resting on a low ledge that went round the room. One day – whether it was because of what I had realized or by chance – I suddenly stopped in surprise in the middle of the room and stared into one of the mirrors, in which I saw my own reflection. A shudder went through me, and I thought something which had never previously occurred to me: That's me! Shy and curious I took a step forward and looked at the narrow translucent child's face, which seemed to consist of nothing but eyes, great astonished eyes, which looked at me enigmatically and searchingly, as I did at them: so those are my eyes, my forehead, my mouth; I have to exist all the time with this face, with these limbs, and experience everything with them. This *frater-corpus* – brother body – which I suddenly saw before me did not seem in any single respect to be my self, but a companion, additional to me, with whom I had now to continue on my way. And I thought that there had been a time when we had had nothing to do with each other. Hitherto I had been conscious of my body only when I had fallen with a bump on to my head or stubbed my toes against a big stone. But it was only a short moment of surprise, when I became aware of this incomprehensible duality.
Isolde Kurz

A RELIGIOUS EXPERIENCE?

In the course of those dim years I can remember a minute of intense delight – I was four or five years old – such as I have never experienced since. Should such things be told, or should they be kept secret? There came a moment in the room when, looking up at the window pane, I saw the dark sky and a few stars shining in it. What words can be used to express what is beyond speech? That minute was perhaps the most important one of my life, and I do not know what to say about it. I was alone in the unlighted room and, my eyes raised towards the sky, I had what I can only call an outburst of love. I have loved on this earth, but never as I did during that short time, and I did not know whom I loved. Yet I knew that he was there and that, seeing me, he loved me too. How did the thought dawn on me? I do not know. I was certain that someone was there and talked to me without words. Having said this, I have said everything. Why must I write that no human speech has given me what I felt for a moment, just long enough to count up to ten, at a time when I was incapable of putting together a few intelligible words and did not even realize that I existed? Why must I write that I forgot that minute for years, that the stream of days and nights all but wiped it out of my consciousness? If only I had preserved it in time of trial! Why is it given back to me now?
Julien Green[3]

The word 'religion' is an expression of the vital bond between man and society and the source of their existence. Religion is the coming into being of a faith, rooted in the experience of the world, but breaking through the world to reach the Other. If it is true that from the beginning of religious experience religion already exists, it is also a task to fulfil and a truth to discover. It is a movement, which changes by way of conflicts, resistances, conversion, identification with examples, integration of the person through the rite, reinterpretation of the world by a personally appropriated faith. Faith has to bridge the gap that divides the personal God from the pre-religious experience of the mystery of existence.

Religion touches the heart of man, the vital kernel of his selfhood, which precedes all the separate functions of thinking, feeling and the will.
Antoine Vergote

Only the committed person is ready for God, because he encounters God's reality with a human reality.
Martin Buber

PARADISE LOST?

One might suppose that on the basis of our life before birth we are homesick for a total unity and complete security, and that this is shown by the myths of paradise and the golden age. Becoming a human being means being driven out of 'Eden' and the interruption of the parasitic form of existence.

Birth is a shock for the child, and a total upsetting of his balance, a metamorphosis. It can be seen as the prototype of all later fear: being completely abandoned, without any realization of what is happening and without any defence or possibility of reacting.
Paul Osterrieth

It is only in the minds of adults that childhood is a paradise, a time of innocence and serene joy. The memory of a Golden Age is a delusion.
Selma Fraiberg[4]

Thank God, we no longer have to suffer as we did when we were young.
Rudyard Kipling

The emotions of a child can go very deep.

A child enjoys and suffers much more strongly because he is completely given over to the experience of the moment; not a care troubles his joy, and not a hope relieves his suffering: the grief of a child is without compare.
Paul Osterrieth

The time of childhood is on the one hand a happy period, which people try to recover with nostalgia, because everything in it is pure, new and joyful; while on the other hand it is a sombre and sad period, because in it one feels the fear of death all the more intensely, because one is still defenceless.
Georges Bernanos

FIRST IMPRESSIONS

Let parents learn to magnify nothing but what is great indeed, and to talk of God to them and of his works and ways before they can either speak or go.
Thomas Traherne, Third Century of Meditations

The only thing in man that is firm and permanent is what is received in the first years of life.
J. A. Comenius

> ... those first affections,
> Those shadowy recollections,
> Which, be they what they may,
> Are yet the fountain-light of all our day,
> Are yet a master-light of all our seeing.

William Wordsworth, 'Ode on Intimations of Immortality'

In the first three years of his life man undergoes a development, the range and scope of which is scarcely less than the development in the whole of his further life.
W. Preyer

THE FORGOTTEN PERIOD

The first memories disappear between the fifth and seventh years, and this sets the child free from an enormous emotional pressure, and this forgetting makes adults quite blind to what they experienced in the first years of their lives.
Paul Osterrieth

THE ROOTS OF FAITH

Children react much less to what grown-ups say than to the imponderables in the surrounding atmosphere. The child unconsciously adapts himself to them.

The peculiar 'religious' ideas that came to me even in my earliest childhood were spontaneous products which can be understood only as reactions to my parental environment and to the spirit of the age.
C. G. Jung[5]

The first seven years constitute the period for laying the foundations of religion. This is the most important period in the whole
of a person's life in determining his later religious attitudes.
R. S. Lee[6]

Clearly religion and life in the early years are so interwoven they
are indistinguishable. 'The entire religious development of the
child has a much slower tempo than the development of any other
field of his experience.'
Ronald Goldman[7]

Sir J. M. Barrie said that 'the God to whom small boys say their
prayers has a face very like their mother's'. In the early years God
does entrust to the mother a very great responsibility, though it
is one which she can only with difficulty discharge unless the father
also understands his most important function. This is surely to
provide a child with security and stability in which to grow,
expressed in the happiness and certainty of the expressed relationship between his parents.
Frances Wilkinson[8]

RECEPTIVENESS TO RELIGION

The child is not yet conscious of itself, nor of others. His laughter is contentment and joy in living. His affectionateness is an expression of his vital dependence. And yet he is in contact with
others. This attitude is already active and is a certain kind of love.
Antoine Vergote

A healthy, lively young child is full of faith. Our greatest concern
must be not to take his faith away from him. He must be wholeheartedly with men and things, and thereby also wholeheartedly
with the origin of all things.
J. H. Huijts

The feeling of the sublime when in the presence of the grand
spectacles of nature, the mystic intuition of the presence of an
invisible and beneficent being, the tragic conviction of shortcom-
ing, are already present in the inner lives of little children; and in
numbers of these experiences we are compelled to recognize with
astonishment that we are dealing with original facts and that
intuition plays no part whatever.

Who, more than [the child], has an inner secret life of reveries
and of aspirations which lie beyond the control of consciousness?

Who, more than he, loves; and, more important still, who, more than he, suffers from the absence of the beings whom he loves? Who, more than he, is in the position of being compelled to obey or to disobey?
Pierre Bovet[9]

The idea of God does not grow spontaneously in the child's soul, but certain mental characteristics can favour an early entry into the religious tradition.

It has been possible to perceive a receptiveness to religion in children.

At four years old a child has no difficulty in conceiving of God. It is the golden age of life with regard to its importance for the world of religion.
Antoine Vergote

No child has ever thought of God by himself, but every child is ready to believe in him.
O. Kroh

4 In the Name of the Father and of the Mother, Amen

The basic experiences of a human child are the origin and principle of what happens in his life and what takes place in his faith. This is particularly true in that there must be a link between the first human contact – father and mother – and the relationship to God. In religious terms, the experience of father and mother is a condition of faith.

Those who say that a young child is still completely taken up with his relationship with his parents, and consequently does not yet need a God, are right to a certain extent. The parents themselves are the first 'gods' to the child. A three-year-old, who had not yet quite got hold of the words that are spoken with the sign of the cross, turned them into: 'In the name of the father and of the mother, Amen.' This was more in accordance with his own experience of life than the incomprehensible theological formula of Christian tradition.

The mother and the father are the representatives of God to the child. This is not only because they seem to be omnipresent, omnipotent and omniscient, but also because the child is still completely dependent upon them. They signify more than they are in reality, because they fulfil a symbolic function. Even though they sometimes fail in their function of mother and father, a human child always goes on seeking *the* mother and *the* father.

The mother symbolizes the one who embraces, is constantly present, and brings tranquillity, protection and care. She signifies safety, trust and consolation. She is the first person, who accompanies the beginning of life and surrounds the child with her care. The first contact with her is the original situation of the child in its mother's womb: safe, tranquil and protected.

But just as a child is born of a man and a woman, so he can only become human through the mother *and* the father. The father is the second person, the other, who breaks into the unity of mother and child. One may even say that the father must inwardly adopt the child who is born of his wife. He is united with the child in a different way from his wife. The father signifies authority, power. He comes home from work out of the world. He is expected to provide leadership.

Odiseria Knechtle has called this contact with the child's parents 'the first school of faith', 'the child's first lesson in religion'.

How can a person come to trust in God without the experience of trust in men and of being accepted into their fellowship? How is it possible to believe in divine mercy without the experience of human forgiveness and acceptance?

Many people have great difficulty with the trust required by faith. They perhaps experience an emotional inability to surrender themselves to God. This may be closely related to the early experiences of their life.

The experience of life can be a fertile or a stony ground for the contact with God. But whatever experiences a child undergoes, deep in every human heart there is a desire for security and certainty about the future, for comfort and recognition, for purpose and fulfilment. He has some idea of it, even though his experiences have been disappointing. In later life some may harden their hearts against a gospel which appeals to this desire, or even become conscious atheists, while others, because of their very lack and loneliness, undertake a passionate search for God.

The link between the dislocation of family life and the growing unbelief of the present day is not accidental. And yet men are becoming obsessed as never before by the search for a God who can put us to rights. To the child, his parents are the first representatives of God, whether they will or not. And yet a child cannot really find his God until he has discovered that God is more than his parents and different from them. What matters is not only the experience of love, but also the liberation from the first and fundamental human dependence.

No person comes to faith by himself. It is not a natural consequence of human growth and development. A contact has to be made with something which is more than human. Faith must be aroused.

The faith of parents is contagious without their ever consciously speaking about it. But the true spark of faith, which can leap over the experience of life, is the story of the love of God which has become a human reality in Christ. The strange and astonishing story, the word which is so human, and yet so different from what men expect, is the seed that falls on the earth (Mark 4.2-9). In human terms the experience in life of contact and fellowship is a condition of being able to come to faith in God. And yet the strange story of Jesus brings to the fore another and completely different possibility.

The seed is the divine word. The good ground into which the root can strike is human reality, which, however, in its very lack and desire, hunger and thirst for love and righteousness, can be receptive to the word. Not only a sound psychological development, a 'good family' and a religious upbringing can form this good ground. The seed of the love of God falls deeper and comes up we know not how.

The great story in the Bible which can bring us to faith, handed down for thousands of years from generation to generation, tells how men have attained to faith. In the Old Testament we see how men were set free from primitive religion. Throughout the world we can recognize in religion the human desire for the mother, for the return to the primitive unity of the womb. Magical actions to make the gods, the forces of nature and destiny, look favourably upon men, are also selfish in their purpose. And man bows his head fatalistically when the powers are against him.

In the midst of this universal religion, in Israel, the first steps were taken towards a new and hitherto unknown faith in a God who is the creator of the universe; who is more than the forces within the world, and calls men away from their primitive union with mother earth, begins the course of a history in association with them, and makes them responsible for the earth. This is the Father-God, who 'moved with pity', comes to meet us and leads us on towards a future and even beyond death.

And in the history of Jesus this became such a present reality that man came to faith through him. He turns out to be the inspirer of faith in a God who is more than any force in the world, and whose love can help us to find ourselves in the uttermost darkness.

This story signifies more than the greatest love of parents for their child, and more than any religious education.

When you are dead will I still be all right?
Girl aged three

Has God got a mummy? Is he all by himself? – No, he has the Lord Jesus. – Oh yes, the Lord Jesus – (*with great relief*).
Girl aged three

God is father, just like Daddy, but God.
Girl aged four

Mum, you say we still have a father in heaven, but that isn't right, is it? We have our own Daddy who looks after us.
Girl aged four

Who is God, then? – It is difficult to say because God is so big. – Is God as big as Daddy?
Girl aged four

On the stairs she is the same height as her mother, who is standing on the ground: Now I am Mummy. She goes up one step: Now I am God.
Girl aged four

At school we had to sing,

> Through their Father's mercy,
> Children big and small,
> Every day are given,
> Food and clothes for all.

I thought it meant my father who had died. When I burst into tears, I was put out of the classroom and got my ears boxed as well.
Girl aged five

I like God best of all.
Girl aged five

Do you want to be God? – One God is enough, I should say. – Well, I don't think so, and then I would make lots of people, but when you are God you can look after all the people, even you. And if I was, I would see that you never died.
Boy aged five

You always say God and he, but I say she.
Girl aged five

The Our Father is the best prayer when you are sad.
Girl aged five

How can that be, one Father and so many children? – That's quite possible with God. – You're kidding, so many children and no mother.
Boy aged six

Would father and mother be cross if I like God better than
father or mother?
Girl aged six

Mummy, is a father better than a mother? – Well, they both love
their children just as much. – Yes, but, God is a father. – God is
father and mother at the same time.
Girl aged seven

My mother told me that God was simply love. I could not imagine
what this was like, and thought that it meant a nice gentleman.
Boy aged seven

You always pray 'Our Father'; isn't there a mother?
Boy aged seven

Is God a man or a woman or both?
Boy aged eight

God is nice and he has a wife called Mary.
Seven-year-old

THE REPRESENTATIVES OF GOD

Thou, O God, thou my Lord, thou my mother, thou my father,
Lord of the mountain and the valleys. Who knows when I will be
able to speak to you again, O my father, O my mother, angel,
Lord of the mountain and the valleys? But I shall pray to you
again, why should I not do so, O my God?
Prayer of the Kekchi before the maize harvest

My parents were – in short – visible powers of nature to me, no
more loved than the sun and the moon: only I should have been
annoyed and puzzled if either of them had gone out; (how much,
now, when both are darkened!) – still less did I love God; not that
I had any quarrel with him, or fear of him; but simply found
what people told me was his service, disagreeable; and what people
told me was his book, not entertaining.
John Ruskin[1]

I must have been a little more than three years old at that time,
and my mother about forty-two. But I had not the smallest idea

of my mother's age; it never entered my head to wonder whether
she were young or old ... No, at that time it was she, and that was
all; as much as to say that the face was to me unique – never to be
compared with any other – from which there beamed on me joy,
safety, and tenderness, from which all good emanated, including
infant faith and prayer.
Pierre Loti[2]

I remember well that I was seized with indignation when I heard a
friend of the family say in conversation that he was older than my
father. 'That is not true! My father is older. Nobody is older than
my father.' (He was then about sixty years of age.)
Quoted by Pierre Bovet[3]

My parents stood for protection, trust, warmth. When I think of my
childhood, I still feel the warmth above, behind and around me, the
wonderful feeling of not yet living on one's own account, but of
leaning body and soul against other people, who accepted the burden. I walked through dangers and terrors like light through a
mirror, borrowing protection for the whole of my life. My parents
stood for heaven. I knew very early – I am certain of this – that in
them another being was taking pity on me, speaking to me. I did
not call this other person God; my parents did not speak of God
until later. I gave him no name at all. He was there and that was
more. Yes, someone stood behind my parents, and my father and
mother simply had the task of passing this on to me at first hand.
This was the beginning of my faith, and explains why I never had
any doubt with regard to the unseen.
Jacques Lusseyran

To rouse the fire into a blaze, a spark had to fall upon me; and
the spark by which my own universe – still only halfway to being
individually personalized – was to succeed in centering itself on
its own fullness, undoubtedly came through my mother to light
up and fire my child's soul.
Pierre Teilhard de Chardin[4]

Long before I could think, long before I understood the name of
God, I had already experienced a Godhead without limits, an
overflowing love, an indescribable blessedness. You are not alone
and you are secure. Father and mother are like bulwarks of
divinity and omnipotence and warmth surrounding you. As soon

as I was three years old, I went to infant school with my elder
brother. After an immensely long day I came back home – how
many hours must it have been? – with my hand in the large hand
of our maid, who always smelt slightly of bleach. I came into the
warmth and luxury of home.

Later they told me how they asked what I had done, and my
vague answer was, 'All sorts of things.' When they asked further,
I said, 'Prayers.' They asked me what, and I was still so small that
I could not pronounce the letter F properly, 'Oh, about our Sader
who art in heaven. I say "My Sader is at home".'

After so many years this sounds like a confession of faith. My
father is at home. There is an infinite goodness all about me, to
which I sometimes return.
Rogier van Aerde

THE FALLEN GODS

The unreasonable outburst he had just witnessed proved one
thing. His father was omnipotent and omniscient, but not wise.
And, once part of it had crumbled away, the whole image soon
collapsed and the omnipotence and omniscience disappeared as
well. His father did not know everything, because the Bible
stories which he used to tell were different in various points from
the stories told by the Sunday school teacher.
Simon Vestdijk

But at last, gradually came a time when we began to feel that our
consciences were our own. We might keep some things secret. We
did not have to expose every fault to the light. I remember a
wonderful feeling of freedom when this attitude first occurred to
me.

At about this time, the feeling that our parents were some
remote deities, always moral and perfect though unintelligible,
began blessedly to give way to the idea that they might be human
like ourselves.
Gwendolen Freeman[5]

My Mother always deferred to my Father, and in his absence
spoke of him to me, as if he were all-wise. I confused him in some
sense with God; at all events I believed that my Father knew
everything and saw everything. One morning in my sixth year, my
Mother and I were alone in the morning-room, when my Father
came in and announced some fact to us. I was standing on the

rug, gazing at him, and when he made his statement, I remember turning quickly, in embarrassment, and looking into the fire. The shock to me was as that of a thunderbolt, for what my Father had said 'was not true'. The shock was not caused by any suspicion that he was not telling the truth, as it appeared to him, but by the awful proof that he was not, as I had supposed, omniscient.

My Father, as a deity, as a natural force of immense prestige, fell in my eyes to a human level.
Edmund Gosse[6]

It was there, I remember, that I received the first terrible impression of nature and of something invisible beyond her. The child has in his life a period – rather a long one – during which he believes that the whole world depends on his parents, or at least upon his father. And so he asks his parents for fine weather just as he might ask for a toy. This period comes to an end when the child one day discovers, to his great surprise, that some events are as unwelcome to his parents as they are to himself. With the ending of this period there vanishes a great part of the mystic charm which gathered about the sacred head of the father. It is at this same moment that a man's true independence begins.

My own eyes were opened to this fact by a terrible storm, accompanied by a thunderclap and a flash of lightning. The maid, as frightened as the tiniest of the children, stood erect, crying 'God is angry!' Then she added didactically, 'It is because you are such bad children!'

This cry, though it issued from a humble source, forced me to look beyond myself and those about me; it kindled in me the spark of religion.

Returning from the school to my home, I found there desolation: our pear-tree had not only lost its fruit, but all its leaves. A superb plum-tree had been deprived of its finest branches, and seemed mutilated and crippled.

And now I suddenly understood why my father went to church every Sunday, and why I must never put on a clean shirt without saying, 'God bless it!' I learnt to know the Lord of lords: his wrathful servants, the thunder and lightning, the hail and the tempest, had opened wide the gates of my heart, and he had entered in all his majesty.

What had happened to me may be briefly stated. One night when the wind whistled loudly in the chimney, and the rain beat vigorously on the roof, at the moment when I was being put to bed, the petition learnt by rote and said with the lips was transformed abruptly into a really serious prayer.

Thus was broken the spiritual bond which till then had linked me to my parents. And very soon I came to make complaints to God about my parents even, when I considered they had behaved unjustly towards me.
F. Hebbel[7]

WHAT MOTHER AND FATHER STAND FOR

Woman conserves; she is tradition, as man is progress.
Frédéric Amiel

The mother is a continual presence, immanence, security, the certainty of human relationship, safety, protection against danger, calm and a quiet life. Mother *is* home.

The father signifies the experience of distance. The father is aloof, comes from afar; father *comes* home. As the one who comes, the father is the one for whom a sharp and eager watch is kept, who will be there 'presently', who changes things. He turns the attention forward, towards a world which is over there: far away and in the future. The father is more the educational person.
N. Beets

The mother symbolizes inwardness, depth, intensity, refuge; she is there with open arms to pick the child up, and signifies emotion, affection, willingness and patience; she surrounds, cares, notices, provides, is always there, is sensitive, and allows the child to exist and shelters him. The father symbolizes authority, law, power, force, the norm; he judges, guides with understanding, stands apart, is strict, firm, dynamic, makes things clear, turns towards the future, instructs, takes the initiative, gives the awareness that you are small, achieves things.

The initiation into the world takes place through the mother. The father represents the reality which lies outside the little world of the child.
Antoine Vergote

We fathers really adopt our children, but mothers bear them.
Fons Jansen

The mother is a mother by nature, but the father must become a father.

Those of our children who are somewhat older have made their father more of a father. To the extent that the father takes an interest in the children and concerns himself with them he feels that he has more and more become a father.

The mother lives continuously with her child, much more intuitively than the father, and understands better what is going on in her child. She has to be the child's mouthpiece to the father. To give children to the father is part of the mother's task.
Parents

THE DYNAMIC FORCES OF BECOMING HUMAN

The images of the parents and the tension between the two are the driving force necessary for becoming a human person.

The essential and definitive structure of man is formed by way of the Oedipus complex, in which is formed the child's emotional pattern and the way in which he orientates himself towards life.

It is the father who drives the child out of the 'paradise' of the undifferentiated unity of feeling with the mother.

He represents the desire, the pattern and the promise, he introduces the principle of reality, distinction, definition and the recognition that there are other persons.

It is the father whom the child recognizes by way of the word. This belongs to a different order from that of affection.

The father becomes the example of an existence in freedom and directed towards the future. Thus the child learns to become itself as a distinct personality.

An emotional drama can take place if the real father and mother do not correspond to their symbolic function. In the case of divorce, the relationship can remain symbolically present in the form of emotional links.
Antoine Vergote

THE RELIGIOUS FUNCTION OF PARENTS

In the early years in particular, the father and mother have a divine authority, a numinous quality. In a manner of speaking, the child never reaches God, because he is still wrapped up in the relationship to others.
H. Faber

As the experience of the world awakens man to the awareness of religious depths, it is the images of his parents which play a mediating role in regard to the person of God.
Antoine Vergote

It is right that in the image of God held by many children one can find features of what their father signified for their own feelings.
   A father and a mother have simply been mediators.
M. J. Langeveld

The character of the attitude of the father to the child is of decisive importance for the nature of the earliest religious development.
Eduard Spranger

It is a tolerably safe assertion that a child who, for some reason, has never worshipped his mother will be so much the less likely ever to worship any other divinity.
Dorothy F. Wilson[8]

When a child is still wholly in the 'mother-period', we already speak about God as the Father. Difficult for him.
An infant teacher

The experience of a childhood, secure in the protection of the father, plays an important role in the feeling of trust and self-surrender. It must not be overlooked that the attitude of trust as the basis of existence, of unconditional commitment to the mystery, that comes to us as an intimately close love, protecting and forgiving, is difficult to find in those who in their childhood have not known the countenance and the heart of a true father.
   It must be true, then, that in most cases only those who have learnt from experience the concepts of 'father' and 'mother', as expressions of a protecting love which one can trust unreservedly, can give the name 'Father' with complete trust to the inexpressible ground of their existence.
Karl Rahner

MORE THAN HUMAN

God the Father is not simply the answer to human desires.
   The fatherhood of God is revealed in all his holiness and in-

visible transcendence – going beyond this present reality – and in all his power to renew human existence.

God is not really the Father except in so far as he offers maternal qualities as well, otherwise two divine functions would be duplicated, which would break down the unique relationship to God.

Between the fifth and seventh year the child consciously begins to distinguish God from his parents. The disappointment of the child, who is beginning to discover the limitations of his parents, cannot be dissociated from the making of this distinction. The parents do not know everything and cannot do everything. Moreover, the child is beginning to come into conflict with them and to discover faults. However important these negative elements are in the formation of the image of God, the transition to the 'Father in heaven' must be prepared by the witness of the parents.

To realize the effect of the witness of this human similarity to God one must see the astonishment of a child of four or five years old, when his parents say 'Father' and 'Mother' to their own parents: the myth of an absolute father and mother is destroyed, sometimes to the dismay of the child.
Antoine Vergote

Parents are thought by their children to have divine-like qualities such as omniscience, omnipotence and omnipresence ... An inevitable disillusionment occurs, ... and results in the child's first religious crisis.
Ronald Goldman[9]

A young child still places a total and complete trust in his mother or his parents, and before he possesses self-consciousness he does not exist without them. They are his safety, he is completely secure with them, they are still in place of God to him. And therefore their affection, their encouragement and their forgiveness are all he needs to be at peace. Only when this original trust has been shaken is there room for real religious experience.
P. Kohnstamm

The concept of God the Father is very difficult for children to grasp, if their home relationships are not good. The story was told how the shepherd looks after his sheep, and in the same way God the Father looks after us. One boy cried out excitedly and actually pushed his way to the front: 'You should have had my father to put up with this morning, he didn't half go on!'
Teachers

Whenever a person has had to spend his early years in uncertainty, he will protest that everything is absurd, that there is no meaning in life, and that God does not exist.

But it is also very probable that the lack of parents, of their presence and their love, is a stimulus to search for the deepest foundation of existence.
Karl Rahner

Does he not already contain within himself, in his earliest experience of a love he can trust and take for granted, the germ of his own understanding? Perhaps to present Christ to a small child is precisely to let his love *be present* to the child in our love and, for a time, nothing more. As the bounds of his small world widen, experience will teach him, long before his mind can grasp the fact, that all love is not contained in the love his parents have for him ...

If by a slow and gradual spiritual growth – *at his own speed* – a child is led to the point where he can dimly begin to formulate the question 'What is the source of this love?' or 'Who is it you trust?', is there not then, and only then, a relevance for him in the category 'God', because there is an element within his own experience to which a name must be put?
Ruth Robinson[10]

It becomes necessary to reverse our way of speaking, and to speak of a 'paternization' of God rather than a 'divinization' of parents.
Pierre Bovet[11]

It is far easier to grow out of ideas about our real parents than to outgrow infantile ideas about God.
R. S. Lee[12]

We live in a culture which – in part – is uprooted from its links with the past. We live in a fatherless society, in which authority as a semi-religious father-figure has been abolished, and it is not surprising that a feeling of alienation creeps over us in a church structure which is simply overloaded with fathers. This puts us into a position of childhood, and our feeling of responsibility tells us that this is not our task.
L. Kuylman-Hoekendijk

Anyone who thinks of God as a woman has a limited image. But so has anyone who thinks of God as a man. Both man and woman can be of use in completing the image.

The mother goddess must be taken seriously, as a symbol – however much difficulty this causes Christians. Like God the Father, she can be more than a naïve projection of childhood experiences.

Anyone who has worked out the full function of human father-hood and has recognized it as a symbol of a divine reality, will not easily regard God as a copy of a limited earthly father. Far less will he see the fatherhood of God as in conflict with human maturity, because it is the father who calls the child to adulthood.
Hans M. M. Fortmann

5   Another World

'The first period of childhood, roughly the first five years of life, is submerged like a buried city, and when we come back to these times with our children we are strangers and cannot easily find our way,' wrote Selma Fraiberg.[1]

We are not conscious of this when we are dealing with children. We take for granted that they understand our words in the sense in which we mean them and that they thereby experience what we experience. We have only just come to realize how much a young child still lives in a different world.

One of the essential characteristics of a child's existence is that his own personality is born only gradually out of its original oneness with his environment. And he is virtually incapable of making any distinction between himself and the outside world.

This explains much which we would not otherwise be able to understand. It explains not only why a child is fretful when his mother is nervous, but also why the table which the child has bumped himself on is 'naughty'. He is busy, with unbelievable seriousness, giving life to a most unpleasant heap of wood as though it were a castle. And what breath-taking reality a dream can take on! For a child it is not 'only a dream'. The world within and the world outside are one, and how can you tell which one you are in?

Just as a child itself lives, breathes and moves, so he thinks that the things round about him live and are moved, as though the world were his own body on a larger scale.

The stars are the eyes which look down on us out of the dark, and the moon is friendly because it goes with us to lighten our way. Thus one can say that a child still exists in a primitive stage. Primitive men also lived in unity with their environment, could project their fears on to evil spirits, and believed that they could influence the course of nature by their own magical actions. The world was also the 'self' on a larger scale.

It would seem an obvious assumption, then, that a child also has this primitive religion. But only remnants of this primitive religion can actually be seen: distinct images in dreams, a certain amount of superstition, magical actions and the attribution of life to objects.

Perhaps the remnants of primitive religion that can be observed in children are no more than are to be found in adults. Who goes under a ladder without reservations? How many people secretly expect to be punished because they have neglected the practice of their religion? A child will even make an agreement with itself to step off the stairs with the right foot. It becomes a sacred necessity, a rite. Even children's reaction to thunderstorms recall the fear of wrathful gods in ancient times. But this is not true of children alone. The flood disaster in Holland brought to light in tragic fashion how deeply even people at the present day still experience a link between natural catastrophes and their own feelings of guilt.

Apart from this, however, we are strangers to children's experience of reality. How innocently busy they are, discovering the world; and in the process they stagger from one surprise to the next. To them, what is strange and unbelievable seems obvious and natural. We say for this reason that a child cannot see a miracle. For the most unlikely things are taken for granted. Life is a fairy tale. Perhaps the reverse is really true. It is we, who describe as a miracle an extraordinary and unnatural phenomenon of which we cannot give a rational explanation – and then we do not believe it – who no longer know what a miracle is.

A child is astonished, as by a miracle, at almost everything it discovers, even the most ordinary things. It lives in a state of wonderment. A miracle is not what is impossible and absurd, but the discovery of reality as something special, unique and unbelievable. A child can teach us to know again what a miracle is, and that the most ordinary and obvious things can be astonishing.

Parents often do not know how to talk to their children about reality which is not part of everyday experience. For their picture of the world is different. It is difficult to speak to the world of their thoughts, because it has lost its truth for us. On this point, the perplexity of educated people is particularly great. We are imprisoned in our educated or scientific world-view and are frightened of an impossible question posed by a five-year-old: 'What would God do if the sky fell down?'

The child thinks of the world in the same way as he experiences space himself. You live in a house, on a floor under a roof. Therefore God, too, has to live on a floor, whether it is of gold or of clouds. And his floor is the roof of our space, or a higher storey of a cosmic house. It is like the world view of antiquity: the sky as the tent roof with the stars fixed in it. The earth is flat. Under the earth is the realm of the dead.

'The earth is flat,' says the child, 'because I can see it with my own eyes.' And, 'I have seen this myself, you don't go to heaven at all when you are dead, they put you under the ground.'

What can you make of the tale that the sun is a star, that the moon does not give light and that the little distant spots of light are so much greater than the sun?

Just as man originally regarded the world as a living being and saw it through his own eyes, so is the child's vision of the world.

But why must we have scientific pangs of conscience whenever we try to talk to children in the truth of their world? We, who live on a flat surface, between height and depth, the world above of light and the world below of darkness and death.

For us this has the purely relative significance of the language of images. For a child this world-view can be a reality, while for us it is the shadow of reality. There is truth behind both, but which is closest to it?

Just ask yourself whether the thoughts and actions of a young child are not much more symbolic than ours. For he is totally involved with them. How very indignant a child can be when parents deny the reality of what their children represent in their games.

When it comes to 'higher things', we are perhaps somewhat hesitant of the homely and even banal way in which a child brings the holy into his everyday world. He himself plays at God, sitting on a table – which is heaven – throwing pencils off on to the floor – which is the rain.

Have we any right to deprive a child of this concrete relationship with the invisible? Children must not be disturbed in the form of their spiritual experience. They bring the all-highest and incomprehensible down to their own level, drag it in their own way into their own world and are occupied with it. What sounds sacrilegious to parents can be deeply serious to a child.

A child once asked her father if God ever had a birthday. The father replied, 'God never has a birthday.' The child left the room deeply disappointed, but came back later full of enthusiasm and cried out, 'Mummy says that God has a birthday every day!'

Which of the two parents gave the best answer? For the child, it was obviously the mother, but was the father closer to the truth? Anyone who talks about God cannot do so except in images; this is what we always do. Why did the child ask if God ever had a birthday?

It was really asking whether there is a link between human experiences and God. Of itself it is not such a silly question. Anyone whose birthday it is, finds himself in a specially fortunate situation. For a child it signifies a high point in his usual existence: you are the centre of attention, you give a party, you get presents, people sing to you, and there is company. It is something splendid to have a birthday. The childish image brings us to the great words of the prayer – which in their turn are simply images of human reality: 'Thine is the kingdom, the power and the glory.' Are we filled with enthusiasm when we utter these words?

Why are we in such a hurry to lead a young child as soon as possible into the 'reality' of hard facts and objective truth?

In the sixth year of their lives, children already have to learn that twice two is four, but it seems as though this is not soon enough. Experiments are being carried out to train children at an even earlier age in the laws and truths of our intellectual culture.

This is bound to be at the expense of what comes from the child himself, of the truth of his child's experience.

Is a child's experience simply an early and primitive stage in the way in which we experience the world after we have been indoctrinated by the knowledge we have learnt at school? Perhaps this first experience of reality is valuable in itself!

It is not for nothing that in the very age of science and technology great importance has come to be given to dreams, even though this is principally in clinical psychology. To come to himself, modern man must once again begin to pay attention to his dreams.

In painting, the world we have learnt to analyse at school is scarcely recognizable.

And when, in dealing with the Bible, we make use of words like demythologization, the reason is that we have wrongly taken the images of biblical history as objective historical facts. We must once again learn that reality is more than bare facts. These biblical images represent a deeper reality and history than can be verified by natural science or history in the academic sense. To understand anything of the language of faith we must re-mythologize, and begin to understand the depth of the images.

Here we need children to remind us of the living testimony of things round about us, the reality of dreams and the truth of stories.

The child still lives in another world, which, however, can be of great significance to us. This is the world of the miracle, the obverse side of our reality, which contains more than we realize. It is a world which is still full of secrets.

THE CHILD AND NATURE

How do the birds know where they have to fly? – God shows them.

Up there the taps are always on. – Lord Jesus, turn the tap off for a bit.
Girl aged four

A little girl with new gloves on: 'If God sees them, I know that he will keep the rain away.'
Girl aged four

God, keep the rain off, because I can't go to the barn.
Girl aged four

Why doesn't God just say: Go away, hailstones!
Girl aged four

God throws the rain with buckets out of the air.
Boy aged five

It isn't raining and I just got a drop on my nose, God must have been washing the windows.
Girl aged five

No, he just lets it rain, he doesn't mind it and it all falls on our heads.
Boy aged five

'It is good for the flowers,' said mother, after it had rained for days. 'Dear Lord, please let it be fine again and we will look after the flowers.'
Girl aged six

A snowstorm. God is throwing that.
Girl aged three

I believe God has quite forgotten the winter has come. – Hush, not so loud, or he will hear you.
Boy aged five

Why is it snowing so hard? Can't God see that I've got my new coat on?
Boy aged four

The first snow. Just look, God doesn't want it any more, he is throwing it all down.

The king in heaven does that, he makes it snow.
Boy aged seven

God can hardly see anything.

A thunderstorm. God must be shovelling.
Boy aged three

A little boy hasn't eaten up his plums. It thunders that night. He comes downstairs in his pyjamas to eat up his plums; he is afraid that God is angry with him.

I'm waiting to see if God is coming.
Girl aged five

I think that it is something to do with God, a message from God. Now he really wants to say something.
Boy aged seven

Now God is angry with me.
Girl aged eight

In the wood. Just stand still, I just want to listen how quiet it is, I feel it in my heart.
Girl aged four

Sometimes I think that the trees themselves are God.
Girl aged six

Whose is the tree? – God's. – No, Our Lord's. – No, the church's.
Conversation

I just went into the wood and it was so nice there, and I felt so

happy that I would have liked to have given God a kiss on the forehead.
Boy aged eight

THE WORLD: HEAVEN AND EARTH

Jet Planes. Look, Daddy, they are making scratches on God's floor!

Yes, heaven is a big black hole.
Boy aged four

A child looked at the sun, thought it was a hole in the sky and that his father, who had died, ought to be able to see through it.

The air never ever stops.
Boy aged four

Is there another world in the air and is there a world under the ground when you dig very deep?
Girl aged five

That's why the sky is so high, isn't it? The air is soft underneath but hard on top, isn't it?
Girl aged five

Is the earth round? And if you come to the edge, do you fall off, and where do you go then?
Boy aged five

It's God's secret, that you go round with the world and don't notice.
Girl aged five

Is the horizon the end of the world? – No, the earth is round. – But don't I see it with my own eyes?

The end of the world is God.
Boy aged five

It's the bird's sky, not God's sky.

I don't believe that heaven comes after the clouds.
Girl aged five

You're making a mistake with your story about heaven and about
God. It can't be like that. Heaven is God.
Girl aged five

Where is the very end of the world? – Nowhere, it goes on and on
for ever, the world is round, you get back to the same place.
Boy aged six

She says that there is no heaven, she says, 'There is no end', and
then I said, 'All right, look at a rocket, that goes as far as the
moon.' – Do you think that the moon is the end? – No, first the
moon and then the sky and that's the end.
Girl aged nine

That sort of thing, a rocket, goes a long way, but however far it
goes, it can never get to God because human beings can never go
as far as God.
Boy aged ten

WHERE IS HEAVEN?

I think that heaven is above us. – Heaven is millions of miles high
in the sky. – Above us, perhaps, I don't really know, I can only
guess. – Above and below us, all over the world. – Everywhere
above, below, above, everywhere where nobody can go.

WHAT DOES HEAVEN LOOK LIKE?

*Answers from the fourth class of a Roman Catholic primary
school*
You cannot see heaven, but it exists, it is behind big clouds up in
the air.
Everybody says that heaven is in the air, but if I went up with the
rocket into the air I still wouldn't see anything and I wouldn't
know where heaven was.
Nobody knows where heaven is and yet heaven exists.
Heaven is everywhere, because nobody knows where heaven is,
only God.
Heaven is everywhere, because nobody knows anything about
heaven.
I have never been to heaven yet, but I tell you that heaven is nice,
that's what I tell you all, that heaven is nice.

Heaven looks nice, but let me get in; if I could see heaven, that would be nice.

Heaven is in the sky and heaven is high, very high, you could go on for hours but you never get there. But one day we go there and that is when we are dead.

Heaven might be a big room but I don't know I have never been there since I was little till now I am nine I have never been there but one day we go there and that is when we are dead then we are there and then our life starts again and then we stay alive for ever.

Heaven is everywhere; where God is, heaven is as well.

Heaven is a glass house that God and the angels live in, it looks just like a castle from the inside.

Heaven looks white – like a palace – full of flowers and full of angels – heaven is all blue and white.

Answers at a school for Christian Popular Education (corresponding to an English church-aided primary school)
Just like a park but much nicer and very big with lots of angels and trees.

It is really fine there it is just like paradise there.

I think that there is a big country there.

I think that there is a big city with everything white.

Perhaps it is a big world where it's always holidays.

Everything is nice there and with lots of light.

White houses and black houses a gap between them for hell and the place of God.

There are trees as well and just like here, just exactly like here.

It is nearly the same as in the world, but it is lighter there.

CHILDREN'S DEFINITIONS

A dragonfly: a helicopter insect.

A caterpillar walks like a mouth organ playing.

A tomcat is a pussy that doesn't have kittens.
Boy aged five

A horse with a white mane: an angel horse.

A germ: A little bit of illness.

A volcano: A mountain that is being sick.

A town child in the country: Look, the trees grow wild here!

Johnny said that the water was autumn, not too hot and not too cold.

A water tower: Mummy, that's a church tower with water.
Boy aged three

The mist rises out of the drainage ditch. Is that snow? Mummy, the air is coming out of the ground.
Girl aged three

Fireworks: Is God doing that?

Are you frightened of cows now? You didn't used to be. – But I was still little then.
Boy aged four

She never looks at her dolls any more: I don't believe in dolls any more.

When we sleep, we make the morning, God makes the morning.

Who makes the days and when are they finished?

Mother, if war comes, I'll shoot the war dead.
Boy aged four

I know a way that only Jesus can go; the Milky Way.

THE WORLD IN HUMAN FORM

O tree, dear tree, how I love you!

Auntie say something, I'm frightened in the dark. – Why have I to say something, you still don't see me? – It doesn't matter. When somebody talks, it gets light.

I've seen an angel in our pear tree in the garden.
Boy aged four

My eyes are as big as the world, because I can see everything!
Five-year-old

The stars are God's eyes, they wink. The stars wink at us.

How did God make man? God lit the cloud with a great big match
and that is man.
Boy aged five

Doesn't God burn his hands when he winds the sun up in the
morning?

At sunrise: Auntie, it's a holiday in heaven, look what a lovely
sky!
Girl aged six

The sun comes through the clouds: God has come down to earth.
– Why. – The sun has come down to earth and God is in the sun.
Boy aged six

A red sunset: That's God's lamp, isn't it?
Boy aged six

I think that the mountains are God's feet.

I think that life, I mean our life, is something like the thoughts
of a giant.
Boy aged five

MAN

If you like something, does God like it just the same as you?
Girl aged three

I've lost my voice, *says Grandma.* – Where is it then? – In Enk-
huizen. – Grandma, tomorrow I will go and get it for you.
Boy aged four

No one: A person who doesn't exist.

Don't you remember how brave the little black children were
when they were bandaged up? – That was only on a picture!

Why is the bride in white? – Because it is the happiest day of her
life? – But why is he in black?
Boy aged four

When you have thought for a long time who are you going to marry, then you get engaged!
Boy aged four

How do I go to sleep? – You lie down nicely and it just happens. – Doesn't God make you sleep? – Yes. – Then he must press a button.
Girl aged five

You can't guess my thoughts, only God can do that.
Five-year-old

What is your soul? – What you think with, feel with and what you can talk with. – Your head then. Up to here. And your eyes as well?
Girl aged five

'Where is your soul? Here?' – pointing to his head – 'Or here?' – pointing to his stomach. He had a cold, and while I was trying to explain that the soul makes itself known in the fact that you live and move and can run and think, and that you can do what you want, he suddenly sneezed hard. He said: 'Today my soul is in my nose.' 'And mine is in my legs,' cried his brother who was jumping about.
Six-year-olds

Miss, I can hear my conscience inside me. – And what does it say? – It doesn't say anything, it sort of bubbles.
Six-year-old

Teacher is explaining what a commandment is. If your mother tells you not to go into the sitting room, that is a commandment. Who can tell me what a commandment is? – If Moses says that you mustn't go into the sitting room, that's a commandment.
Girl aged six

I think it's a pity they found words for kicking and killing. If they hadn't found the words, the things wouldn't have existed.
Boy aged six

Father is a station-master. What was it like at school? – Just the usual, first class and wooden seats.

Mummy, it looks like your heart goes by atoms, and it runs out

very slowly and then it doesn't exist any more, and then you are
dead, and nothing can be done about it.
Boy aged eight

Where is your soul really? – In your everything.
Girl aged ten

I don't want to be a sheep, but a big boy.

You say that we are all God's sheep. But that can't be so, because
we can't eat grass.

Undertaker's man in long coat: Mister, are you dead?

WHAT IS A SOUL?

*Answers given in the fourth class of a Roman Catholic primary
school.*
The soul is in my body.
You soul is mainly in your stomach.
My soul is white and round.
A soul is a big round ball.
A round ball with a cross, in the middle of the soul there is a
cross.
Your soul is God.
I think nothing but air; it is inside you.
It is something of your body; if you die it goes to heaven, hell, or
purgatory.
Your soul is just next to your heart, round the soul is a little cup-
board, when you die your soul goes to heaven but you go into the
grave so all of you doesn't go to heaven only your soul; the rest
stays here you yourself go into the grave.
The soul is god. I have never seen the soul but I will never see
the soul but it doesn't do any harm I don't ever need to see it. We
have a body and a soul if we swear and tell lies these are sins and
if we go to confession everything is all right again.

ANGELS

I don't want to be a little angel, I'm afraid it will hurt when you
get the wings.
Four-year-old

He says it and it is.
His brother

What is an angel, what does he look like? – It's not a he, it is a light from inside and then you start singing (*after a moment's thought*) or skipping.

One evening when I was saying my prayers before going to sleep, the room got very light. I thought it was an angel, then it disappeared.
Girl aged eleven

FAIRY TALES AND HUMAN CONTACT

A story about a little boy who was four or five years old. On principle, his mother told him no fairy tales. However, an acquaintance gave him a gramophone record of Red Riding Hood and played it to the child. His mother was not there. He heard it without any contact with his mother.

For a long time the child was nervous and no one understood what was the matter. After three months he said to his mother, pointing to a fly, 'What do flies eat?' A stream of questions followed, 'What does this animal eat, what does that animal eat?' The food eaten by an endless series of animals had to be specified. Then he was silent. When he had gone upstairs, on his way to bed, he finally got out the question that mattered: 'And what do wolves eat, do wolves eat children?' From that day on, the child was at peace again and the tension was broken.

THE IMPRESSION MADE BY NATURE

Religious awe is the same organic thrill which we feel in a forest at twilight.
William James[2]

My Zulu nurse-girl, Catherine, ... had wheeled me further than usual on our morning outing. We had been skirting hedges ... when a hedge suddenly stopped, and we came to an empty railed-in site, on a ridge of the Berea, overlooking the Indian Ocean. A horse had its head over the wire fence, and as we rounded the hedge and surprised it, it reared up and turned away; and I, looking down the grassy slope through its legs, saw a huge living

expanse of glittering azure, like a peacock's tail, electrified with winds and solar fire. It took my breath away and when Catherine told me what it was, that Zulu word for the sea, 'Lwandhla', which in two syllables Homerically expressed the pride and glory of the ocean and the plunge of its breakers, struck my mind with a force which no other word or line in poetry has ever had for me since. I went on repeating the word 'lwandhla' for days. It is the first word I remember *learning*.
Roy Campbell[3]

Up to the age of five nature did not exist for me. All that I remember happened in a bed or in a room. Neither grass, nor leaves, nor sky, nor sun existed for me. It cannot be that no one gave me flowers and leaves to play with, or that I did not see the grass and was not sheltered from the sun, but up to the age of five or six I have no recollection of what is called 'nature'. Probably it is necessary to be separate from it in order to see it, and I was then part of nature.
Leo Tolstoy[4]

One fine Sunday morning – I must have been getting on for six years old – I ran out after breakfast to the side of the drainage ditch and sat down there. The church bells began to sound in the distance and a feeling of total joy descended on me, so immense and making me so happy that I have never forgotten it. I was a nervous and fearful child by nature.
Recollections of a man of fifty-six

One night my mother woke me and took me out on to the street. People were standing together, murmuring to each other a little, and looking up at the sky. A hand turned my head in the direction in which they were all looking and a voice said, 'Can you see the comet?' There was a long arch of white light in the midst of the dark night that covered the village. The way the people stood gazing up, their almost fearful whispering, the way the shining curve of light stayed far away in the distance, all made a deep and lasting impression on me, and later had a much more powerful effect on my memory than on that night. Though I was only three years old, I was still old enough to be frightened or delighted. I sat up on my mother's arm and through her was aware of the mighty course of nature.

Being with animals brought me to a condition of unthinking and sorrowful expectation, which I have never experienced

amongst men. I used to have the feeling of being alone in the world with my emotions. At those moments, whenever the thought of father or mother, lessons or prayers came into my mind, I rejected the recollection as unbearably alien, as though under the spell of nature I wanted to be nothing more than a creature myself, and not be distinct from the guiltless and sombre background of the animal world.
Hans Carossa

As far back as I can remember I was saddened by the amount of misery I saw in the world around me. Youth's unqualified *joie de vivre* I never really knew, and I believe that to be the case with many children, even though they appear outwardly merry and quite free from care.

One thing that specially saddened me was that the unfortunate animals had to suffer so much pain and misery. The sight of an old limping horse, tugged forward by one man while another kept beating it with a stick to get it to the knacker's yard at Colmar, haunted me for weeks.

It was quite incomprehensible to me – this was before I began going to school – why in my evening prayers I should pray for human beings only. So when my mother had prayed with me and kissed me good-night, I used to add silently a prayer that I had composed myself for all living creatures. It ran thus: 'O heavenly Father, protect and bless all things that have breath; guard them from all evil, and let them sleep in peace.'

The science teaching had something peculiarly stimulating for me. I could not get rid of the feeling that it was never made clear to us how little we really understand of the processes of Nature. For the scientific school-books I felt a positive hatred. Their confident explanations – carefully shaped and trimmed with a view to being learnt by heart, and, I soon observed, already somewhat out of date – satisfied me in no respect. It seemed to me laughable that the wind, the rain, the snow, the hail, the formation of clouds, the spontaneous combustion of hay, the trade-winds, the Gulf Stream, thunder and lightning, should all have found their proper explanation. The formation of drops of rain, of snowflakes and of hailstones had always been a special puzzle to me. It hurt me to think that we never acknowledge the absolutely mysterious character of Nature, but always speak so confidently of explaining her, whereas all that we have really done is to go into fuller and more complicated descriptions, which only make the mysterious more mysterious than ever. Even at that age, it became

clear to me that what we label Force or 'Life' remains in its own
essential nature for ever inexplicable.
Albert Schweitzer[5]

I had been told that all iron attracts lightning, and as soon as
the first dark clouds with their shining edges appeared over
the horizon, my superstitious activity would begin. I would gather
all the axes, saws, hammers and tongs into the inner yard and
carry them to the farthest barn; I picked up all the nails from
the outside window sills, and could not rest until the last needle
from my mother's sewing table was put in an isolated place. I
was calmed by my exertion, and when the lightning struck in the
wood and the thunder shook the house, and sometimes an old tree
was struck by lightning and flared up like a torch, I used to sit in
my little corner by the stove, shaking like any other creature and
devoutly subject to the majesty of God, but without fear, because
I had done my bit to appease God's anger.
Ernst Wiechert

He was four years old when fear, which hitherto had never had
any opportunity, paid its first visit. He had great difficulty in going
to sleep. Often his father sat by him and held his hand tight.
Through the open door was a distant contact with his mother.

Whenever the full moon shone in through the open window
at the east side, the young Anton lifted his head up, and, however
drowsy and soothed he was by his father's presence, manifested
by his heavy breathing, the light of his cigar and a warm, heavy
hand, he would say, clearly and audibly, 'Bye bye moon!', sometimes ten times over, until he fell asleep.

In reality he was fearful by nature. The first visit of fear came
from an infinite distance, in the form of a pale yellow sphere,
which rolled smoothly into a bedroom.
Simon Vestdijk

A WORLD OF THEIR OWN

The child says to us: 'Come down close to me, otherwise you
won't be able to understand me. I don't stand where you grown-
ups stand. You may stand on the ground, but your minds have
long grown far above it. You are no longer in contact with the
ground, like us. That is why we are really different people. You
talk so much over my head, and you think that the same word
means the same idea to me as it does to you. Your horizon is

wide, mine is small and narrow. Give us little ones time to experience.'
Odiseria Knechtle

The child only reveals himself fully in his own world; only there can one really get alongside him.

'Don't you understand adults?' 'No, I really don't, because I've never been an adult.'
The child's point of view is always different from ours. It could not be otherwise, for he lacks our experience.
Most misunderstandings begin with an unwillingness to take the bother to hear the child's side of the story ... Nor can children ever be treated as if they were undersized adults ... The Child's World is very real ... Rightfully they regard it as a *world of their own*, and there is good reason to believe that there are times when they like to be alone there ... Parents should not feel shunted aside if they don't succeed in getting into this other world with their own children. There are times when children can be aided by their staying out.
Helen Parkhurst[6]

Anyone who really puts himself in the child's place enters a world where things have different colours, different shapes, and different proportions and meanings. The child inhabits a different space in the house he shares with his parents. The distance that divides adulthood from childhood makes it difficult for adults to remember how they themselves experienced house and town.
Adults are usually too ready to suppose that they can see things from the point of view of the existence the child lives. They are usually not aware that at the present day children live in a totally different reality.
J. H. van den Berg

Not a single fiction was read or told to me during my infancy. The rapture of the child who delays the process of going to bed by cajoling 'a story' out of his mother or his nurse, as he sits upon her knee, well tucked up, at the corner of the nursery fire – this was unknown to me. Never in all my early childhood did anyone address to me the affecting preamble 'Once upon a time!' I was told about missionaries, but never about pirates; I was familiar with humming birds, but I never heard about fairies. Jack the Giant Killer, Rumpelstiltskin and Robin Hood were not of

my acquaintance, and though I understood about wolves, Little Red Ridinghood was a stranger even by name. So far as my 'dedication' was concerned, I can but think that my parents were in error thus to exclude the imaginary from my outlook upon facts. They desired to make me truthful; the tendency was to make me positive and sceptical. Had they wrapped me in the soft folds of supernatural fancy, my mind might have been longer content to follow their traditions in an unquestioning spirit.
Edmund Gosse[7]

THE EXPERIENCE OF SELFHOOD

A child lives outside himself in his environment, and has no consciousness of being in himself. He asks about things he sees, not about inner experiences. There is no contradiction between imagination and reality.

The child is believing and optimistic. Just as fairy tales bring the world to the child so he naturally lives in his imagination and emotions. Children draw the unexpected down inside themselves, even with regard to religion.

In play they can deal seriously with things that are sacred to us.
Charlotte Bühler

They know the world on the basis of the world of their own experience, just as the poet peoples the world on the basis of what he has experienced. It is still a warm and living view of the world, not yet spoilt by cold, sober knowledge, the world they learn about at school.
Fons Jansen

We are all visionaries; and what we see is our own soul in things.
Frédéric Amiel

There is no such thing amongst children as real magic, such as we find in the world-view of adults who belong to primitive races. The child sees the world in a light determined by his own self. His self is the world as he senses it and feels about it.
M. J. Langeveld

THE DISCOVERY OF REALITY

A child left to himself is sometimes faced with areas of unex-

plored country, no man's land, which no one has ever mapped. He
creates for himself a world accessible to him in the uttermost
corners of existence. A story, a trick of behaviour to overcome a
fear, a strange conception which makes an unexplained piece of
the world accessible to him.
M. J. Langeveld

The child is the architect of his own intellectual growth, and this
rests on the principle of continuous interaction between the child
and the world around him; it is this that furnishes all the
material, as well as the motive force for his intellectual advance.
Nathan Isaacs[8]

The infant is dependent on adults, who make the world reliable
for him. The greatest fear is that of the loss of love. The discovery
of the world is always the source of fear and uncertainty. The child
experiences the world as a totality, largely through his emotions,
without the protection of rational control, and is sensitive and
vulnerable. The infant does not analyse, but is subject to what
happens. The form in which he undergoes his experiences is that
of concrete, emotionally laden images.
    There is an urge to know. 'What is yesterday? Will I get small
again when I am big? What is dying?' But these questions about
life are strictly related to his own self. The infant explores the
world in his play.
Nijmegen Catechetical Institute

THE WORLD IS A WONDER

The child lives in a fairy-tale world where everything is possible.
Plants and animals have the same feelings as the child, but it is
an ordinary world in which nothing miraculous or supernatural
happens, as it does for adults, who live in a different world, where
there is a precise boundary between what is possible and what is
impossible, between imagination and reality.
P. Osterrieth

So-called common things are not common for him; all is penetrated with mystery. Perhaps if we grown folk wondered more,
we might understand the children better. Perhaps with the
'Renaissance of Wonder' might come a Renaissance of Religion.
    To the little child, the unseen is not necessarily unreal. He
cannot see the wind, but he can see what the wind *does*. He learns
more of fatherhood – in both human and divine – from what we

are than from anything we may *say*.
E. Read Mumford[9]

For the child, the world is just beginning when he opens his eyes, and he experiences as it were a second time the wonders of the event of creation, the greatest of all miracles, which it has ceased to be for us, because it has become the regularly repeated events of every day. For the child, God is still separating the light from the darkness every new day.
Alexander Rodenberg

Anyone who thinks that a child's soul is clear and transparent and open is in error. There are areas which every child anxiously keeps sacred and into which no one, even in the deepest intimacy of love or friendship, is ever allowed to open the door.

But their deepest feelings are stirred by the apprehension of the unbelievable possibilities lying behind things, and therefore the child is closer to the eternal mystery than the adult.
August Miehle

To love is to let yourself be astonished, because what was dead routine has been made new and striking by children.

The realm of the fairy tale and of the divine are one and the same for children. Anything can happen in a fairy tale, and anything can happen with God.

It is remarkable that a child feels quite at home with the mysteries of birth and death. The whole of life is mysterious; to die is really no more mysterious than flowers which just appear from the bud.
Fons Jansen

THINKING IN IMAGES

What are images to us can be realities with a purpose for a child.
M. J. Langeveld

Anyone who has seen children playing spontaneously, or heard their stories of the wonders seen on their daily walks, can have no doubt of the tremendous part played by a free and unfettered imagination in their lives. Life lies before them and imagination provides the forecast and rehearsal of it; lack of experience of

what life really is leaves fancy as yet unchecked, at times almost unbounded.
Dorothy F. Wilson[10]

In the dreams of three- and four-year-old children there are some which are so pregnant with mythology and significance that one would immediately regard them as the dreams of adults. Primitive people live to a large degree in the collective unconscious. Children too live in close proximity to this inner world, which is why they possess so rich an imagination and believe so easily in mythological beings.

In his own inner world lie embryonic the phantasy building powers of the collective unconscious. From them he often weaves for himself strange explanations of the newly discovered world ... We may laugh at these phantasies. By doing so we cut ourselves off from one of the most vital sources of relationship with the child ... We must keep this door of communication open between us so that his phantasy may not be used as a retreat from reality and a barrier between him and ourselves.

The imagination contains an indication of the direction in which unconscious forces are acting.
Frances Wickes[11]

What does it mean to be a child? 'It is to be something very different from the man of today. It is to be so little that the elves can reach to whisper in your ears; it is to turn pumpkins into coaches, mice into horses, lowness into loftiness, and nothing into everything, for each child has his fairy godmother in his own soul.'
Francis Thompson[12]

Fairy tales arise when children and adults part company. The great importance of fairy tales for the Romantic Movement is associated with the great increase in the distance between adult and child which was taking place just at that period. It is no accident that the fairy tales are cruel. By being cruel they show the remote and even repulsive character of adulthood, and that is their purpose.

But anyone who now reads the fairy tales of the past to his children will soon realize that they trouble them. The reason for the change is obvious. If the fairy tale, not least by its cruelty, was able to keep children away from adulthood that was all too close, by now the distance between adult and child is so great that the middle ground is lacking. The cruelty which once pushed

the child gently back, now terrifies him. In the vacuum which now separates young and old they are sources of fear and disturbance.
J. H. van den Berg

At this stage the child is wide open to miracles, which are encountered not as miracles, but as something natural and normal. In the same way fairy tales are understood as a totality. For it is not the case that whoever can give the best rational explanation of a fairy tale has best understood it, but he who encounters it in its wholeness as a reality. Thus it is wrong to cheat children with explanations of fairy tales, as some people so readily suppose. The same is true of fairy tales about birth. When children are told that the baby was brought to the parents from fairyland by a stork or picked off a bush in a faraway garden or grew out of a cabbage, these strange stories, because they find an echo in unfathomable deep associations, reflect the whole of reality – which is wholly penetrated by mystery – no less than semi-accurate accounts, almost always rather ridiculous, of the technique and physiology of reproduction. The same is true of myth, of the creation story, of God and the angels, of hell and the devil. For the child they have a charming and terrible reality.

All this changes around the seventh year. A new interest is attained in the meaning of reality. The child becomes receptive to the scientific explanation of relationships in the world. The child must be helped in his need for objective scientific explanations and should not be given indigestible religious nourishment instead. This intellectualist and rationalist stage is followed in puberty by a new high point of sensitivity to the irrational. The age of the first personal religious experience is beginning.
H. C. Rümke

Has Dr Robinson not observed that our technological world is beginning to long for a return to the resources of nature, is eager to 'get away' in order to dream, to be idle, to indulge in fantasy and create new 'myths'?
E. Schillebeeckx[13]

THE PICTURE OF THE WORLD

Just as time is 'the time of the child', so space is 'the space of the child'. They are experienced only as they affect him, and only in this experience is there a relationship to space. Time is identical with intensity of experience. The child lives in the present to such

an extent that the concepts of past and future have no meaning for him, unless they are very close and are connected with a direct experience.
M. W. Steenmeyer-van Rij

The *rêve éveillé* of Robert Desoille emphasizes the recovery of the areas of 'height' and 'depth', because no others carry such symbolic weight and have consequently such directive significance for real life as they do. Everybody has a very distinctive personal affinity to rising and going down. Those who are mentally healthy can very easily be made in one way or another to sink into the lowest depths or to rise up to the utmost heights. A non-believing patient can find himself somewhat embarrassed and surprised when he sees himself so directly confronted with heaven and hell, God and the angels. One of my patients could never let slip an opportunity of uttering the necessary correction: 'But I don't believe in a heaven and I don't believe in angels.'

This throws a striking light on the pre-conscious structure of the inhabited human world, which in spite of Copernicus has hell beneath and heaven above.
J. H. van den Berg

FEAR

Now my little heart goes beating like a drum,
With the breath of the Bogie in my hair;
And all around the candle the crooked shadows come,
And go marching along up the stair;
The shadow of the balusters, the shadow of the lamp,
The shadow of the child that goes to bed –
All the wicked shadows coming tramp, tramp, tramp,
With the black night overhead.
Robert Louis Stevenson, A Child's Garden of Verses

The flood rose and the storm would not slacken. I felt it was a punishment because I had been naughty, although my parents had never aroused feelings of guilt. It came from within and can probably be regarded as a primitive superstition.
A reminiscence

PLAY

Perhaps, as adults, we forget the intense consciousness of what is

real to a child in a game he has 'made up'. In much of his play he is 're-presenting' reality, and within the context of the game to refer to it as 'pretence' is an affront to the depths of his conception. None knows better than he that the actual play is made up, though it represents something very real. In childhood he plays at 'mothers and fathers'; in adult life he will discard the play and live out for himself the relationship he has begun to apprehend and express through childhood play. He is, in fact, capable of a very high doctrine of myth – that is, he is able to value it not simply for itself, for he can accept it as expendable, but for the reality it embodies upon which he sets an enduring value.
Ruth Robinson[14]

It is well known that the play of some children is necessary to overcome their fear following a shock. Things that are powerful, terrible and incomprehensible must be brought into a framework of safety and security, if they are to be prototype experiences of a religious nature.
M. W. Steenmeyer-van Rij

In children's liking for little things, in the way they hide things and play hide and seek, we can see a feature of childhood: the unconscious striving for something that is their own, separate from the world of adults.
Erika Hoffmann

There is also a link between play and religious reality. It is a sign of this that a child will even bring something extremely serious, even sacred, into his child's world. That is why it is wrong to regard children's games about religion as profanation.

Two small children were playing with a box of blocks. The two-year-old said: 'That isn't God, it's a block!' His four-year-old sister began to cry and said, 'Can't you see that that's God?'
August Miehle

Play serves a physical and social end; it develops the child's body muscles and he needs other children for its happy fulfilment; but it goes deeper than this. He is also expressing an individual psychology; his own conflicts, his own perceptions, his own incipient reasoning. When he is building with bricks, we do not know merely by watching him what deep desire is being satisfied by the towering summits of his castle.
Marjorie Hourd[15]

A study of children's dramatic play indicates how they may be

wrestling with conceptions of such mysteries as birth and death. Sometimes such ideas may be dramatized in a straightforward manner, as when six-year-old Richard commanded me to 'go dead', signifying that I should lie down and close my eyes. After a few moments he announced: 'You can come alive now.' But the resurrection was shortlived, for within moments I was commanded to 'go dead' again. Then roles were exchanged, as Richard lay on the floor with closed eyes instructing me to make him come alive. Two children, who lived on a farm, were observed enacting the birth of puppies which they had recently witnessed. The boy, aged five years, said to his five-year-old girl companion: 'You lie down and I'll crawl out of your tummy and be borned.'
Violet Madge[16]

6   When the Questions Come

Man is the creature who asks questions. He is incapable of simply existing. He does not take for granted the world into which he is born. He sets out to investigate what lies behind things, where they come from and what they are for.

In Dutch and English and in German too, interrogatives begin with a W: what, where, who, when, whence, whither, why, which. The underlying form of this sound of astonishment is the Germanic *hwa*, represented by the *wh* of English. And throughout the world, questions are marked by a rising tone in the voice. A question contains more musical note than an answer, and perhaps portrays more emotion by virtue of its uncertainty.

Even before children can really talk, their questions are unmistakable: a pointing finger, an interrogative note in their voices. For they still know nothing and begin their lives looking at others with big questioning eyes. Everything is still puzzling or frightening. What is there behind things, people, events?

'A child who is growing up,' wrote Fons Jansen, 'is an explorer. Very slowly they have woken up out of the darkness of the time when they did not exist. It is in my view no fun to come into existence on this planet. The question, "What is going on round about me?" is a reasonable one in every respect. Education is scarcely more than to give an answer to questions and to introduce the child to the world just as one introduces two strangers to one another. Slowly but surely they gain trust in our world because day in, day out they experience that the world tallies with what we tell them about it.'

The first interrogative word a child uses is 'What?'. 'What is that?' He has noticed that persons and things have a name, that they signify something, and that you can talk about them. He discovers the hidden link between things and words. This is the beginning of his intellectual voyage of discovery. With indefatigable enthusiasm the child takes its first steps on the long journey of human knowledge. It is a long way from the first 'What?' to the whole complicated system of our language and our world of thought.

The second question is, 'Where?' It is not enough just to give a name. It is important whether something is far away or near by, that is, whether you can control it, whether it affects you. This is a major problem of life for the two-year-old child.

A three-year-old child is already a philosopher. He is not satisfied with things as they are or as they are called, and almost drives the grown-ups mad with his continual 'Why?' They have long resigned themselves to things and for them almost everything is taken for granted.

An infant still has almost no past. The great unknown lies before him. This is perhaps why he first asks about the purpose of things and only then about their origin. But when he begins to ask, 'Where does that come from?', he never rests until he has asked the question about the beginning of everything. Anyone who thinks that the last word has been said with a reference to God who is the beginning, has underestimated the questioner. The inevitable question comes, 'And where did God come from then?' or, 'Well, who made God?'

In their questions they are above all seeking contact, in order to discover the world with the aid of older people. It is most unwise of Daddy to give an impatient grunt behind his newspaper when his youngest child asks him something. Why should Mummy be the only person to hold a conversation with the child?

But what their questions really amount to is what it means to be born into this world, whether there is anywhere on this earth where you can be safe, what you can expect later on when you are grown up, and whether there is someone more powerful than all men. They are asking about this contact with the great Unknown.

How often are they fobbed off, silenced with a deliberately false answer, just to get them to keep quiet? When children get no answer to their little questions, how are they later to ask the great questions of life? When their questions are brushed away like tiresome flies, children can easily go round for years believing the most curious ideas or conclusions, which can actually cause them much fear. There are some childhood reminiscences which bear witness to this.

In the first few years of his life, a human child probably asks more questions than he does later. Psychologists and educators have a tendency to deny that these questions and ideas of children have any deep significance or religious meaning. In their view, these questions are simply to be ascribed to a general curiosity.

We, however, would prefer to remain in reverent silence before the unbelievable miracle that a child who has only recently come into the world, cannot stand up on his feet and has learned only a few words, is already beginning to ask about the secrets of existence.

It would be much more obvious that a child should first begin to ask about what is concrete, visible and close by, and near at hand, and then, after many years experience of life – for example in the years of puberty – should go on to ask about origin and purpose, life and death, and the riddle of suffering. But astonishingly, we find that four- and five-year-old children already ask about these things. And this is not simply because they have heard about them, and are imitating adults. They go into the matter and are capable of being a partner in dialogue. They can react to answers, digest them in their own way and come to their own conclusions. It is unbelievable that this should be possible after four years' experience of life!

This enquiry into the mysteries and background of existence between the third and sixth year is perhaps unique. The first investigation of the questions of life, this innocent receptiveness, never returns in the same form. It is the period of questioning. Questioning reappears in the years of puberty, but in a different form. But at that age the same themes return: 'Where do we come from and where are we going, what is the meaning of life, is there a God?'

That the questioning of young children more or less ceases when their first schooling begins may be related to their indoctrination by our materialistic, rationalistic and technical culture, in which calculation takes the primary place and reality is burst asunder into numbers, measurements, weights, laws, rules, verbs, battles and place names.

It is understandable that parents suddenly get the feeling that they must do something about religious education when their three- or four-year-old child produces its questions. God and death seem to be the main themes.

In our collection of children's remarks we list the following themes: The existence of God, his nature and form, his greatness, invisibility, omniscience, eternity and presence, his transcendence and immanence, the creation, how God came into being, man and his purpose, birth and death, God's guidance and providence, human responsibility, suffering, contact with God, his love and salvation, prayer, the Trinity, the birth of Christ, Jesus and what he did, his death and resurrection, his presence here and now, the

end of the world, heaven and hell, good and evil, angels and the
devil, the Bible and the church, ecumenism and mission.

This is enough to fill the programme of studies of a faculty of
theology! All this in the words of children of four or five years?
The obvious conclusion is that these are not really original ideas
of the children's own, but an echo of what is of interest to parents
and teachers. 'Children talk about the very things which I am
interested in,' wrote one mother, 'they feel that it is the real thing.'
Parents undoubtedly influence their children more than they
know, not to speak of school.

When we glance over this 'children's theology' one thing is
abundantly clear. How we have burdened young children, all too
soon, with the problems of our theology! But have they not asked
about them? Yes and no. It may be that children's questions are
connected with what men have thought for centuries and the
answers they have given, with what has been handed down from
generation to generation. They drive their parents willy-nilly to
the uttermost reaches of dogmatic theology!

Protestant parents do not realize that they give their children
answers which can actually be found in the old Roman Catholic
catechism:

 5. Who is God?
    God is our Father who lives in heaven.
10. Has God always existed?
    God has always existed. He is eternal.
11. Can God do everything?
    God can do everything. He is omnipotent.
12. Where is God?
    God is in Heaven, on earth and in every place. He is
    everywhere.
13. Does God know and see everything?
    God knows and sees everything, good, but also evil. He is
    omniscient.

And from the old Protestant Children's Bible there sounds like
a refrain occurring again and again, the question and answer:

14. Is God just?
    God is just: according to merit he rewards good and
    punishes evil.

Out of these answers from the Roman Catholic catechism
tradition there has now developed a standardized creed for
children, passed on almost involuntarily from generation to
generation, a body of doctrine taken for granted in Roman Catho-

lic and Protestant schools alike: God is in heaven, he is everywhere. He can do everything, he sees everything, he hears everything; he rewards the good, protects religious people, and punishes the wicked.

But we do not do justice to 'children's theology' if we characterize it solely as an echo of a catechism which has been inculcated for centuries. The whole pattern of thought of Christian tradition is changed in conversation with children, and is reproduced in children's own words. The formulation is sometimes so original that there is no parallel to it in the whole of church history. From children's reactions we can even tell where a crucial difficulty lies in our theological thinking!

How many parents would find a 'shorter catechism' useful in their conversations with their children, giving questions and answers! But is it right to give children answers 'out of the book'? How much more valuable it is when parents try to find an answer themselves for their child. And sometimes it is not even necessary to answer. The question, 'What do you think about it yourself?' may even receive an answer which we ourselves would never have been able to think up.

It is naturally not good to allow a small child to perceive our own uncertainty too clearly. For he is asking for a firm support in this puzzling world. How much better it is to translate this uncertainty into positive terms and thereby come even closer to the truth: 'We do not know, this is something which is a mystery to human beings.' A child is aware of what a mystery is. It is not a sign of inner poverty to point out that there is a mystery. The deeper our faith becomes, the more we begin to realize the unbelievable mystery. A mother was once talking to her little daughter about God and said: 'But I cannot understand it.' 'Neither can I,' answered the little girl, 'but I understand it better than you because I am nearer it.' This is why children's questions are good for us. It is not only because we are forced to reflect on them and because our faith and our hope are called into question, but also because children can bring us to think new thoughts. They are 'nearer it'. They can sometimes give an answer to our questions themselves. In any case they bring us to what is real and original, to that on which our life is really based.

WHO IS GOD?

He makes people and animals and looks after you when you are dead.
Girl aged five

If God existed, I would know all right.

Daddy, has God got eyes as well? – No. – Is God only as if?
Girl aged four

God is the dearest of all, but I don't know him.

God was first a little heart. He loved people so much that he grew up and then he was God.

WHERE IS GOD?

God is everywhere. – Everywhere, I don't know where that is, I can't find it.
Boy aged four

God used to live a long way away in heaven above the stars. So one fine evening I went up and stood on the hedge to see if I could discover God amongst all the stars.
Girl aged six

THE ALMIGHTY

Why, if God can do everything, can't he just let it rain on the trees and the flowers and not where I'm cycling on my tricycle?
Boy aged four

THE OMNISCIENT

Why do you tell God that you are ill? Doesn't he know that already? Doesn't he know everything?

GOD'S PROVIDENCE

When you get lost, God knows the way back, doesn't he? Then he lets you think of the right way, doesn't he, Mummy?

I think God's unfair. He lets people die, but he stays alive himself.
Boy aged seven

HUMAN RESPONSIBILITY

At the death of Martin Luther King. Has God got to do everything himself now?

COMMUNION WITH GOD

A summer evening. She grew quieter and quieter, and I thought she was tired from cycling. Mummy, isn't it nice, just as if you could hear God speaking.
Girl aged six

PRAYER

Together your hands.
Three-year-old

Can I go and pray in the church? I pray for God to make people better first and then send the baby Jesus again.
Girl aged four

JESUS CHRIST

Why do we celebrate Christmas? – Jesus was born then. Where? – *Suddenly he knew the answer:* In a book.

At Christmas we all go to the new earth.
Girl aged six

If God will have me, then I will crawl quickly behind Jesus.

Jesus, poor man, did they kill him? They can't have done!
Girl aged five

Easter. A brighter dawn is breaking. – I haven't noticed!

THE TRINITY

There is only one God and the Lord Jesus is in God's heart.
Boy aged four

Dost thou know the Holy Ghost? – O yes, he's disguised as a dove, isn't he?
Boy aged five

THE CREATION

Mummy, there is something I have to talk to you about. Why did God create the world? I know, first there was nothing, then everything was white, oh no, when there is nothing everything is black, and then God was so lonely, that he thought, 'I shall make a world'.

Why doesn't God make more trees? Because God is much too tired, and if there are too many trees. God can't find the people in the wood.

When God existed, before the world was made, where did he go?
Six-year-old

BIRTH

Then I didn't exist, then I was still dead, and then I started to live, and after I will die again.
Boy aged five

DEATH

Everybody dies in the end. Only God is left. He began by himself as well.
Boy aged five

When you are dead, have you nothing left? – No, you've nothing left. – But you must keep your mouth and your ears, because you have to be able to hear what God says and answer him, don't you?
Boy aged four

Why do we go to heaven? It's because God is lonely, isn't it?
Girl aged nine

GOOD AND EVIL

The Lord says to you, if you are naughty: you must be good. –
I'm good by myself.

Listen, Mummy, as soon as I'm good again, that's when I can say
I am sorry.
Four-year-old

Why aren't we committing original sin if we eat an apple?
Four-year-old

Loving yourself is all you have to do, because if you love yourself
completely you wouldn't have any faults.
Boy aged ten

THE BIBLE

I don't know what the Bible means to me.
Boy aged seven

A pity for Adam that he was never a boy!

THE CHURCH AND SACRAMENTS

What is baptism? – You get a good heart in your tummy.

Why can't we run in church, can't we play there?
Boy aged four

How can all of Jesus get into that piece of bread?

RELIGIOUS INSTRUCTION

What happens in a church school? Do they teach you: one
shepherd plus one shepherd equals two shepherds?
Girl aged eight

ECUMENISM

What she calls Almighty God and she calls Lord Jesus and I call God is all the same.
Conversation between four-year-olds, Catholic, Reformed and Remonstrant

Are the kids at the state school our neighbours as well?
Boy aged ten

MISSION

Grandpa, why doesn't everybody tell everybody else about God and the Lord Jesus?
Boy aged seven

THE LAST THINGS

If an atom bomb destroyed the world, God would make a new world, he knows what it's got to be like.
Boy aged six

Yes, he's coming again to make all things new, but by then I shall be dead.
Girl aged eight

Why do you keep peering out? – To see if Jesus is coming. He's probably coming soon.
Boy aged eight

THINKING BEGINS WITH QUESTIONS

Because they are surprised, people begin to reflect. They have been surprised at the incomprehensible things about everyday life and are faced step by step with ever greater questions.
Aristotle

Perhaps the most obvious way in which young children seek understanding is through the questions which they ask adults and other children. These make clear children's concern with everyday situations regarding themselves, other people, and things in their immediate environment.

Although verbal questions are certainly one way in which children reach out for understanding, such enquiries inevitably spring from the child's predominating mode of discovery through action. This may be seen in simple speculative behaviour involving sensory experience and physical movement in which, though questions may not be voiced, they are implicit.
Violet Madge[1]

The time-question 'when', the causal question 'why' ... are, for the main part, not the expression of unmixed desire for knowledge on the child's part, but are most intimately connected with his small ego and its practical needs; for this reason the first 'why' meets the parents' ears in the annoyed expression, 'Why not, then?', if some wish of the child's is forbidden or withheld. And 'When?' the child asks to find out when the earnestly desired meal-time is to come at last.
W. Stern[2]

A child's questions signify a contact with the remarkable, not wholly comprehensible and therefore ultimately inaccessible world of adults.
J. H. van den Berg

CONTACT AND SECURITY

Primarily, the child asks. He is readily satisfied with an answer.

The pattern of a child's life is characterized amongst other things by the basic fact that the child can live only in a world which is safe. Therefore he wants to know a lot, because he hopes ultimately to obtain certainty and therefore security.

The pattern of a child's life is ultimately irreconcilable with a picture of the world which in the end seems meaningless and dangerous.
M. J. Langeveld

Questions signify a need for information, but at the same time they have an emotional function: to call on adults for attention and to obtain assurance about a world which spreads out before his eyes and which every day presents him with the unexpected. What the child is looking for is a link between what he is asking and what concerns his desires and fears. His curiosity is real and justified. He is eager to know who he is and where he comes from. Unhealthy curiosity is never caused by a bold certainty, but by

fearful ignorance.
P. Osterrieth

Children ask questions in order to make contact and look for
contact in order to ask questions. To refuse a child an answer
is to refuse a dialogue and to disappoint the child in his confident approach to you. We can never know how much valuable
activity is being resisted, how much hope and courage is being
crushed.

In a world which is a constant source of surprise the mother
holds a central position. It is she who kindles a questioning
attitude. From this starting point the child turns hesitantly and
cautiously towards the world, asking his mother continual
questions.

At this stage of his development it must have considerable
consequences for the child whether he is left alone with his
questions or whether there is a partner, who is interested in them
and willingly answers his questions and gives him, in a world
which is still too large for him to take in, certainty, clarity and
security.
Oskar Rieder

For a child, an answer to his questions is a means of defining
his place in a world which surprises him. He is not interested in
a rational answer, but in a firm footing in reality. His whole self
is affected by the question and the answer. And therefore, too, he
does not always need a logical answer, but a reassuring answer.
Ultimately the question behind all other questions asked by
young children is: 'What does the world mean for me?'
N. Snijders-Oomen

DISCOVERING ONESELF

Every object and every thing becomes a reality for the child
through the word. Before the word it did not yet exist for the
child, although it was able to perceive it.
Friedrich Fröbel

The most valuable work of infant teachers is to stimulate them to
inquire, explore and examine all aspects of the world about which
they are so naturally curious.
Ronald Goldman[3]

Learning can be said to consist of learning to ask questions, which embrace increasingly wider areas of life and finally the whole of life. A child does not expect us to know everything. He does expect us to be genuine. He himself likes to make discoveries. We must learn to listen to what the child himself has to say.
J. van Haaren

DO THE GROWN-UPS KNOW EVERYTHING?

We are walking encyclopedias.
There are a great many things which we do not understand, and neither do children. They really feel that we possess the last word. They make the important discovery that adults do not know everything either.
Fons Jansen

In the many questions that children ask at this age, it is necessary, we believe, to recognize in addition to the 'desire to know', the 'desire to know if the grown-ups know'.
Pierre Bovet[4]

He thought that when people grow up, they are not surprised by anything, and that when they are strong they know everything; and he would try to be grown up himself, and hide his curiosity, and appear to be indifferent.
Romain Rolland[5]

NOT GIVING A CHILD MORE THAN HE CAN DIGEST

An answer which he does not understand or misunderstands is as little use to a child as a lie or a reply that shows him up. A child may be too small for your words – in which case you have to look for simpler words or clearer parallels – but he is not too small for the truth that he is asking about.
Rogier van Aerde

Although a rational explanation signifies order and therefore security, the same explanation can arouse fear, because it brings the child face to face with facts which he yet cannot fit into his present pattern of life. From the point of view of religious education it is in no way a misfortune that everything cannot be explained with absolute logic to a child.
M. J. Langeveld

THE GREAT QUESTIONS OF FAITH

Children's questions are the great questions of faith. In part this
is due to the fact that our language introduces the child to things
which the thought of centuries suddenly lays before him in a
single word.
M. J. Langeveld

Children ask about God. They ask with awkward words which
sometimes disturb and sometimes frighten us, and which to adult
ears sound sometimes deeply reverent, sometimes merely curious
and sometimes utterly profane. Children ask about God. They
ask with their heart, their eyes, with their whole being. They
ask questions without words or concealed in words which
apparently refer to quite different things.
H. J. W. Modderman

7 Who is God?

There is a firmly rooted view about children's conception of God. A child is supposed to think of God as an old man with a beard, sitting on a throne above the clouds. It may be added that this image of God is no longer tenable by the parent and that often faith in God disappears as a result.

But we must ask whether this is really true. It has become a kind of dogma about the faith of children. Does a child think of God as he is represented in old churches? Or was it adults themselves who have passed on this image of God from generation to generation, even if it was only by the distribution of religious pictures?

What is the source of this concept of God?

It is reminiscent of the prophet Daniel (7.9-14): 'As I looked, thrones were placed and one that was ancient of days took his seat; his raiment was white as snow, and the hair of his head like pure wool; his throne was fiery flames, its wheels were burning fire ... a thousand thousands served him.'

By way of Byzantine art this description of God penetrated the Christian church, but not until a thousand years later. Before that it was in fact a dreadful thing to portray God. People drew only a hand sticking out of a cloud, or words of God coming out of a shining cloud.

This dread can be derived from the second of the ten commandments in Exodus 20.4, 5: You shall not make for yourself a graven image, or any likeness of anything that is in heaven above, or is in the earth beneath, or that is in the water under the earth; you shall not bow down to them or serve them.' But this commandment does not refer so much to God as to false gods. It is a basic rejection of nature religion, of superstition, of the magical control of natural forces, which were brought close in the form of images. On the other hand, one of the most typical characteristics of the Old Testament is in the fact that with great freedom it speaks of God in images and in human terms. It gives throughout the appearance of 'anthropomorphism' – the representation of God in human form – and presents a contrast

with the typical Jewish reluctance even to speak the name of
Yahweh.

The confessor of Henry V, Thomas Nettex of Walden, said:
'What men permit themselves in speaking need not be forbidden
to the painter's brush.'

Towards the end of the Middle Ages the number of portrayals
of God increased. He was first pictured as a heavenly pope with
a tiara or as an emperor with the orb in his hand. Then, under
the influence of the Renaissance, this developed into a representation of a Christian Jupiter.

This may have been an attempt to express the majesty of the
All Highest, but it gradually came to be the respresentation given
to children.

The intention was clearly to come closer to children by making
this portrayal of God more childish. In pictures for children, even
in modern children's Bibles, God is no longer distinguishable
from human beings. The only difference is that the little human
figure is drawn in a cloud.

And now for children themselves. At a first hearing, we are
inclined to dismiss their statements about God with a smile. They
are so very childish! What misunderstanding and lack of comprehension! How naïve, banal and superficial! Are not the people
right who say, 'You must not talk too soon to children about
God. They are not yet ready for it. You cannot give them any
real understanding of such an exalted, holy being'?

But it is difficult to keep the name of God from them for long.
Whether we will or not, it is bound to be mentioned some time.
The word itself is still used in all kinds of arbitrary ways, and a
child will ask, 'Who is that?' This is the start. It begins with
something passed on by the next-door-neighbour's daughter or at
school. And whenever God represents a living reality for the
parents, the child is all the more fascinated by this Unknown:
'Who is he?' However dechristianized the society we live in, the
name of God is just as intensely topical. Because God cannot be
seen, felt or heard, one might think it obvious that after his first
request for information, a child would show no further interest.
But the reverse seems to be true. Just because of God's invisibility and mysterious presence, the child is fascinated by him. He
goes on asking, and without his parents having anticipated or
wished it, they find themselves once again treading the hard path
of theology.

In the meantime, the child has appropriated the strange word
'God' and is preoccupied with it. He thinks further about it, and

portrays him mentally. He asks more questions, but above all he is taken up with the idea; perhaps as with a strange fairy tale, but not a fairy tale of the 'once upon a time' kind, because he tries to locate God in his own world, 'at the bottom of the garden', or as the shining weathercock on the church roof. He has seen him really and truly, upstairs in an attic or in front of a church. Isn't the church his house? There is one thing that a child has obviously understood: 'He really exists.'

Certain experiences or emotions recall the word 'God' to him. It is remarkable, for example, that a child will make a connection between the mysterious mist in a wood and God: I ran through God. The mysterious stillness of a wood in the mist, in which the trees are like dim, almost unreal spirits; this is different from ordinary, clear concrete reality: it is as though we were outside the ordinary world. All this can make a child say, 'I ran through God.'

This is a long way from the old man with a beard, although it is not yet very close to 'God our Father'. Yet there is already a realization of God here: he is strange, different, mysterious and not concrete in the ordinary sense.

Another child thinks that God comes near to him in the shining white cloud, which seems to float up to the window against a leaden black background. Here again we have the mysterious, strange, startling, holy, white apparition, seen against the dull mass of clouds which seem to threaten the earth.

Thus it is not always true that children conceive of God as a human being. The idea of God also occurs as a mysterious natural phenomenon or a mysterious word, a name out of the distance.

Mostly, however, a child will speak of God as a human being. What else could he be expected to do within the Christian tradition, which believes that God does not come to us in fire, in the wind, nor even in the stillness, but in a human being, in Christ?

A child sees God as a human being. He cannot yet connect the experience of something different, strange and mysterious in the wood with the divine being who knows us, and with whom we can speak. The conception is still a very human one, but very moving, when a child asks whether God ever hurts himself or whether he is tired of caring for the world. This is not a God who sits exalted and untroubled in heaven; how human the way in which he suffers with men!

Is the thinking of children in this respect still 'primitive and anthropomorphic', and still far removed from true theology? Will the child eventually have to reject this image in order to come to religious faith?

We are somewhat ashamed of this childlike and all too human image of God. And yet we too, in our faith, our prayer and our hymns, seek human contact with God in human images. Why are we frightened to use the very symbols of humanity for contact with the greatest Mystery, so incomprehensible and exalted above all things, to such an extent that many people even give up thinking and speaking about him? Perhaps this happens because we have a feeling of inferiority about what is human. And therefore we consider it wrong to refer to God with images drawn from this questionable reality. A human being is good but evil as well, limited and fallible, and, in his tiny form, so obviously a creature of this earth.

Where did we get the wicked audacity to think of God according to our own image and likeness? This has actually been called a projection on to the great Unknown, and God the Father has been described as a wish fulfilment dream, an infantile relic of the world of childish emotion. Thus there are people who prefer to speak of 'the ground of our being' or 'Life'. These, too, are images, but chosen from a pre-human or sub-human reality. In our world, the impersonal is not higher than the personal. The evolution of the earth and of history has taught us otherwise. The ground on which we walk does not know us. The wind which rustles through the trees cannot speak to us. The life force which makes plants grow does not show us what to do. As far as our experience goes, the image of the human and personal is more living and more full of meaning than that of matter, energy or vital force.

It could well be that human images show more of the purpose of creation and the nature of God than we realize.

In his book *Exploration into God* Bishop Robinson has given a free translation of the beginning of the Gospel of John:

> The clue to the universe as personal was present from the beginning ... It is that light which illumines the darkness of the sub-personal creation ... And this divine personal principle found embodiment in a man and took habitation in our midst ... The ultimate reality of God no one has ever seen. But the one who has lived closest to it, in the unique relationship of son to father, has laid it bare.[1]

Why does the Bible speak in such human images about God? It must be due to the experience of his living reality. It is not an abstract idea of God, not a dogmatic construction, but a demonstration of the living God in the concern and the life which he shares with history and with mankind. It shows not a distant and inaccessible mystery, but God who comes close.

No other images can be found for language which must speak 'as though seeing the invisible'. In the Old Testament in particular, this language may well strike us as childish and primitive, but God is at least alive and concerned for us. He is not dead, not a shadow, not a projection of humanity, but he who overwhelms men with his love and righteousness. He is the First; not man, who thinks himself a god.

And only in human images can this living God become familiar to us, and be the God who calls us and gives us grace. The only relationship we can have with God is a human relationship.

If God is God, he must be infinitely more than man, and that means more living, more personal, more active and the source of all love.

When children ask, 'Who is God?', the answer they usually receive is taken from the old catechism: 'God is our Father, who lives in Heaven.'

It is remarkable that the creation is often referred to: 'He created the whole world', while there is seldom or never a reference to the essence of Christian faith. For Christians, the most living and meaningful answer to the question, 'Who is God?' is to be found in the man Jesus of Nazareth. It is he who has convinced us of the living God, who has brought us into contact with the heart of the universe, with the ground of our being, the meaning of our life, and has called him 'Our Father'. This is a very intimate and personal image.

And how naturally Jesus himself used human images when he spoke in parables to convince us of this God: 'But when he was yet at a distance, his father saw him and had compassion, and ran and embraced him and kissed him' (Luke 15.20).

One cannot be more human than that.

In modern theology we are asked to give our attention to Jesus, but to be silent about God. But in fact any one who concentrates in all seriousness on Jesus and lets the words and actions of Jesus sink in upon himself, can surely not be silent about God as the great Unknown or as an inaccessible mystery. Jesus was not only 'the man for others', but asserted above all the authority, love and glory of the living God. Not only in his words, but above all in the way in which he gave himself for men in life and death, he showed that in fact God is with us, and shares our humanity and that this is his nature.

But it is also made terribly clear that God is infinitely more than, and different from, our common humanity!

And when people nowadays assert so loudly that 'the old God' of the Christians is dead, that 'centuries-old images of God have disappeared' and that most people 'can no longer make anything of this God', which God do they mean? Not the living God of Jesus. Are not such claims really a rebellious reaction against what has been passed on to children from generation to generation? This theological rebellion is like a crisis of adolescence, a resistance to one's own youth.

'The old man on the throne', who 'sees everything' and 'can do everything', who 'rewards the good and punishes the wicked' and 'changes the fortunes of the devout when they pray to him for it', is in fact the God who has been portrayed to children!

When your child asks you, 'Who is God?', what can you reply? How can we transform the child's concern that God should be visible and take shape, in the direction of what really matters: that he is our God, and that we are his and can trust him to the uttermost degree?

'Who is God?' None of us has ever seen God, but we believe in him. How else could we live? How could the earth, the sun and the stars have come to exist? Could he who invented love not care himself for everything he has created?

Jesus assures us how much God cares for us; much more than a father and a mother. The people who knew him said, 'How can we come to understand who God is? We can belong to him as his children, however far away we have gone or however much wrong we have done. There is no end to God's love.' And Jesus said. 'Call him "Our Father".'

We human beings cannot see God, and to us he remains the greatest mystery. But we can believe in him all the same, even though we do not see him. And Jesus helps us to go on trusting in him, even when bad things happen.

IS THERE A GOD?

Of course there is a God, because he's got a name.

What does God mean? Why is God called God? Nobody knows what he is really called.
Boy aged five

Mum, does God really exist? – Yes, of course. – Oh, I thought that was just a story.
Boy aged five

A boy rang up his uncle: Can you tell me who God is? They don't know here at home.
Boy aged five

Look, you know who God is, because you talk to him.
Boy aged six

'I HAVE SEEN GOD'

I have seen God. It's a lady.
Boy aged three

You can't see God. He is everywhere. He's with you as well.
His brother aged four

When she had said grace, Mother had prayed that God would make Daddy better again and bring him home in the car. Has God got a car as well? – No, but Mr M. has. *When the car stopped outside the house, there was someone else in it as well. Beaming, she shouted,* I've seen God, he was sitting next to Mr M.
Girl aged three

You feel God in your heart. *Looking at the heart of a dead chicken. he said,* Is that God then?
Boy aged four

In Indonesia the caretaker was sitting in front of the church. 'the house of God'. – Is that God?
Boy aged four

A man with a beard was walking along the street. Mummy, is that God? – No. *A young man with a beard got on to the bus.* Is that God then? – No! – Oh well, it must be Joseph.
Girl aged five

A boy has Catholic friends. Now I know what God looks like, *he says, standing with his hand raised to give a blessing.*
Boy aged five

The teacher prayed that our Lord would go with us on the school trip. When they had returned: I didn't see Jesus anywhere, he must have been sitting upstairs in the tram.
Boy aged six

A little girl repeatedly drew a king on his throne: God. This figure also appeared in the flower garden she drew. Who is that? – God, but he's not like that really. He's much nicer, you can't really draw him, but I do it because he's really there.
Girl aged six

IS GOD A MAN?

What sort of person is God? – He isn't a person. – What sort of person is he, though? – He's in the clouds. Well, is he in an aeroplane?
Boy aged four

Is God a man? – No. – Then did God become a man and then become God?
Boy aged four

You mustn't say 'God', that's a naughty word. *Later,* I know that God must be a naughty old man.
Boy aged five

What does God look like? – We don't know. – What sort of clothes does he have on? – We don't know. – But the man in the shop, who sold him the clothes, he knows, doesn't he?
Boy aged six

What does our Lord look like? – I don't know, you can't see him. – Is he like a man? – I don't know. – Is he like an animal? Well, I think he's like a man.
Boy aged six

Is God a boy or a girl? – No. – Then he's something in between.
Girl aged six

Is God a girl? No, he can't be, can he, but a sort of father, not like Daddy, only the angels must be girls. because they are very pretty.
Boy aged six

Is God a man or a woman or both?
Boy aged eight

A good man, a person like us, but much more handsome, I can't imagine him very well. Like a person, but I know that he exists.
Boy aged eight

I used to think of a bad man with a whip.
Boy aged eleven

God is a person that we can't see.
Eleven-year-old

Grandma, do you believe that there is a man sitting above the clouds, called God? – Yes. – How can that be? – He's not a man. – What is he then? – The great, holy and almighty God, that we know so little about, and we won't know until later. – But you are seventy-two, do you still not know? – No. – I don't understand any of this.
Boy aged eleven

Does pussy think that God looks like a pussy?

THE HUMANITY OF GOD

Mummy, I've drawn God and he's crying. – Why? – He hasn't got a father or a mother and no children, only a man who's dead. And he would love a father and mother and children. But the real God never cries, does he, because it wouldn't do for God to cry. God is nice. It is very sad if God dies. – But surely God can't die? – No, he can't die, because he's in heaven.
Girl aged three

Is God ever ill?
Girl aged four

A little boy burnt himself: Grandma, does God ever hurt himself? Not even if he falls out of a big tree? Not even if he pinches himself hard?
Boy aged four

I think that God must go on a holiday sometime, he needs it.
Four-year-old

Does God live in heaven? How does he eat and sleep?
Girl aged five

Does God ever go to sleep? Does God ever cough?
Girl aged five

God never has to sleep, it's always morning in heaven. When we
sleep, we make the morning. God makes the morning.
Girl aged five

Hasn't God got a wife? Oh no, he wouldn't have much use for
one, because he hasn't got a body.
Boy aged seven

God is even older than Santa Claus. That's why he never comes
to people. He's too old for that. He can't walk any more. Did you
know that, Mummy? – How do you know that? – By myself, of
course, it's got to be like that, hasn't it? He is so terribly old!
But he never dies. That's fine. – How do you know that? – By
myself, of course, it's got to be like that, hasn't it? If God died,
the whole world would be finished. So that can't happen. So he
doesn't die, but he's sometimes tired, you see. I think that's very
sad.
Girl aged nine

IF I COULD BE GOD

A little girl wanted to play at God: You can't. God is different
from people. – But if I'm very good to B. can I then?
Girl aged four

I wish I could be God for once, then I could pinch out of all the
sugar bowls.
Boy aged six

God is infinitely good, infinitely wise, almighty and present
everywhere. – Gosh, I wish I could be God.

Conversation at table: I should like to be God. – Listen, my girl,
you wouldn't be any good at it at all, you haven't any idea about
God.

NOT LIKE A HUMAN BEING

A little girl looks at the moon while she is going to bed: Look, Mummy, there's God.
Girl aged three

Like a cloud. Like a mist.

I think that God is like a cloud with an eye and a mouth.

God is like a cloud, but he can speak.

I think that God is a coloured cloud.

God is a big cloud, so that you can't see whether he is there or not.
Four-year-old

Mummy, look a minute, God is coming into my bedroom! *He points to a little white cloud, standing out against the heavier dark clouds, which seems to be moving towards his window.*
Boy aged four

Mist in the wood: I ran through God.
Boy aged five

God is an egg. Everybody eats from it and it never runs out.
Boy aged five

Is God not a man? So can you not see him? Then he is a pane of glass.
Boy aged five

Is God really a bird?
Girl aged five

THE GREATNESS OF GOD

The bridge over the Waal was being opened. In the trolley bus we were talking about it. Our Lord is big, isn't he? – Yes, our Lord is very big. – Bigger than our house? – Yes, much bigger than our house. – But not bigger than the Waal bridge, is he,

Mummy? – Yes, bigger than the Waal bridge and bigger than the sky that hangs above it, bigger than the air and bigger than everything that you can think.
Boy aged three

Is God as big as the room? Can God see Austria and America at the same time? God must have big eyes, mustn't he? Can God hear you if you are right under the ground, right down under the ground? What big ears God must have and big eardrums and really great big thick legs.
Girl aged five

I don't know how big God is, as big as the whole air. – Look kid, that isn't God, that's his power.
Girls seven- and eight-years-old

Is God really big? – How many people on top of each other is God?
Girl aged eight

I thought that God was a great giant, twice as big as the whole world.

If God is a giant, a man is a grain of sand, isn't he?
Girl aged nine

I thought, God is so big, and I'm just a little tiny baby, but he counts me in as well.
Girl aged ten

THE ETERNAL

God can't die, can he, Mummy? Where is he? – You can't see him, but I know that he exists and looks after us. – But don't you look after us? – But someone has to look after me and grandma and everybody. – Does he build houses for you? – No, but he makes sure that we can live and die and lots more. – Why have we got to die?
Boy aged five

If war comes, you can't kill God, can you?
Boy aged five

The king of all men is born. – Yes, that is God. – Where is he? – Above in the sky and if you shoot God dead, he usually still goes on walking.

But he doesn't die. If God died, that would be the end of the whole world.
Girl aged nine

What do you think would be the worst thing that could happen? – For God to die.
Girl aged ten

Do you know why God doesn't die? Because what God does with people when they are old, people can't do with God, and so God always goes on living.
Boy aged seven

CHILDREN'S DOUBTS

But God doesn't really exist, because you can't see him.
Girl aged five

I can't believe that Santa Claus and God really exist. But you sometimes see Santa and then you recognize him, but you never see God and I can't believe that he is in the sky. Nor can you, can you, Mummy, it's the same with everybody, isn't it?
Girl aged five

What if it isn't true about heaven? – I sometimes think that, there are lots of people who think it isn't true. – Sometimes I think that the trees themselves are God.
Girl aged six

Look, Mummy, now you've told me Santa Claus doesn't exist. Will you tell me sometime soon that God doesn't exist?
Six-year-old

I don't believe in God. They only make those stories up to believe in. Perhaps in Jesus. – Who made you then? – Jesus. No, you are born by yourself.
Boy aged seven

God made us, but who actually made God? I can't understand

that and if I can't understand it, I can't believe it either. Will I
be able to make my first communion?
Girl aged seven

*One evening a little girl wanted to read Donald Duck instead of
saying her prayers.* I've no idea, I really don't believe it, I don't
believe it, how can it be like that: living in your heart. God isn't
a little dwarf, is he? God is big. Who is God then? What is heaven,
there isn't a house there, but it's close by. But God is much
higher ... I don't want to believe, I believe – *she burst into tears.*
Girl aged nine

God never answers when you ask him something. I can't see anything of him at all. When was God born? There's lots I can't
believe. – Believe it because Mummy does. – Not on your life!
Girl aged nine

I really don't think you can tell that God exists. You don't feel
that God exists. Your father seems to be stronger than him. I
really think that when you go to communion, you don't feel that
he is with you. People have got used to it. My mother says, 'If
God does not exist, we wouldn't be alive.'
Girl aged nine

How do you know that God exists? How can God hear you talking, and why does he not speak any more? How can God live in
heaven?
Boy aged eleven

Sometimes when I lie in bed I think that God really doesn't
exist because why had my father to go away so soon and then I
really don't understand it any more and then I usually have to
bite my lip so as not to cry.
Girl aged eleven

You don't see anything of God. He might just as well not exist.
Girl aged twelve

A QUESTION AT SCHOOL: 'HOW DO YOU THINK OF GOD?'

God looks almost like a man but a man looks a bit different from
God. And God has different clothes on and no stockings. God

does have shoes on and a very long robe.

God looks the same as us, but Jesus doesn't have such good shoes there aren't any shoemakers.

Poor God, he is divided into three persons, the father the son and the holy spirit.

God looks quite handsome God made people come on to the earth.

When we make the sign of the cross then we hear clearly what God looks like.

God looks about the same as a person, when he was crucified he felt pain just the same as a person, because Christ could feel as well.

He is the father of all of us of all the world and he is powerful too. God is the almightiest in the whole world and God has a nose and two arms and two eyes and a mouth and two arms and a body and two legs and a head.

I have never seen God but one day I will go to him and that will be nice when I go to God it will be nice.

Third class, Roman Catholic primary school

God is a man. – I think that the Lord is an ordinary man, who wears a white robe. – Ordinary. – An ordinary man not big not little but very powerful. – Just like Jesus looks. – A young man. – God is young. – A young man with a cloak I can make a drawing of him. – Like a young man with a beard and Jesus at his right hand with angels all around him. – A fairly old man. – God is old and invisible. – God is invisible and God is a flame of fire. – With a crown on and a cloak and a sceptre in his hand. – Like a strong powerful man who understands a lot and who is somebody, a glory for people, for example we are his marionettes and he is the man who moves us. – I have no idea.

Sixth class, Protestant school

When was God born? – Pastor, is God invisible? – Can God change himself into a man? – What sort of person is God? – How did God come to the world? – Do they really know that God exists? – Does God know what we are thinking as well? – How did they get the name of God? – Who is God's king? – Is the devil under God as well? – Why did God plant the tree? – Pastor, does God decide the shape he's in? – Is God married, because he has Jesus as well? – Does God rule over the whole universe as well? – Does God ever die? – Pastor, does God know what I think? – What does God look like?

Pupils' questions

The Lord God sits on a golden throne. He has a golden cloak, he has a long beard, he is great, holy, beautiful and strong. He has many angels round about him.
First class

I think of God as a big man who sees that everything is in order. But when he comes down to earth, he makes himself invisible.
Seventh class

It seems to me that the way he is drawn on a throne and with a great cloak with a book bound in gold is wrong. For me God is without dimensions.
Ninth class, recorded by A. Stückelberger

God has a beard and his son is a very good healer and God is braver as a lion and someone is Gods mother.
God wears white clothes God is the Holy Ghost God is Love God likes me Gods star is the biggest star every Christmas is Gods Birthday he is more than 1,000 years old.
God is a very nice man he had a very good mind to he maid flowers and the sky and us he was nice when he was little to and he was nice to little children becuse he read them lots of stories all out of his own miand and he is very chental to older peapol and maid the sun to he is a very Good man.
Recorded by Violet Madge[2]

THE IMAGE OF GOD IN CHILDHOOD REMEMBERED

Now Anselm ... when he was a small boy lent a ready ear to his mother's conversation, so far as his age allowed. And hearing that there is one God in heaven who rules all things and comprehends all things, he – being a boy bred among mountains – imagined that heaven rested on the mountains, that the court of God was there, and that the approach to it was through the mountains. When he had turned this over often in his mind, it happened one night that he saw a vision, in which he was bidden to climb to the top of the mountain and hasten to the court of the great king, God. But then, before he began to climb, he saw in the plain through which he was approaching the foot of the mountain, women – serfs of the king – who were reaping the corn, but doing so carelessly and idly. The boy was grieved and indignant at their laziness, and resolved to accuse them before their lord the king. Then he climbed the mountain and came to the royal

court, where he found God alone with his steward. For, as he imagined, since it was autumn he had sent his household to collect the harvest. The boy entered and was summoned by the Lord. He approached and sat at his feet. The Lord asked him in a pleasant and friendly way who he was, where he came from, and what he wanted. He replied to the question as best he could. Then, at God's command, the whitest of bread was brought him by the steward, and he refreshed himself with it in God's presence. The next day therefore, when he recalled to his mind's eye all that he had seen, like a simple and innocent boy he believed that he had been in heaven and that he had been fed with the bread of God, and he asserted as much to others in public.
Eadmer[3]

He learnt his first prayer in his father's workplace. 'Fear God, dear child, God the Lord knows and sees all things. Amen.' In these words his father spoke the prayer to him. Without understanding, the child repeated and learnt them. They became a game to him, it was like walking over a plank bridge across a stream, when five steps bring you to the other side. The unfamiliar High German of the words made them all the more strange. Between the obscure parts, 'Fear God, God the Lord', came the familiar 'dear child' and 'sees and knows', benevolent, a token of affection. The child experienced 'knows' as light and clear, while 'sees' signified something dark. 'All things' (*alle Dingen*) reminded him of Tuesday (*Dienstag*), and the 'Amen' was a cry of joy on arriving at the other side after a dangerous crossing.

The name of God was not much mentioned in his parents' house, more from reverence than from indifference. The first encounter with the name of God in a curse faded from his mind. But the call of the divine took the form in the child of the experience of mystery, at various levels. It appeared first in the name of the neighbouring village of Westedt. The sound of the word affected the child as if he was being called by it, and therefore one day he asked for his boots: he had to go to Westedt. His mother laughed at him. 'The outright refusal of my mother and her laughter, by which she certainly meant no harm, taught me very early that it is better to conceal the call of mystery from other people.' Then he set off one day in his wooden clogs, but was caught by his grandmother, and once again the grown-ups laughed because he wanted to go to Westedt.

This desire disappeared when he discovered mystery in the immediate neighbourhood. He climbed for the first time over a wall which separated his father's piece of ground from their neighbour's. He had expected to find there the end, the abyss, and to his surprise a world lay open before him. At the edge of the new horizon he was struck by a tree with a remarkable shape, which now became the place where the mysterious was located.

The boy called it 'lion'. Strangeness, fear and attraction radiated simultaneously from the lion. It had to be overcome. The whole of the mystery was concentrated in the lion, grew dark in it, was established in it, and gazed vigilantly from it over the world.
K. P. Moritz

The thing I found most remarkable was God the Father hovering above the globe, not only because it was enviable to be able to hover like that; but I also did my best to recall his face exactly, so that I would know what he looked like when I was saying my prayers.
Wilhelm von Kügelchen

By my tenth year I had still heard nothing of God. When I could no longer ascribe something to my father, I ascribed it to the sun. For me the sun was more than all human beings put together, it was God for me, although I did not know the word 'God'. Everything that happened at night also came from the sun, as the result of the fact that it existed during the day. My father once found me in the garden, kneeling before the rising sun. What did he do? One clear night he explained that all the stars were suns, and even greater than my sun. To me, this was like a death blow. I no longer knew where to direct my worship. I could have shared it out amongst all these suns, but this did not respond to my need: for a long time I had devoted the whole of my worship to a single sun, and I had lost a joy.

My father told me more about astronomy. The marvellous link between the infinite universe and the unity made a profound impression upon me. A question occurred to me: 'Father, I drew the sun down to my eyes; and was joined with it and believed that from it we had life, joy and blessing, myself and all things. Tell me which of all these suns ...' Then my father interrupted me, taught me about the sun of all suns, the original sun, the invisible and unique, the eternal cause of the union between all suns, who himself cannot be in only one of the suns. As soon as he finished, I rushed to embrace him. From that moment I was once again as happy as I had been, and happier than ever.
C. F. Sintenis

I was just five years old when I ran away from my friends and the children of my own age to go into the wood, to wander through the open fields, to sit on the little hills in the fields, where I spent hours brooding over the question: Is there a God? Has God a wife, children? What does he eat, what does he drink, where does he come from? Who are his parents? Why is he God, he and not someone else? Why am I not God? What am I, why do I walk, shake my head, talk, eat, drink, sit, sleep, while the trees, plants and flowers cannot do so?

The phenomenon which for a long time made a profound impression upon me was the sun and the stars at night. I could simply not understand how they moved. There were days when I was so fascinated by the sun that when I went to sleep I thought: I will get up early in the morning, and somehow or other I must go where it comes from. I would only have to take a piece of bread with me, and Mamma would not have to see me.

I was no less interested in the stars. I did not understand why they only shone at night. What are they? Do they live like people or are they lights set in the sky? I shall never forget the feeling of ecstasy and joy whenever I looked at the sun and the milky way.

Archimandrite Spiridou

As the far-off, snowy mountains were visible to me now veiled in mist, now brighter, now darker, now white, now red, I naturally thought of them as living things, marvellous and mighty, like the clouds, and I would bestow the name 'cloud' and 'mountain' upon other things as well, if they inspired me with awe and curiosity. Thus I called the first female figure which pleased me, a girl living near us, 'the white cloud' because of the impression she made on me, wearing a white dress. With more justification, I preferred to call a long, high church roof that towered, gigantic, above all the housetops, 'the mountain'. Its vast surface, sloping towards the west, was to my eyes an immeasurably large tract, on which my eyes rested with ever fresh delight whenever the last rays of the sun illuminated it, and for me this slanting plain, glowing red above the dark town, was in very truth what the imagination understands by green pastures or heavenly meadows. Upon this roof stood a slender, pointed spire within which a little bell hung and on whose tip a shining, golden weathercock turned in the wind. When this little bell rang at twilight, my mother would speak of God and teach me to pray. 'What is God?' I asked. 'Is it a man?' and she answered, 'No, God is a Spirit!' The church roof sank gradually deeper into the grey shadow, the light climbed higher, to the little spire, until at last it sparkled only on the

golden weathercock, and suddenly one evening I came to the fixed
belief that this weathercock was God. It had its place too in the
childish prayers which I knew by heart and took pleasure in repeating. But when, one day, I was given a picture book in which
was a magnificently striped stately tiger, my conception of God
was gradually transferred to this tiger, although I never expressed
my opinion about it, any more than I did about the weathercock.
They were absolutely subjective ideas, and only if the name of
God was mentioned, first the shining bird and later the beautiful
tiger hovered before my vision. Gradually there took shape in my
thoughts another conception, not, it is true, a more definite, but
a nobler one. The Lord's Prayer, whose division into clauses, with
its symmetry, had made the learning of it easy for me and its repetition a pleasant exercise, I would say with masterly skill and
many variations. From this prayer a notion had taken root in me
that God must be a Being, to whom, perhaps, one could express
oneself in rational fashion more easily than to those animal
creatures.
Godfried Keller[4]

For my childish imagination it was first of all the king who sat
on a golden throne; then, on a much more beautiful and much
higher and much more golden throne far, far away in the blue
sky, sat God and Lord Jesus, with golden crowns and white robes.

While it became increasingly impossible for me to adopt a
positive attitude to Lord Jesus, I remember that from the time I
was eleven the idea of God began to interest me. I took to praying
to God ... God was not complicated by my distrust. Moreover he
was not a person in a black robe, and not Lord Jesus of the pictures, draped with brightly coloured clothes, with whom people
behaved so familiarly.

Rather, he was a unique being of whom, so I heard, it was impossible to form any correct conception. He was, to be sure, something like a very powerful old man. But to my great satisfaction
there was a commandment to the effect that 'Thou shalt not make
unto thee any graven image or any likeness of any thing.' Therefore one could not deal with him as familiarly as with Lord Jesus,
who was no 'secret'.
C. J. Jung[5]

THE CHILD'S IMAGE OF GOD CONSIDERED

Children see God in the form of a child, a being like themselves.
Bernard Mailhiot

To tell the truth, we have never found any trace of a God with a beard.
Jean Pierre Deconchy

All that the child attributes to God and his capacities are of this world. God 'lives in heaven', to be sure, but this only means that he is difficult to reach.

Moreover, God has a special place in the child's world. He has greater capacities than other men, greater even than the child's father.

For children he represents the high-point of greatness, power and goodness. The really 'wholly other' of the supernatural world is still beyond his comprehension.
W. Hansen

Is the mentality of the child with regard to God as infantile as we think?
J. van Haaren

All children, both those who live in a religious environment and those who have had what one might call a completely free-thinking education, come into contact with 'figures' which rise up behind the words which they hear. Who can say when he first heard the word 'God', 'Jesus Christ', 'heaven', 'hell', and 'cross', and who can say what was the effect of these words upon him? One cannot think of any words which have nearly as much power as these.

The discovery of faith is a difficult journey through words, the mysterious signs, the ultimate lighthouses leading us to a harbour which is not of this world. Behind the words there stand, dimly or clearly outlined, sometimes misleading, the figures. God, Jesus Christ, the devil, paradise ... Who does not possess, hidden somewhere within him, the image of the garden of gardens?
H. C. Rümke

Children who do not hear about God at home often cling firmly to Santa Claus, to something familiar, something they would have been concerned with if they had heard of God at Sunday school.

God is always with them, but in the years of childhood they have really no other idea about him than my little brother, who was always accompanied by a dream figure called Jan Pieters who always made things right. Jan Pieters was a giant, Jan Pieters could also go through the keyhole.

There seems to be no way of avoiding giving children at first the impression that God is a human being, a very special father, an angelic being, and in any case something quite concrete. It is later very difficult to make it clear that things are not so simple. Is there any alternative? In any case it is enthralling to be involved with your children in all this.

I sent her to Sunday school because I believe in God, therefore I cannot neglect letting her share in my belief. But I hesitated for a long time because I am so afraid that she will learn things there – intellectually – which are hindrances to true faith in God. 'Where does God live? In what country? Did God make himself as well? Is it nice to be dead with God?' I wouldn't dare to answer questions of this kind from a six-year-old child. Faith in God is something for the more mature soul. She finds the idea that God is everywhere horrifying. Do you understand how I hesitate to impart these things to her in this form?
Parents

It is unnecessary and sometimes incomprehensible to speak of God as a spirit to young children. It signifies very little to them. They would probably come to regard God as something unreal, illusory.
Herman J. Sweet

DOUBTS ABOUT CHILDREN'S FAITH

When a child says that he believes in God, he does not believe in God, but in Peter and James who tell him that there is something which is called God.
Jean Jacques Rousseau

Since the time of Rousseau the repeated theme of the philosophy of religion has been that a child's religion is not something of its own, something original and spontaneous, but is an echo of what is heard and learnt.
Theophil Thun

IN THE LANGUAGE OF HUMAN IMAGES

The tendency in young children to anthropomorphise the deity ... is a natural result of egocentric thinking...
Ronald Goldman[6]

God is first of all the superlative of man. The 'wholly other' is a separate discovery.
M. J. Langeveld

Religious anthropomorphism represents man's attempt to conceive of the reality of God. At the same time, as the result of feelings of reverence, trust, astonishment and fear, God is conceived of as more than human, so that his image takes on a symbolic value.

A child conceives of God in a human image and thinks of him likewise as in reality a human being, but at the same time he separates God from what is human and places him in another reality.
Antoine Vergote

It is principally adults and the illustrations which they suppose are suitable for children which allow the child to become stuck in the inevitable transitional phase of anthropomorphism.
Theophil Thun

Holy scripture makes no apology for speaking of God in human form.
H. M. Kuitert

Anthropomorphism is to be found on every page of the Old Testament in a wealth of detail, unashamed and even drastic. God speaks, converses, calls. He hears, sees, smells, laughs, and hisses. He has eyes ... hands ... fingers, an arm, ears, feet, a mouth, lips and a tongue, a head, a face, a back, a heart and emotions.

He also has feelings and passions like those of a man. He feels delight, shows favour, rejoices. But He also rebukes, hates, rejects, abhors, feels disgust, is provoked to anger and can be jealous.

He rides, goes forth, treads, comes down, walks. He bends Judah as a bow. He is like a moth, a lion, a panther and the dew. Through the anthropomorphisms of the Old Testament God stands before men as the personal and living God, who meets him with will and with works, who directs His will and His words towards men and draws near to men. God is the living God.
L. Köhler[7]

The presentation of Yahweh in human form is a description of his role as a partner in the covenant and not an indication of his personality.
H. M. Kuitert

THE DEATH OF GOD

Have you ever heard of the madman who on a bright morning lighted a lantern and ran to the market place calling out unceasingly: 'I seek God! I seek God!' As there were many people standing about who did not believe in God, he caused a great deal of amusement. 'Why! is he lost?' said one. 'Has he strayed away like a child?' said another. 'Or does he keep himself hidden?' 'Is he afraid of us?' 'Has he taken a sea voyage?' 'Has he emigrated?' – the people cried out laughingly, all in a hubbub. The insane man jumped into their midst and transfixed them with his glances. 'Where is God gone?' he called out. 'I mean to tell you! *We have killed him* – you and I! We are all his murderers! God is dead! God remains dead! And we have killed him! ... How shall we console ourselves, the most murderous of all murderers? ... Is not the magnitude of this deed too great for us? Shall we not ourselves have to become Gods, merely to seem worthy of it? There never was a greater event, and on account of it all, all who are born after us belong to a higher history than any history hitherto!'

Here the madman was silent and looked again at his hearers; they also were silent and looked at him in surprise. At last he threw his lantern on the ground so that it broke in pieces and was extinguished. 'I come too early,' he then said, 'I am not yet at the right time. This prodigious event is still on its way, and is travelling – it has not yet reached men's ears.'

F. Nietzsche[8]

Life is completed, for some, by the addition of God. Most others wonder why they should add this extra storey. In any case, the effect is a displacement of him as God. He has ceased by definition to be ... the most real thing in the world. He is on or off the edge of the map.

And it is in this sense that men in the Bible say, 'There is no God': he is not operative, he does not function, he is not real. And that lies behind ... the current proclamation by *Christian* theologians of 'the death of God'. Drained gradually but irrevocably of reality, he has become a shadow ... 'God' is a dead word ... It does not signify, or add anything, or bring any illumination ... From having been the sun of the universe it is now more like the moon. It is still around, somewhere in most people's consciousness, but fundamentally as dead matter.

J. A. T. Robinson[9]

'GOD'

[The word 'God'] is the most heavyladen of all human words. None has become so soiled, so mutilated. Just for this reason I may not abandon it. Generations of men have laid the burden of their anxious lives upon this word and weighed it to the ground; it lies in the dust and bears their whole burden. The races of men with their religious factions have torn the word to pieces; they have killed for it and died for it, and it bears their finger marks and their blood. Where might I find a word like it to describe the highest! If I took the purest, most sparkling concept from the inner treasure-chamber of the philosophers, I could only capture thereby an unbinding product of thought. I could not capture the presence of Him whom hell-tormented and heaven-storming generations of men have honoured and degraded with their awesome living and dying. I do indeed mean Him whom hell-tormented and heaven-storming generations of men mean. Certainly, they draw caricatures and write 'God' underneath; they murder one another and say 'in God's name'. But when all madness and delusion fall to dust, when they stand over against Him in the loneliest darkness and no longer say 'He, He', but rather sigh 'Thou', shout 'Thou' ... and when they then add 'God', is it not the real God whom they all implore, the One Living God, the God of all the children of men?
M. Buber[10]

We now find that the various uses of the word God, once conveniently fused, are coming unstuck. Historical change and social differentiation have combined to make the word the most equivocal term in the English language.
Harvey Cox[11]

God – or, just as much, the absence of God – exercises a continuing fascination, like a candle to the moth.
J. A. T. Robinson[12]

God is a word surrounded by clouds of associations: childhood reminiscences, church services, a particular suit of clothes, a particular feeling on Sunday, a voice in the ether; the old man on the throne dream, the absolute invisible force, a misconception from primitive times, a question mark, a stop-gap, a stern father figure.

[He is] not a monument of imaginative power, a magnificent, subtle and poetic divine image. You shall make no graven image of me, he says to us. He has a name, but is unnameable and dark: I shall be there before you.

He is supposed to be far away and very close at the same time, he is not tied and does not react mechanically.

The only language ... which does justice to him and gives him proper scope is the language of myth and poetry. The language of concealment: to say what cannot be said and yet must be said, and said every time anew.

[God] gives me his name as a song and a story, in images and likenesses ... Language into which a person can grow and which has time, a whole life long.
Huub Oosterhuis

And if [that word 'God'] has not much meaning for you, translate it, and speak of the depths of your life, of the source of your being, of your ultimate concern, of what you take seriously without any reservation. Perhaps, in order to do so, you must forget everything traditional that you have learned about God, perhaps even that word itself. For if you know that God means depth, you know much about him.
Paul Tillich[13]

No one who is old enough to think for himself supposes that God lives in a local heaven.
Rudolf Bultmann[14]

The world appears to be something distinct against the background of a reality of a different order, which remains a mystery, and shrouded in silence. In spite of everything, man suspects that there is a thread of meaning uniting the whole. Existence is sustained by someone Other. The Other is the foundation, giver, fulfilment and inspiration. The Wholly Other sustains existence, is the horizon of the true reality, towards which the transitory phenomena of this life point; the proprietor to whom human existence belongs.
Antoine Vergote

The relationship to man is an essential part of God's being God.
H. M. Kuitert

THE ENCOUNTER WITH GOD

Perhaps you ask yourself: why waste time on fruitless puzzling about God, while the world is on fire and human beings are in need, while there is such an appalling amount to do? But have you not yet understood that to ask about God is to ask about man, about his place and purpose? Do you not see that it is the world and man themselves which force you to look for a meaning?
Rogier van Aerde

In pure personal relationship we have the nearest clue to the nature of ultimate reality.

It comes, as it were, from beyond him with an unconditional claim upon his life. The fact that life is conceived as a relationship of openness, response, obedience to this overmastering reality is what distinguishes the man who is constrained to use the word 'God' ...

It is a relationship in which a man knows himself bound, in which he is not his own, and yet in which alone he knows that his true freedom is to be found. It is this ineluctable relatedness, this being held by something to which one's whole life is *response* ... that is the reality, I suggest, to which the language of God points.

It is to say that 'deep down things' ... we can trust the universe not only at the level of certain mathematical regularities but at the level of utterly personal reliability that Jesus indicated by the word '*Abba*, Father!' It is the faith that is as true and objective a picture of reality as that described by natural sciences, and more fundamental.

We can say that, however much of this awareness seems to come to us from within, from the ground of our very being, it confronts also with an otherness to which we can only respond as 'I' to 'Thou'.
J. A. T. Robinson[15]

What is most divine is one to whom we can pray with the language of the heart, with the symbols of personality – even though he is more than mere words can express. But we cannot speak of God otherwise than in our best, most existential language, that is, the language in which we speak *to* him.
H. J. Heering

Jesus our mediator is in the most literal sense the image of God. There God is revealed to us as he never was revealed elsewhere. The Bible itself demands that we should not project for ourselves a God 'above' or 'outside', but that we should look for him within the horizon of the reality we experience, where he manifests himself as renewing our existence.

H. Berkhof

8 Where is God?

When a little child asks 'What is that?', the next question is, 'Where is it?' The latter expresses not so much a need to localize something as to know: 'What is it to me? Have I anything to do with it? Can I get hold of it? Does it affect me?'

Thus everyone who has told a child anything about God can expect the question, 'Where is he, then?'

For he is talked about as though he were an acquaintance and yet he is not there. The grown-ups smile in an embarrassed way when a child suggests that perhaps God can come by tram to visit them.

It is this very mysteriousness which provokes the question, 'Where is God?'

For everything in this life has a fixed place, a child thinks. You can see it, or if it is further away you can go closer to it. And when evening comes and it grows dark, the vital question to the parents is, 'Where are you going?' This 'where' is concerned with contact, accessibility, and security; you want to know where you are.

'Where is God?'

Here we are with almost twenty centuries of Christian theology behind us, and we do not really have any answer. We ourselves never ask the question. As believers, we live consciously or unconsciously in the trust that God is near us, that a contact with him is possible and that there is no need to localize him anywhere. Moreover, we understand that God cannot be contained within our concepts of space and time.

But when a child asks these questions, we involuntarily answer in the words of the catechism: 'God is in Heaven' or 'God is everywhere'. The admission that 'God is in your heart' comes from a different tradition from that of the catechism. It is a relic of a stage in Christian theology, found particularly in the last century, in which it was supposed that the principal seat of religion was in man's inner thoughts and feelings.

To a child we are giving a complicated answer to a simple question. 'In heaven.' How far away and high beyond reach! 'In our heart.' That is terribly close! 'Everywhere.' That is so general.

And does a child know where he stands after this threefold answer to his innocent question?

Should he let the wind carry a letter off to God into the air? Or, when his heart beats violently after a fight, should he be afraid that God will come out of it? Or can he get hold of God in the sugar dish, because he is everywhere?

'God is in Heaven.' There he sits, the ruler on his throne, at the end of the Middle Ages. His all-seeing eye looks down on men and rewards them according to their deeds.

'Here is the old image of God again,' Bishop Robinson would say. For modern men this image is supposed to be finished. Does this mean we are now concerned solely and definitively with the earth?

Moreover, for a child heaven is so far away, and his concern is to feel protected in the close presence of God.

By this expression a child probably understands simply the spatial definition: 'above the clouds'.

But is this the purpose of the ancient biblical expression, which we also know from the Lord's Prayer? Is God dismissed 'upstairs' by this expression and is a place outside the world being attributed to him?

Rather, the purpose is to affirm that God is not identical with his creation, and is not an earthly force, but extends beyond and above his creation in the fulness of his divine authority. Heaven as the 'dwelling place' of God signifies his majesty, holiness and glory.

Modern religious jargon actually plays about with the word 'God' without respect of persons. He appears as a little figure in cartoons. It is 'with it' to have buried him like a troublesome old Santa Claus. 'The old man in the sky' is for those who are traditional and therefore backward. People want to reject the old images. But do they then succeed in keeping what these old images contained?

Who is coming forward with a new image which can express the majesty, holiness and glory of God as well as the old? Parents probably do not realize that in conversation with their children they are re-living the whole history of Christian thought. Before they know it, they have passed through the Middle Ages into the age of the enlightenment and pietism: 'God is the little voice inside you' and 'God is in your heart'.

How many adults live with the notion that God lives in their hearts? And even if they believe it, which of them is conscious of this in his daily life? How many adults feel themselves continually under the all-seeing eye of God? Then why subject children to this religious high pressure? Moreover, they take it literally. How is it possible for the great and mighty God to live in such a tiny space as your heart? 'Is he a little dwarf?' or 'Then there must be lots of little Gods in all the hearts!'

What are we trying to tell a child with this expression? That a contact is possible with God, that we can be affected in the very depths of our heart by a spirit and a love which does not derive from ourselves? Fair enough, but is this not a pretty rare experience, and do not many believers have an unsatisfied longing for an inner experience which they have obviously never undergone? But if, then, our own experience of God is so meagre, why should we tell children that God himself 'dwells' in their heart? 'I don't notice it,' a child could reply. Other children feel this knowledge as a burden.

And when we go on to identify God with the 'little voice inside you', our own conscience, we are completely on the wrong track. For the conscience of a little child is no more than an echo of 'what he can do and what he can't', of what his parents forbid or allow, exaggerated by primitive fears and feelings of guilt which are remote in the uttermost degree from what is really good or evil, and even further from the judgment of God.

The child's question, 'Where is God?' evidently leads us astray. Is this because in the literal sense it is not an essential question?

When we answer, 'God is everywhere', once again following the catechism or the Sunday school hymn, 'In the hills and in the valleys', we find ourselves before we know where we are in the midst of the central dogma of Hinduism or, in more general terms, in pantheism: everything in its deepest being is the deity itself. If God is everywhere, then the water is a part of him, and he becomes identified with the cosmos, and we ourselves are 'God in the depths of our thoughts'.

With children, this theology, too, becomes an absurdity: 'Then he is in the table as well,' or, 'Can I get hold of him when I reach into the air?' Isn't he everywhere? 'Just look, I am jumping over God,' says the child.

How remarkable it is that a child works his idea out in his own way. He explains the 'immanence' – the being in the world – of God with embryonic images or by analogy with the food which becomes invisible in the body. And in this respect it is notable that the child thinks that the world is in God rather than that God is in the world.

'God has such a big stomach that everything can go into it.'

'The world is God's tummy.' 'I think that we live in one of God's legs because he is so big.'

'God is everywhere' is an unbiblical expression because in the Bible God is not identified with anything, neither with the life force, nor with the earth. He is always the Creator of everything. He is not the sun and he is not man. He is not everywhere precisely because he has made room for his creatures, for others. He does not force them aside by wanting to be where they are. A nine-year-old boy said: 'Is God in the rain too? No, he cannot be in the rain, because he made it himself. So he can't be inside it.'

Moreover, can we speak of God – 'the most special of all', as a child once called him – in such general terms? 'Is God everywhere?' asked a four-year-old boy, 'because I don't know where that is, I can't find it.' Another boy, who had to go up to fetch an iron from the attic, where the wind was making the tiles rattle, and stopped halfway up the stairs from fright, was told, 'Why are you frightened, you know that God is everywhere, don't you?' He answered, 'But I want him to hold my hand!' In other words, What does such a generalization mean to me? I want him to hold my hand, that is, I want him to be for me the most special of all that is near me. The child asks for contact with God. 'God is everywhere' is a brush-off. We say it, but we do not experience it, in the high tension of his presence. And so when we say it, it is a superficiality, a truism, we laugh it off.

In the Bible the presence of God is on the whole not taken for granted, and is certainly not a commonplace. It is something quite special, something extraordinary! The Bible in fact describes the way in which God sometimes came too close to men, and sometimes seemed 'far' from them. If it can be taken for granted that God is 'everywhere', why should a person have to seek God, how can he then be found by his God, and how could the person whose faith was greatest of all cry out, 'My God, why hast thou forsaken me?'

In the Bible we also find the expectation that God encounters us in history and that his kingdom is ever more immanent. In short, the presence of God is an event, in which we can be involved.

Man's experience of life, too, is a history of belief and doubt, security and abandonment, longing and unbelief, certainty and forlornness. Let us therefore not be too ready to say, 'God is everywhere'.

In modern theology, in which we have to forswear heaven, and are redirected to the earth, we are called upon to look for God in our fellow men. We encounter him in our neighbour, and in

particular in the Biafran child, the oppressed black man or the
rebellious youth who yearns for a better world. God is not in a
distant heaven but here on earth. He is wherever injustice is resisted and peace is made. He suffers with the hungry and the
despised.

The ancient image of the majesty of God on the heavenly
throne is replaced by that of Christ from Matthew 25.35: 'I was
hungry and you gave me food, I was thirsty and you gave me
drink, I was a stranger and you welcomed me, I was naked and you
clothed me. I was sick and you visited me, I was in prison and you
came to me.' 'As you did it to one of the least of these my brethren,
you did it to me.'

A passionate appeal is made to this gospel at the present day.
This is a healthy reaction to the unworldly faith of earlier ages,
in which all devotion was directed towards 'heaven'. But these
words were spoken by someone who taught us to pray to 'Our
Father who art in heaven', and the text itself occurs in a context
which speaks of 'his glorious throne'. Here we have the biblical
tension between earthly and human events and the reality of the
kingdom of God which (in spite of all) goes beyond these events.
Only in this tension can our encounter with our neighbour become a divine encounter. Those who at the present day seek to
keep silent about God, and identify faith with our common
humanity, can get stuck in human activism or become involved in
a political campaign, as if the only way left for the presence of
God to be recognized or verified in the world is in a social programme.

Is it reasonable, then, to reject the ancient biblical image of
God in heaven without further ado? He who has a sacred authority
over the creation, he is God and we are men. He is God, and
escapes from every human attempt to localize him somewhere
in a church, in a creed, or in a social programme.

'Where is God?'

The question 'where' leads us into a superficial error, because
we try to give an answer in the form of a spatial definition. God
cannot be defined spatially, but only by the intensity of his relationship to his creatures. For he must always be involved, in a very
special way, with his creatures, through a love and a compassion
which is beyond human understanding. That is what we read in
Psalm 139, that we can never escape from this love, that it keeps
hold of us even in death. God's presence with us is an event: 'I
will be with you', you can rely on me (Ex. 3.12).

This is the mystery of God, that he will not occupy our place, that he makes room for us, does not thrust himself upon us with his visible presence, which would overwhelm us with his glory; that he remains hidden, in concealment, can only be perceived by faith and is our companion precisely in this liberating absence. He is present in a different way from men and things, in a divine way. He is not a human being, infinitely multiplied by the word 'everywhere' and 'all', a kind of superman who 'sees everything' and 'hears everything', 'is everywhere', and 'can do everything'. 'To us God was a policeman who always had his eye on us,' someone once cried. God does not see the same as we men see with our eyes, he sees the essence of things, what it is all about, what we are in reality. That is why it is extremely dangerous to give children the idea that 'God sees everything', because for centuries now a moralistic threat has always been implied: 'Watch you don't pinch anything out of the sugar bowl!' The eye of love sees differently.

What matters is that we should let our children feel something of the total transcendence of God and his otherness over against what he has created; and also something of the unbelievable love which means infinitely more than that he can hold our hand.

'Where is God?'

We should be able to answer that we do not know and that we cannot understand either, because we are only men and he is God. It does not matter where he is.

People of course say that God 'lives in heaven'.

What they mean by this is that God is highest of all, that he is King, that he is so much more than the world, and that he is very different from men. With him there is such light and glory that it cannot be compared with the light of the sun or the glory of the earth. This glory is still hidden from us, for we would not be able to bear it.

And yet it does not mean that God is far away. This cannot be, because it is he who has made us and given us life, and who cares for us so much that he wants to be with us.

When you ask, 'Where is God?', think only, 'He is with us.'

We have no need to know more.

IS GOD EVERYWHERE?

God is very hot, he is just as hot as the sun, yes he is though, because God is in the sun.
Boy aged four

In him we live and move and have our being. – God has such a big tummy that everything can get into it.
Girl aged five

Mother is reading the New Testament. Is God in your tummy reading the New Testament as well?
Girl aged five

Is God everywhere? – Yes. – Is he in my tummy as well?
Boy aged five

I understand best, the world is God's tummy.
His brother

If God is everywhere, I can get hold of him like this, now I have God in my hands.

If God is everywhere, is he in this vitamin tablet as well? He must be awfully crushed up!

Is God under the ground? Well, aren't you put under the ground when you are dead?
Boy aged five

I see everywhere God's hands, all hands, because God is everywhere, teacher says.
Boy aged six

God isn't in the mud, is he?
Boy aged seven

Is God divided up into pieces, so that he can be everywhere?
Girl aged eight

Perhaps God could be in the sea, couldn't he?
Girl aged eight

Does God take on the shape of where he is?
Girl aged eight

Mother, that God exists right past the stars and so on, perhaps he does, but it doesn't really mean anything. God is here – *pointing to his stomach* – here is everything, the earth, the stars and God.
Boy aged eight

He cannot be in the rain, because he made it himself. So he can't
be inside it.
Boy aged nine

Looking at the aquarium: Who eats us up when we die?

IN OUR HEART

Daddy, where does the Lord God live? – In heaven and in our
heart. – Then, where does the Lord Jesus live? Does he live in my
tummy?
Boy aged three

Where does God live on earth, Mother? – God does not just live
in a particular country, he wants to live here on earth in the
hearts of people and children who really do their best to be good
and don't think just of themselves. – Does he run about from one
heart to another? – God can live everywhere at the same time.

God lives in your heart. – No he doesn't, God is far too big, the
Lord Jesus lives in your heart.
Two five-year-old boys

A few months later one of them was frightened by something that
had happened, and lay crying fearfully in bed: Oh, Mummy, I
am so frightened that the Lord Jesus will come out of my heart, it
is beating so hard!

Dear Lord inside me, though I don't know how you can be with
all the eating pipes.
Girl aged five

Have you hurt yourself? – No, I haven't, but what a smack Jesus
must have got!
Six-year-old

Can God live even in a plastic heart?
Boy aged eight

How can he live in your heart? God is not a little dwarf, God is
big!
Girl aged nine

IN HEAVEN

If he lived here, it wouldn't be so far, but he lives a long way away in heaven. – Would you like to live in heaven? – I wouldn't, oh no, I'd rather stay here. I don't ever want to die. Perhaps ten weeks there and ten weeks here.
Girl aged four

If we run a long way through the wood, will we come in the end to God?
Boy aged four

I would like to go to God. – You can't, he's in heaven. – Let's go and get a ladder off the window cleaner, and then I'll climb up there.
Boy aged four

Is God deep down there, where the clouds are all piled up? Do the clouds hurt God? Can you get hold of God if you go right down in the clouds? When people start fighting, what does God do then? Does he get angry? Does he come out of heaven? What if you went up above with a ladder? When people start arguing about a car, what does God do then?
Boy aged four

Daddy, when there wasn't any air, there wasn't any God either, because there was nowhere for him to live.
Boy aged four

Why does God stay in heaven? If he really loves us, he ought to come down to us on earth to help us!
Boy aged four

How can God be in heaven? You can't stay in the air, there's no ground there, is there?
Boy aged five

If you stand on the top of the highest mountain, are you right by the Lord?
He is even higher, but he comes to be with you.
Boys aged five and six

Hey, Father, is God in heaven? No, God is on the earth, because everything grows there, trees and flowers.
Girl aged six

Surely God has a big telescope, because God lives in heaven and that is a long way away. – Where is heaven then? – In the air. – So God lives in the air? – Yes, I think he lives on a cloud, just like Pooh Bear. – But what if it rains? – He has a very old house. – Why has he a very old house? – Because the builders can't build a house in the air. – And how did this old house get there? – Oh, Daddy, the house was already there, God has always had it. – Oh, I didn't know that.
Girl aged six

God is everywhere. – No, Grandma, God is in heaven and Jesus is on earth. God is right above your head and above my head and above everybody's.
Girl aged six

They say that God lives in the sky, so when the rockets go up why don't people see him?
Nine-year-old

THE INVISIBLE

Where is God? I should so like to see him!
Boy aged four

We can't see God, but God lands at night.
Boy aged four

I used to imagine that it was a little man who always sat on your shoulder, never left you and was invisible.

God is transparent.
Girl aged five

Teacher's fibbing when she says that God is always with you. I looked secretly when we were praying, but I never saw anything.
Six-year-old

How can we not see God? – It is just like a bare garden newly dug over, even if you don't put any seeds in, after a while weeds

grow. And in the same way, you can't see God, but he is there all the time. – Oh, Mummy, really, God isn't a weed!
Girl aged seven

ALL-SEEING AND ALL-KNOWING

Wandering in the wood: Can you see us, God?
Boy aged three

Why can't you see God? – I think, because God is too big for us. – But how can God see me then, how can he? Has he glasses or does he look through a hole in the roof? – No, God is everywhere. – How can he be?

Conversation in the sand pit. God can see you, of course he can! – I don't believe it. – When we are sitting here in the sand pit, he can see you and if you went up into the attic, he could still see you. – No, he can't because he can't see through the roof, can he?
Boys aged three and four

Has God got eyes? – No, something else, so that he can see.
Boy aged four

Has God got eyes? Why can't we see him if he has real eyes?
Boy aged four

A lady went past wearing a veil. Look, Mummy, God's going past. – Why do you think that's God? – Because she can see us and we can't see her.
Four-year-old

I won't shoot you dead, nor Daddy, but I'll shoot God dead because he sees everything!
Boy aged four

What does God look like? – I don't know, because no one has ever seen him. – Does he hear when I say bad words? – Yes. – Then he has ears, big ones? – It's not hearing, just knowing.
Girls aged four and six

Bad luck on God today, isn't it? – Why? – It's such bad weather outside, he can't see us at all.

Why can't I see God? Look, Mummy, here at the window I can
see the pigeons and you say they are a long way away. Why can't I
see God, who's close? – For that you would have to have quite
different eyes, to see God, not human eyes. – God's eyes?
Girl aged five

Does God see everything, Mummy? But why can't we see God,
then?
Don't you see God with your heart?
Boy aged five

If I knew what everybody was feeling and thinking, I would be
the dolls' God.
Five-year-old

God knows that I already go to school and that I have eaten
three slices of bread and butter.
Boy aged five

God knows everything, he knows how the trees grow and what you
look like. He also knows what your heart looks like.
Six-year-old

Does God know everything? He doesn't know what you are going
to be later, not if you have just been born.

Has God got hundreds of eyes, so that he can see everybody?

Holding his basket in front of his eyes: Now I am God, I can see
you and you can't see me!
Boy aged seven

God isn't a hedgehog, is he, with eyes on stalks everywhere? I
think that's just horrible.
Girl aged eight

THE EXALTED GOD

The transcendence of God is probably easier for the child to con-
ceptualize about than the immanence of the divine.
Ronald Goldman[1]

In fact, we do not realize how crudely spatial much of the Biblical terminology is ... In fact the number of people who instinctively seem to feel that it is no longer possible to believe in God in the space-age shows how crudely physical much of this thinking about a God 'out there' has been ... Every one of us lives with some mental picture of a God 'out there', a God who 'exists' above and beyond the world he made.

God as the ground, source and goal of our being cannot but be represented at one and the same time as removed from the shallow, sinful surface of our lives by infinite distance and depth, and yet as nearer to us than our own selves. This is the significance of the traditional categories of transcendence and immanence. God is not outside us, yet he is profoundly transcendent.
J. A. T. Robinson[2]

That the whole area of his life is filled by God is for the Israelite, more than for any other oriental, an essential assumption of his religion and a powerful reality, because he couples it with a profound concept of the distance of God. Just because Yahweh cannot be localized in any earthly phenomenon or contained in any human category, he is an all embracing and all penetrating reality.
H. Renckens

I WILL BE WITH YOU

Because and as God is one, unique and simple, He is for this reason omnipresent. Omnipresence ... is the sovereignty on the basis of which everything that exists cannot exist without Him, but only with Him.

The whole divine sovereignty is based on the fact that for God nothing exists which is only remote, i.e. which is not near even as it is remote, so that there is no remoteness beside and outside him which is remoteness without his proximity.
K. Barth[3]

WHERE WE LET HIM IN

Where does God live? – What are you talking about? The world is filled with his glory. – God lives where we let him in.
A rabbi

God is beyond in the midst of our life.

The beyond is not what is infinitely remote, but what is nearest
at hand.
Dietrich Bonhoeffer[4]

Faith does not look for any way out into inwardness or into
heaven. It is concerned with the Kingdom on earth, with becoming man in freedom.
J. Sperna Weiland

When you turn to the truth which must be done, then you have
reached reality. Because the truth is not an illusion – even though
you might never succeed in doing it – it is real, concrete, and you
cannot doubt its existence, even if you have never seen it anywhere. It is as though by the bare act of setting out towards the
truth that has to be done, God is admitted, as if a highly oppress-
ive emptiness if filled to overflowing, all your life overflows, and
the whole world is filled with him.

If this is true, then we can not only see him, but talk with him,
give him our hand and do something for him.
Rogier van Aerde

9 Can God Do Everything?

'God can do everything, he is omnipotent.' Answer 11 from the Catechism.

Is there any point in quoting a document which is no longer in force? Certainly, because even now many children, even Protestant children, are educated with the aid of the teaching of this catechism. A little boy was once complaining to his mother of the way she told Bible stories. 'The master at school tells them much better, because he says that God can do everything!' What an ideal for a young person, that a being should exist which can do everything, but absolutely everything!

Alas, before we know what is happening, the bottom drops out of our theology. 'If I drop this cup, God can see that it doesn't fall,' says the child. The cup falls and breaks in pieces.

Have we not once again misled children with theories by which we do not live ourselves! 'God can do everything' is nonsense, as plainly as 'God is everywhere'. Can God tie my shoelaces, breathe for us, wage war, or make the sun stand still? Is he sitting up above the clouds on his medieval throne, a heavenly potentate from whom one can expect everything, absolutely everything? A Christian may believe in a God who cannot actually do everything, who of his nature is incapable of doing what is evil or ungodly, and who can only and exclusively be who he is: God, the Father, true to his nature for eternity.

One might even say that 'God can do everything' is a blasphemy. We cannot attribute and ascribe everything to God. A child takes this expression as a literal truth because of the magical world of his experience. God as the great magician, from whom you can expect anything, even what is utterly impossible. And why should God not be able to manage all the forces of nature: 'Can't he see that I've got my new mittens on?'

It is remarkable that 'God can do everything' has become a central article of the child's creed. This may be connected with the fact that parents themselves snatch eagerly at this dogma in front of the children, because it corresponds to an egocentric religious desire, a certain immaturity, which fights shy of personal creative freedom. God must be able to intervene, to step in and intercept the terrible risk of life in this world. How much piety is determined by this hope!

We no longer share the superstitious belief of primitive religion, in so far as we no longer seek God in the forces of nature. But we have not been wholly converted from this religion in so far as we still look secretly for God within what happens. Has he not determined and sent everything, especially when something happens that brings us misfortune or suffering? And people try to explain by saying that God has done this or that to us: it was a trial, a punishment, we must learn from it. How many people react by sighing: 'What have I done to deserve this?', whenever anything bad happens to them? Or they say, 'It had to be!'

The latter expression is a clear statement that everything that happens, especially adversity, comes from God, and that there's nothing to be done about it. But children, on the other hand, are taught that there is a clear connection between one's lot in life and one's own good or bad deeds, one's belief or unbelief. Read the children's Bible of your youth over again and see. You would get the impression that by his actions and his religion man decides his lot upon earth and even his eternal destiny. Anyone who does not love the Lord runs the risk of being punished in this life with misfortune and will not go to heaven. But those who believe can be sure of God's protection, and do go to heaven.

In this way immense moral pressure is imposed on children. It must have caused great conflicts in the minds of innumerable people as they grew up, or have driven them into unbelief.

However much biblical theology is preached in church, deep in the minds of the congregation what they were taught as children remains indelible. Just because what is at issue here is the explanation of adversity and suffering, it seems to be man's most sensitive point, the point where unbelief is born.

We live in a period of world history in which men seem to be intoxicated with their omnipotence, with unknown possibilities of dominating the earth and of determining life and death, although the problems seem to be growing beyond our capacity.

One of the most important themes of the 'new theology', therefore, is that of human responsibility. It is advanced in reaction against 'the old image of God' of the Almighty on his heavenly throne. This concept of God has always played into the hands of a Christian fatalism. It has been one of the reasons for ecclesiastical conservatism, which allowed social injustice to exist for so long. The church has not been a progressive movement in the world. Here is a quotation from a Protestant catechism – the

answers for the ninth and tenth Sundays in the Heidelberg Catechism: 'God maintains and rules the creation. It is he who provides us with all the needs of body and soul, and who will turn
all the evil which he sends us in this vale of tears to the best,
because he can do this as an omnipotent God and will do so as
devoted father.'

'What do you understand by the providence of God?'

'The omnipotent and omnipresent power of God, by which he
still maintains heaven and earth, together with all creatures, as
by his hand, and therefore ensures that trees and grass, rain and
drought, fruitful and unfruitful years, food and drink, health and
sickness, riches and poverty do not come to us by chance, but
from his fatherly hand.'

Creatures are in his hand in such a way that 'they cannot move
or stir without his will'.

In the violent present-day reaction against the Christian image
of God, it ought to be recalled that this conception of things was
more that of the Middle Ages than of primitive Christianity.

In the Bible the word omnipotence never seems to occur. God
is of course called 'the Almighty', but Buber translates the Hebrew
word by 'the powerful', 'the overwhelming'. God is described in
this way particularly in the books of Job and Revelation, but
otherwise infrequently.

The very beginning of the Bible tells us that God renounced
his omnipotence. He created the universe, another reality, a place
for the forces of nature. According to the old creation story, on
the first page, we learn that God gave up his omnipotence even
further, by creating man and entrusting the earth to him. A considerable risk. As we turn the page, we find that things went even
further, because evil was there for man to seize hold of. This was
the consequence of a free, thinking being: man.

Have these primitive Israelite stories ever been excelled by any
philosophy of life whatsoever?

The whole of biblical history is the dramatic history of God
and the men he created, and how he did not change them magically into helpless puppets, but wanted to let them come freely
along the way to his Kingdom. This God, who did not wish to
use his omnipotence to shatter man in his freedom, appears in
the person of Jesus, the Messiah, as a God who was defeated by the
power of the world. Defenceless, Jesus gave himself up as Messiah
into the hands of men. And this very event led to the primitive
Christian witness that no power in the world can separate us from
the love of God, of which Jesus of Nazareth was the personification
(Rom. 8.39).

This is a very different gospel from what has been spoon-fed to children for centuries, that 'God can do everything'.

At the present day we are experiencing a late revolt against a patriarchal omnipotence; it is at the same time a revolt against a God before whom we human beings have nothing to say. Is it, however, a protest against a Christian image of God, against Christ himself. It was he himself who made up the story of which modern theology supposes it is the author! 'For it will be as when a man going on a journey called his servants and entrusted to them his property' (Matt. 25.14).

The lord here gives responsibility, delegates, and in this very way exercises his divine guidance. He refrains from telling his servants in advance what to do with the part of his property they have received and how this is to take place. Look what is entrusted to the servants themselves in this story: invention, initiative, activity!

What scope, what opportunities God has given to men, and indeed to the whole of his creation! How little he obtrudes himself or takes things out of the hands of his people. The whole drama of human history is the consequence of this risk taken by God.

Anything can happen, even the very worst. The responsibility of man goes so far that he is even capable of extinguishing life on earth, and bringing to an end universal history on this planet.

'Is everything that happens, then, not God's will?'

Of course not. A lot happens which can never be his will: wrongdoing, war, the damaging of the creation. What about an earthquake, a flood, and natural disasters? It is not man alone who has been given scope to act in creation, but also the forces of the cosmos. We live on earth. The earth's crust has not yet completely settled down. Who can stop an earthquake? Is it God himself who sends poverty or riches, sickness or health, rain or drought? Is what happens on earth directly determined by God? Such a belief can only be a relic of the primitive religion of mankind, in which it was believed that rain and drought, fertility or misfortune were the result of the interventions of the gods or other powers.

God does not send sickness, but his grace, not floods, but Christ. We can believe that he is not to be identified with events, but encounters us in them. He breaks through the fatal course of destiny.

This can perhaps be confirmed by the experience of many people who have to reconcile themselves to a great suffering. Others, who have seen this happening from a distance, may grow rebellious and bitterly ask themselves how God can permit this.

But those who endure it themselves experience that through this grievous misfortune they change, come to think differently, and are driven into a life which is more meaningful and profound and closer to God in their faith. They perceive that through contact with God they are brought into a different ordering of life from that of fate, of nature or of good and evil. God did not will what happened, and perhaps human guilt or the forces of nature were involved, even though he originally made it possible for such things to happen by setting the cosmos and man free.

God's will now, in this situation, must be for one to break through and overcome fate: not by calm acquiescence, but by rising out of suffering, forgiving guilt, renewing life, rising from the dead. It is more, let us say, a liberating breaking through events than a fatalist determination of them. God's will must be the breaking through of his kingdom into human history.

Therefore it is better that the centuries-old image of God as the disposer of all things should be left to decorate old churches as a relic of the history of art.

And when your child asks you, 'Why did this or that happen? Can't God do everything?', can you not answer that this is the greatest riddle of life on earth, which we shall never be able to understand. It is a matter of making it clear to children that God cannot prevent nature and men from being and acting as he originally made possible. God lets everything happen. He stands above it. It is not his fault. Just as God is not within the earth he created, so he is not within the events of man and nature. But just as he is with us in an unknown way because he must love us more than any human being in the world can love us, so it must also be that he is with us when something happens, only not like the storm, not like the earthquake, not like our fellow man who does something to us, but as God. His obvious concern is simply to set us free from the powers of the world, from the destiny that overtakes us, from death. The more we are in accord with him, the greater is our freedom, though it is still relative.

It naturally depends upon the age of a child, how much of this one can get over to him. But a child will certainly have a feeling for human responsibility, that things happen which are men's fault, and why should he not accept that God cannot help it when storms blow?

Should God not have made the darkness, because we could get lost in the darkness? Then we would never have seen the stars... Should God not have made water, because we can drown in it? But we would have died of thirst.

Should God not have made the wind, because a storm can even blow down houses and trees? But what would then move the clouds?

Should not God have made fire, because fire can burn things? But doesn't fire keep you warm?

Should God not have given men life, because they can die? But who would then have cared for the earth? Darkness, water, the storm, fire, animals and men can signify both good fortune and misfortune to us.

But can God stop the wind which he himself set in motion, the water, which he made to flow, or man, to whom he gave freedom to do his will?

Does God think it good when terrible and fearful things happen? He must find it much worse than we do, especially when men destroy what he has given. And yet he cannot do for us what he expects us to do. We ourselves must so change the world that it is more like what God meant it to be. It is God's will to set up his kingdom together with us. He has not only given us life on this earth, but also wishes to share his glory with all his creatures. This is the meaning of the prayer: 'For yours is the kingdom, the power and the glory, now and for ever.'

In a long history of darkness and light this will come true. But we cannot yet understand why this history has to be so arduous. Apparently God still has so much more for us than we experience here and now. What we find worst at the moment is from the point of view of the glory of God perhaps no more than a shadow that passes away. And we can believe that God will overcome evil and darkness not on his own, as an almighty ruler, but only together with his creatures. And this is the great difference between him and a magician.

THE CARE AND GUIDANCE OF GOD

People get burnt, but then God makes them new again. New Mummies and new ladies.
Girl aged three

A little girl was away from home, and had quite forgotten her prayers: But he looked after me all right, though. There was a gnat just once, but it didn't do anything.
Girl aged four

She was sent with a message after six o'clock. Weren't you afraid?

– Yes, Mummy, I was afraid, but then I thought: God can see me walking along and he looks after me.
Girl aged four

Are you home already? – I heard the voice of God, which said: 'The little girl in the blue coat can cross now.' (*The loud-speaker in the traffic control box.*)
Girl aged four

Grandma is by herself now grandfather has died, but God will look after her all right, because he looked after Joseph in prison and Daniel in the lions' den.
Girl aged four

What made the sore place better? – The ointment and God.
Boy aged four

How is the dog going to get better? – God must do it, because God helps us.
Boy aged four

Why have you stepped on that beetle and killed it, you can't make it alive, can you? – Well, perhaps God will come along again this evening.
Girl aged four

God can make Mummy better. – Yes, if he wants to. – And if he doesn't want to, he will do another time.
Boys aged four and six

God can do magic. If your eye doesn't work, then God gives you another instead, doesn't he?

A tooth has to be pulled out. Pray that you will be brave. *Not a sound.* But God is very brave!

Why doesn't God let it always be summer?
Boy aged five

Mummy, God looks after me, doesn't he? But what does God do if burglars come?
Boy aged five

After the Lord's Prayer: You mustn't say and ask everything that

God has to do. He can do what he wants and he will make a good job of it too.
Boy aged five

This storm is a nuisance, but never mind, God still exists.
Boy aged six

When you are crossing the road you should pray to your angel that you don't have an accident and sometimes he says: 'Look out!' – My angel always says: 'You can just make it!'
Girl

Olympic winter sports. A girl crosses herself on the way down. Why does she do that? – She is asking if she can win. *Then she falls.* The Lord Jesus didn't push hard enough!
Girl aged six

Have you ever noticed God's voice? – No, I haven't, but I was once lost in a big wood and my mother went to look for me, but I didn't know and mother called me, but I couldn't hear and then in the meantime I heard a little voice that said: You are being called.
Girl aged six

A little boy is frightened in the dark and prays: And Lord Jesus will you stand with all your angels round my bed, so that there isn't a single crack left open, so that not even a pin could get between them?
Boy aged six

God is rotten and I am not praying any more. Yesterday teacher said that God can do everything and today she says: 'You must bring something for the children in Africa, they are hungry.' Well, if God can do everything and doesn't give the children anything to eat, isn't it rotten of him? – God needs people to help him – Well, that's easy too: helping and letting somebody else pay.
Boy aged six

I don't understand. I ask him to keep watch over me and other children ask the same, but which does he keep watch over?
Boy aged six

If God sees that father arrives safely, then other people will be all right too.
Girl aged eight

Would you like to be God's boss? – No, I couldn't do that, doing all the hard things. – Well, I couldn't think of so many things at once: three thousand million thoughts at the same time and that's just for people, and then there is all the rest!
Boy aged nine

How is it that however powerful he is, God can't get all the people to listen to him?
Twelve-year-old

GOD'S GUIDANCE AND HUMAN RESPONSIBILITY

Pray that the operation comes all right and that she does not have too much pain. – Look, Daddy, the doctor looks after the operation, the aspirin looks after the pain, where do you think that God comes in?
Girl aged three

It's good that God doesn't let you be ill any more. – Yes, but we took anti-malaria pills as well. – God sees that we take the pills.
Boys aged four and five

What nice writing! – I didn't do that, God does it.
Boy aged seven

Are you undressed at last? – Yes, Grandma, I told God and he helps me, but you have to do the best you can yourself, otherwise he doesn't help you.
Boy aged seven

Pray that you don't have an accident. – God can't do that, because if I do have an accident, he doesn't do that either. People do that, people think about it.
Girl aged eight

Why did God make it so difficult and make people a bit good and a bit bad and when it went wrong, he had to come to earth to save us?
Boy aged eight

Lord, take care of Daddy in B. – Are there pavements in B.? –
Let Daddy take care of himself then!
Boy aged nine

THE RIDDLE OF SUFFERING

His brother, a mongol, has died. Why does God give him if he
takes him away again? God can do everything, knows everything,
did he make a mistake, did he make him wrong?
Boy aged four

Why have you only three fingers? – I was born like that. – Perhaps
the Lord didn't have any more fingers, perhaps they had run
out.
Boy aged four

Why does God give some people no children, when they would
like to have them? Why does God sometimes give children to
people who don't look after them properly?

Daddy, does God do it, does God make it happen, when there's a
war?
Girl aged five

A little boy sees disabled children. Does God think it's fun to make
them like that?
Boy aged five

'Say, K, we got Mummy from the Lord to look after us, so why is
she so often ill? – I'm not sure, but I think it is because we have
to think of the Lord more and love him.
Five- and seven-year-olds

Looking at the crippled hand of the playground attendant: I do
think that's bad. If I was God, I would give you a new hand.
Boy aged six

*An aeroplane crashes on a school. A number of children are killed.
She wonders why for days. Finally she says:* How can that have
happened? It was a church school, wasn't it!
Girl aged six

Why does God let some children be born so ill that they can't walk?
Girl aged eight

My Mother got a dead child. Why did God make her happy first and then sad? God is mean!
Nine-year-old

PROVIDENCE

The children were taught that God cares for you everywhere, that no one should persuade them to worry, that he always helps them. 'Does God take care of me, does he see everything, even when I am doing a wee-wee?'

All responsibility is placed on God. Then I say, 'No, God is not concerned with every detail, he has given you your body, eyes, ears and fingers to use, you don't pray to God for him to help you in everything, for example in tying your shoelaces. God trusts you to do this or that well.'
A mother

She walked out into the farmyard praying fervently, her hands folded and her eyes closed. A moment later she fell into an open drain which took the dirty water away from the house. She was so indignant with God who sees everything and can do everything, but did not stop her walking straight into the drain, that she was never able to trust him any more.
Childhood reminiscence

There was an old peasant among them who said that God knew everything, both what had happened and what was going to happen, words which made a deep impression on me. They constantly occupied my thoughts, and towards evening, as I was walking alone some distance from the house, I came to a deep ford. I crawled out on to one of the big stones in the water, and in some strange way the thought entered my mind whether God really knew everything which was to happen. 'Hm, now He has decided that I shall live to be a very old man,' I thought, 'but if I jump out into the water now and drown myself then it will not turn out as He wants it to.' And all at once I was firmly and resolutely determined to drown myself . . . and then a new thought passed through my soul; 'It is the Devil who wants to have me in his power!'
Hans Christian Andersen[1]

I cannot persuade myself that a beneficient and omnipotent God would have designedly created the Ichneumonidae with the express intention of their feeding within the living bodies of Caterpillars, or that a cat should play with mice. Not believing this, I see no necessity in the belief that the eye was expressly designed. On the other hand ... I am inclined to look at everything as resulting from designed laws, with the details, whether good or bad, left to the working out of what we may call chance ... The lightning kills a man, whether a good one or bad one, owing to the excessively complex action of natural laws, ... and I can see no reason why ... all these laws may have been expressly designed by an omniscient Creator, who foresaw every future event and consequence.
Charles Darwin[2]

I meant to speak of the suffering of mankind generally, but we had better confine ourselves to the sufferings of the children. But, in the first place, children can be loved even at close quarters, even when they are dirty, even when they are ugly (I fancy, though, children are never ugly). The second reason why I won't speak of grown-up people is that, besides being disgusting and unworthy of love, they have a compensation – they've eaten the apple and know good and evil. But the children haven't eaten anything, and are so far innocent. Are you fond of children, Aloysha? Children while they are quite little – up to seven, for instance – are so remote from grown-up people; they are different creatures, as it were, of a different species.

This poor child of five was subjected to every possible torture by those 'cultivated' parents ... Then they went to greater refinements of cruelty – shut her up all night in the cold and frost in a privy. Can you understand why a little creature, who can't even understand what's done to her, should beat her aching little heart with her tiny fists in the dark and the cold, and weep her meek unresentful tears to dear, kind God to protect her? Do you understand that, friend and brother, you pious and humble novice? Do you understand why this infamy must be and is permitted? I say nothing of the suffering of grown-up people, they have eaten the apple, damn them, and the devil take them all! But these little ones! ...

I must have justice ... And not justice in some remote infinite time and space, but here on earth, and that I could see myself. I want to see with my own eyes the hind lie down with the lion and the victim rise up and embrace his murderer. I want to be there when everyone suddenly understands what it has all been for.

I renounce the higher harmony altogether. It's not worth the tears of that one tortured child who beat itself on the breast with its little fist and prayed to 'dear, kind God'!

I would rather be left with the unavenged suffering. I would rather remain with my unavenged suffering and unsatisfied indignation, even *if I were wrong*. Besides, too high a price is asked for harmony.

It's not God that I don't accept, Alyosha, only I most respectfully return Him the ticket.
Fyodor Dostoevsky[3]

A GOD WHO CAN DO EVERYTHING

God is the existence corresponding to my wishes and feelings; he is the just one, the good, who fulfils my wishes.
Ludwig Feuerbach[4]

Because God can do everything.
What God says always happens, no one can alter it.
What the Lord does not want, cannot happen.
W. G. van de Hulst

ANYONE WHO BELIEVES AND DOES GOOD WILL PROSPER

Faith alone makes one rich and prosperous.
No one needs to be afraid any more, no evil could happen to them.
God's children would always be safe under God's protection.
Anne de Vries

God cares for all who love him.
W. G. van de Hulst

He loves God, oh, then he will always prosper.
They must be wholly obedient, they must love God, and love each other very much, then they will always be happy and contented, then God will always care for them, then they will always be God's people.

Whoever listens to him and loves him, will prosper, but whoever does not listen to him and does not love him will not prosper.
Sunday school teaching

THE GOD WHO PUNISHES

Now they were being punished because they had not believed the Lord.

They were all being killed by the wicked people of that country.

But men had done evil, and as a punishment they could not go to heaven.
Anne de Vries

I have done much wrong, and now God has punished me.

If you do not love God, you will not prosper, and you are punished.
W. G. van de Hulst

He knew that the man had committed many sins and that this was why he was ill.
Anne de Vries

One day they would have to die, and it was their own fault.
W. G. van de Hulst

A six-year-old child is convinced that a misdemeanour is automatically punished by misfortune. As he grows older, this belief in automatic punishment grows weaker.

Clinical psychology shows how it continues in the sub-conscious mind.
Antoine Vergote

IT HAD TO BE

What could a human being do when everything was in the hand of God? Why should he exert himself? For everything happened as God had determined it. A human being could do no more than struggle a little in the hand of him who provides ...

One day he would have to recognize that a human being could do nothing against the will of God. Will God perhaps show in his life that man can do nothing and needs to do nothing to bring God's kingdom upon earth? Nothing more than to trust as a child in the heavenly Father who rules all things?
Anne de Vries

We experience the world and the things that happen in the world, we observe the way things are all related and identify the process we have established with the providence of God and learn once again that the world and what happens in it is not identical with providence. God rules over the world and all that happens in it. The causal relationship between things is not providence, but the material of God's providence. We are not spectators of God's dispensation, nor the plaything of God's discretion, but co-operate actively in the history which he shares with us children of men.

K. H. Miskotte

A false God has been preached to us. Who said that God made our circumstances? That he decides our fortunes from on high? This is no more than a god of blind fate. But God is not in what happens to us, not in misfortune, nor even in good fortune. These are things which we do to each other. God is at work with us in and through these things. 'Even though I walk through the valley of the shadow of death ... thou art with me; thy rod and thy staff they comfort me.' God is our right of way through this valley.

As a mature and responsible being, man is taken seriously. God never works outside us, nor automatically, nor magically.

L. Kuylman-Hoekendijk

Not a single sparrow will fall to the ground without your Father. It does not say the Father willed the fall of the sparrow. Matthew asserts that the sparrow is safe in the hands of God, even if it falls.

There are things in the world which God has not wished, and yet they happen. We cannot make God responsible for the consequences of our responsibility.

H. J. Heering

Popular faith spontaneously thinks of Providence in connection with escapes from accidents, misfortune, suffering and all that threatens earthly well-being. 'It had to be.' Certainly this can have an authentically Christian meaning, but in itself it is un-Christian, and often so is the emotional atmosphere from which this kind of consolation and resignation stems. It sounds so matter-of-fact, as if an impersonal authority ruled over our lives like a fate.

E. Schillebeeckx[5]

WHY DOES NOT GOD INTERVENE?

We must begin with a change in our thinking, and first of all
with the abandonment of the concept of God as the one who
'intervenes according to his own good pleasure' or at least could
so intervene.
H. J. Heering

Providence is not interference.
Paul Tillich[6]

GOD'S OMNIPOTENCE

This does not mean that we attribute to God to a superlative
degree what we call power. In Jesus Christ his omnipotence is at
the same time the breaking down of what we call power. For it is
also his ability to set aside his power and his self-humiliation.
O. Weber

If we would describe the Omnipotence of God, we would have
to do it the way in which Rembrandt depicts the Passion. Everything which might otherwise be described as 'Omnipotence'
would have to be left wholly or half dark, and all the light would
be concentrated on this One point: the love of the Crucified.
    That One who has suffered defeat in the service of God, whose
enemies crucified and mocked Him, One who out of the depths
of dereliction cried aloud to God, could reveal the Almighty
power of God – what human understanding, or what human
imagination could have conceived such an idea?
E. Brunner[7]

THE ENCOUNTER WITH GOD IN EVENTS

The confession that God is love comes to us from a people who
between slavery and pogrom have experienced in reality the
disastrous violation of their existence.
H. J. Heering

In our journey and in our life with our neighbour, there is present
the experience of a grace which we human beings cannot resist.
We do not become aware of an almighty and eternal controller

behind events, but encounter God in events.
J. Sperna Weiland

Confronted by a personal tragedy or a large-scale disaster, it
never really occurs to me to regard it as the work of a Being who
'allows' (let alone 'sends') such terrible things ...

There is no intention in an earthquake or an accident. 'The
Spirit cooperates for good with those who love God' (Rom. 8.28) –
that is to say, for those who make the response of love, in every
concatenation of circumstance, however pointless and indeed
intention-less, there is to be met the graciousness of a 'Thou'
capable of transforming and liberating even the most baffling
and opaque into meaning and purpose.
J. A. T. Robinson[8]

God acts in and through the actions of men, and even through
their sins. This faith is no faint-hearted resignation to whatever
must inevitably come about, but is a victory.
G. C. van Niftrik

Children's questions such as, 'Who is God?', 'Where is he?', 'What does he do?' and 'What does he do for us?' arise because they are concerned to have contact with this God who is mysterious, strange and at the same time trusted.

Many parents teach their children to pray at a very early age. One may even say that seeing others pray provokes the first question, 'What are you doing? Who are you talking to?' Nothing pleases the child more than to make the same gestures, even though it does not understand what it is all about. Odiseria Knechtle has described the child's feelings as follows: 'I feel, before I understand it, that there is something special about God. I still do not understand what it is about, but I join in like a fish swimming in the water.'

Children are appreciative of rites and ceremonies and especially of their regular repetition. It is as though in them they still experience something of the rhythm of life in their mother's womb, which was security. In constantly repeated rites a child feels safe. He loses an inner balance when the regularity is interrupted. Evening prayers can be regarded as a protection against the darkness, the night and loneliness, and can even be experienced as a magical necessity.

By means of gestures and rites, a child can also become familiar with the world of faith. But it is quite possible that growing up, he has not altogether ceased to experience the religious ceremonies in a magical way. Then, but not until then, are we faced with a relic of primitive religion. For a child this is part of a natural development.

How the church has promoted this mentality! How many people's emotional lives have been led in a sphere of legalism! If only you could fulfil the rites, and carry out your religious duties! And woe upon you if you should step out of the safe line! The consequence of this was feelings of guilt and anxiety. How religious education in the past was oppressed by the heavy burden of the law! A child once expressed this briefly and to the point: 'If you don't pray and don't go to church, you go to hell!' But who told him that?

It is not hard to teach a child to pray. He takes to it enthusiastically and is easily led. The child can even help an uncertain mother over the threshold by asking about it. The innocent trust which parents so painfully lack is something the child naturally possesses. What matters is not to destroy his trust.

As far as the child is concerned it is not difficult to teach him to pray. The difficulty lies with the parents themselves. They mostly take refuge in infantile children's prayers from the past, although these are evidently incapable of translating their own belief to the child. And when they buy a book with children's prayers, they do not realize how questionable these often are. How important these texts are to the child's experience! They can influence his personal attitude to God for a long time.

The most likely thing, however, is that prayer itself is a problem of faith for many who have to do with children. This is naturally connected with the different apprehension of life of modern man, with the uncertainty of his faith. But it undoubtedly also goes to the way in which this generation itself learned to pray.

In the Roman Catholic world magical prayer used to be a typical phenomenon, and for many it still is. Making the sign of the Cross when there is a flash of lightning, ejaculatory prayers, the frequent repetition of a prayer, all give the impression that prayer is a protection against evil or a device to assure success.

In the case of Protestants, who have virtually no fixed prayers, praying for many different things is characteristic. God is informed about the coming meeting or the purpose of the committee, and his blessing is asked upon numerous human activities. This is called 'beginning' and 'ending' with prayer.

In some circles it is even regarded as the height of piety to regard nothing as too unimportant to place before God. Financial worries? One 'has recourse to prayer', and behold, the next day someone is at the door with a cheque book. And yet it is perhaps more probable to attribute this to telepathy rather to the intervention of God in the course of human affairs. Does God want us to ask him about things which he expects us to see to ourselves? Does God want to give his blessing to our separate ecclesiastical institutions? Especially when a bare five minutes after praying we are behaving in our church council as though no God or Christ existed! It could very well be that the prayers are frequently heathen prayers, even in the most devout communities and churches! But what is more important is that in prayer we break through our organizations and activities to what really matters, to the purpose of God.

Prayer is aimed at what really matters, God's purpose for our existence, his rule over the world. It is digging down to the rock on which our existence is built, opening our hearts to what is more than life, being thrown back upon the other dimension of our existence, where the meaning of life is concealed; continually exercising our faith, seeking intensively for power in weakness, for life in death, for Christ, God with us upon earth. Anyone who is really in touch with God passes from 'many things' to the 'one thing that is needful' (Luke 10.41), from our little world with its concerns into the world called into being by Christ. From the point of view of Christ, however, the 'little things' of men can be of the utmost importance.

One might compare prayer to a dialogue between two people. Someone is in need and goes to talk to a good friend, who, however, can offer no direct help. But the conversation is meaningful. Although the need is still just as great, something in it has changed as a result of the conversation. It was a liberation, and one's ideas are changed by it. In much greater measure prayer signifies a change, a turning towards the 'one thing that is needful'. If we were to look at all our prayers with this in mind, we would perhaps omit a good deal, for the sake of faith itself. 'O God give us ... make ... care for ... help us ... bring us ... be with ...'

How have children been taught to pray up to now? Most children's prayers can be classified as thanksgiving for food and requests for protection at night. These are the main themes.

The first theme seems to be a relic of agricultural life in the past, yet it is a very concrete introduction to an awareness of what it means to be able to live. In an age of prosperity it seems a strange tradition. It could well be that in times of abundance we do not pray in the same way from the heart, and can only utter prayers from the depths of our heart when we no longer know where our next meal is coming from. But amid the affluence of the Western world we might remember for a short moment in the day how thankful we can be that we can do ourselves well.

In any case a child can easily understand this prayer. Thanksgiving for food is a contact with the mystery of creation.

But it is remarkable that this should happen almost exclusively by way of thanksgiving for food. Sometimes the flowers and the sun are introduced into children's prayers, but never thanksgiving for life itself. But this is much more fundamental than 'food and drink'. And why should one not also give thanks for light, water, warmth and the earth! We teach a child to give thanks for his food, although he would rather not give thanks for green vegetables, which he doesn't like. At infant school the children give thanks for their dear father and mother, even though there may be a child there who has no mother or whose father is far from dear to him. The moment comes when a child stops in the middle of the thanksgiving, because how can you give thanks for life when there seems to be so much misery! Traditional children's prayers are concerned with human needs. Seldom or never do we find any element of adoration, the glorification of God with no further purpose.

But prayers of thanksgiving are almost entirely swamped by the petitions. We are so used to this emphasis in prayer that we do not realize that we can arouse too many expectations in children which cannot be fulfilled, or at least not by God. No one who teaches a child to ask for things in prayer can expect the child to pray for the kingdom of God of his own accord. He asks for a new scooter, a baby sister and for the ice to come. The great Augustine tells how in his youth he prayed fervently that he might not be beaten at school. He had apparently good reason to be afraid of this.

A young child thinks of God as an even more powerful Santa Claus, though 'Santa Claus is nicer, because he gives presents'. We must be aware of what we are doing when we teach a child to ask for things in prayer. It is perhaps no problem for us that we are speaking to someone who hears us, but who is silent and remains silent. And if it is a problem to us, then we are immediately thrown off our balance, 'can no longer bother', 'can no longer believe' and become grist to the mill of those who declare that God is dead for modern man. But is this not due to the way in which we learned to pray in our childhood?

For the child this is quite a problem: 'You can't hear God's voice.' 'The Lord Jesus never says anything back.'

What a disappointment it must be for a child, after many unanswered prayers for a little brother, when he sees that a little brother is not going to come. But it is marvellous how a child then looks for a solution himself: 'It is better if you don't ask for anything and only say thank you for what you get,' or 'Grandpa has died now and we prayed that he might stay alive, but now Grandma can laugh again.' Professor Langeveld has written about a little boy who had only one eye, 'Mother, if Daddy and you made me you would have seen to it that there

was nothing wrong with my eye.' Then, a few days later, 'Mother,
it isn't clever to see when your eyes are good. And at the resurrection God will say: Have you always seen with that one eye?
That's right. And then God can at least see that you have done
what he wanted.'

It is wrong to give children the impression that nine-tenths of
prayer is asking for things, although Karl Barth says most empha-
tically that a Christian has a right to ask. But then he adds that
he should ask for something that only God can give him.
Experience with infants shows that of themselves they are more
inclined to tell God things.

How are children taught to pray in traditional children's
prayers?

Unfortunately adults have clearly regarded children's prayers
as a teaching aid. At a time when a child's conscience has barely
begun to function, he already has to pray 'Although my sins are
many', 'Forgive me all the evil' and at the same time he has to
declare that he will 'be good and obedient', 'do everything Mother
asks' or 'what God asks of us', 'always follow him', and 'honour
him in every act'. The child has to pray for a 'pure heart' and that
he may 'consecrate himself wholly to God'.

Naturally, a child has an understanding of regret and a desire
for forgiveness, especially as he grows older, but do not these
prayers exercise too great a pressure on the child? Do adults
know what it means 'to follow God' in their daily life or 'to do
what God asks of us'?

It cannot be said too often that we have got to think about the
effect we have on children in this respect, and how we intend to
introduce them to a particular religious tradition. And how
unevangelical it is to let a child excuse himself to God every day
for 'still being only little' and then ask him – 'Yet!' – to have
mercy on this little person. 'Even though(!) I am still so small,
let me be a child of thine', or 'let me yet be Jesus' child', 'accept me
though I am so small'. Here is a real contrast with the children's
gospel of Mark 10.13-16!

The theology of children's prayers also contain a continuous
reference to heaven, especially in German children's prayers:
'Dear God, make me good, so that I may go to heaven.' 'Let me be
a grain of wheat and gather me into the heavenly barn.' Is this
what a child really wants? And all the angels round the child's
bed, when Protestant parents perhaps do not believe in guardian
angels. In one prayer there are fourteen. There once was a child
who was frightened by them.

Anyone who looks closely at children's prayers of petition, will quickly notice that there is one dominant theme in them. Almost all the prayers are a request for protection. Because they are often evening prayers, they ask for protection from the night. This is of course remarkable in itself, because the day is more dangerous for a child than the night. For a child is so active, and inattentive, and takes risks because he does not see the dangers. In human terms, he is nowhere safer than in bed, and nowhere so touchingly attractive and good. Such evening prayers, however, correspond to a primitive feeling of fear of darkness. We have no conception of the dreadful fears which children can undergo in this dark side of reality. Children still live in primitive demonic depths, in which things can become ghosts, in spite of all prayers and night-lights. Thus for a child a prayer against the darkness and against the night can be important.

Is it the helplessness of the child which has inspired adults to create these children's prayers, and their concern that nothing shall happen to them? It is not unlikely.

But for adults it is a strange idea to ask for special protection against the night. Is it perhaps a relic of former and more dangerous times?

God is portrayed to children as the great defender, guardian and protector. People even go so far as to get children to pray, 'Protect us in the heavy traffic, and take hold of our hand yourself.' Or, 'When we cross the street, let us see all the cars.'

For little children this kind of prayer can be dangerous. They can take it too literally, and suppose that God will protect them wherever they go, and consequently cross the street quite unconcernedly. It is probably better from the point of view of faith for a mother to tell her child that God has given us eyes to look round with and so that we can be most careful ourselves.

The whole of this kind of prayer seems to have been inspired by the words of Psalm 91.11, 12: 'He will give his angels charge of you to guard you in all your ways. On their hands they will bear you up, lest you dash your foot against a stone.'

But according to the story of the temptation in the wilderness, Jesus refused to appeal to this verse. Even as the Messiah he would not lay claim to this protection for the believer. And a great deal more happened to him than merely dashing his foot against a stone!

Is it then a religious temptation to expect God to protect the believer against 'the terror of the night', 'the arrow that flies by day', 'the pestilence that stalks the darkness', 'the destruction', 'the wild beasts', or 'war' (Psalm 91)?

We protect ourselves against the night in our houses, against

sickness, against wild animals, which we keep behind bars; it is
men who wage war and no one is safe in wartime.

We cannot ask God to intervene in the events of nature or in
the sphere of human responsibility. But what if someone is ill or
we are moved by the fate of someone who is dear to us? What
Christian does not then think of asking – probably against all
medical knowledge – even for something which is impossible for
man? Then one is fighting together with God for life and for
healing, even though God sees a different life and a different
kind of healing from those we see in our shortsightedness. To us
death can seem to be the worst thing; for God things may be
different. We do not even know what we should pray for, but
in any case we can pray for light in darkness, power in weakness,
and 'that he will raise something up out of all the misery, Amen',
as a child once wrote.

If we are really involved with God in a history, then the hearing
of prayer must take place in a different reality from that which is
immediately obvious to us. From God's point of view our history
has a completely different appearance. And if God is also the
God of our world, then he must have power over all the powers
in the world and the utmost activity must proceed from him.
Otherwise the universe would long ago have fallen into confusion.
But because his actions are hidden from us, we human beings
are thereby made free and responsible. We are taken seriously
by him, more seriously than by anyone else in the world. We
cannot yet see how immensely busy God is with his creation and
for what future he is heading with his creatures. And therefore
we still pray for the little things, which often do not matter very
much. We do not ask too much but too little.

Prayer for children. We have not consulted children themselves
enough. They have not been allowed to participate. They ought
to help us to formulate the prayers.

Here follow a number of prayers for younger and older children
and for the family. They are not meant simply to be used in whole
or in part, but above all to provide a stimulus for parents to work
out for themselves, together with their children, words of thanksgiving, adoration, trust, security, guilt, promise, desire and hope.
The themes are creation, the glory of the earth, light and darkness,
creatureliness, life, humanity, living, eating, sleeping, love, the
riddle of existence, evil and suffering, God's revelation in Jesus
Christ, human responsibility, peace on earth and the coming

kingdom of God. The first themes have been chosen for the younger children.

A child badly needs a fixed prayer. This may even be a prayer out of the tradition of the church, into which it can grow and which it does not need to reject later as infantile.

In any case, prayer for children must be seriously thought out. It matters that it should be true, real, genuinely Christian and evangelical. In fact it forms the essence of what we are trying to inculcate in them. It is the principal touchstone of our faith.

God, our Father, here I am.
I thank you for letting me live.
Thank you for all the people
who love me
and for a safe home.
Thank you for the sun and the flowers,
for everything that makes life good. Amen.

God, our Father,
I thank you because I can live and
because I am your child, protected by your love,
whatever happens. Amen.

Lord, our God,
we eat and drink,
in thanksgiving for your goodness. Amen.

As we eat and drink
what the good earth has given,
we will not forget you, O God,
because you created the earth
in all its glory. Amen.

When we eat of the bread
formed from the grain
that grew in the broad fields,
we think of you, O God,
because through you we live,
move and exist. Amen.

We are going to sleep, O God,
because it is getting dark.

We close our eyes tight,
finish our games and talking,
and wake in the morning with the light.
Please keep us safe this night,
great God, who are called our Father,
not us alone, but all men,
now and forever.

Dear God,
it is good to be alive,
to breathe, to sing,
and to go about everywhere in the world.
There is so much to see and so much happens!
I like the light
and not the darkness,
but you are with us
and the light is with you,
so that we are safe even in the night
and can go to sleep in confidence. Amen.

God, our Father,
I thank you for my birth;
that I was given eyes
to see the beautiful earth;
ears to hear the wind blowing
and a mouth to say
what has happened to me and what I think
and to sing
because life is good.
I thank you that I can walk.
I thank you for my hands,
which can make things
and because I can love people with my heart.
You have made me, God,
and you know who I am.
I cannot see you,
but I can talk to you
with my eyes closed
in blind trust
that you are with me.
Dear God, may we one day
see your glory? Amen.

God, our Father, because you love me, I am alive

Because you know me,
I am here and you watch me,
to see if I make something good of my life.
I cannot see you, but I trust you,
even though I do not understand everything.
You will never leave us. Amen.

Dear God, we thank you
that you are our God and Father
and we belong to you
as your own children.
You have given us the earth
to live on.
Because you love us so much
that you want to give us your glory,
help us to love men,
so that peace may come on earth. Amen.

O God, Jesus called you 'our Father',
because he knew you as your own son.
Through him we can trust you
whatever happens.
In light and darkness you are still our God
and your light shines in the darkness,
and no power in the world can ever put it out.
You have called us
to be children of the light,
to do your will and to live for each other
and to go on hoping that one day everything will be all right.
Amen.

God, our Father, you have given us so much:
life, love, the wide world,
and people do so much harm
and are not good to each other.
There is no peace on earth.
You know that I too am to blame
and it is as though it gets dark in me.
You understand that better than people do
Forgive me for it, O God,
I can often not help it.
Sometimes I want the darkness
more than the light,
but I can always come home to you

in the light of your love
and you accept me as your child.
If I believe that, I can live better
and love people more. Amen.

God, our Father, here we are:
little people in the big world.
So much happens that we do not understand.
Will there ever be peace on earth?
But it is your world
and though unseen,
you are busy, together with the people
making a new world.
We want to help you with this,
though we often do wrong,
but you have called us
for your kingdom.
We hope in you,
because the power and the glory are yours. Amen.

O God, through whom we live
and all things exist.
Your love, given to us,
wants us to be human.

We thank you for this life,
that you want us to have.
The earth that is given to us
Can be our world.

O help us to live
And exist for each other.
Your love, given to us,
must be for the world.

O God, we worship you,
although our eyes cannot see you.
But because the world is so wonderful,
and the stars which shine in the night,
how much greater your glory must be
and the light of your unending love.
We thank you because you have made us
and we were born on this earth.
Although the world is dark.

and life sometimes difficult,
we entrust ourselves to you in light and darkness,
because you are our Father and will never leave us.
You are more powerful than all the powers in the world,
although we do not yet see this.
Your kingdom will come.
For yours is the power and the glory
now and for ever. Amen.

COMMUNION WITH GOD

Daddy, I want to whisper something. *She whispers in his ear:*
Shall I tell you something? God is nice.
Girl aged three

I think God is nice, because he has such a nice little baby.
Boy aged three

God is the Father of all men, he cares for us and loves us. – Can
we go to him sometime? – That is difficult because God lives a
long way away. – Well, he can come by tram and see us sometime,
can't he?
Girl aged three

I think God is nicest of all.
Boy aged five

God the Holy Spirit, he makes you clever and holy. – What is
holy? – Good, good all through.
Boy aged five

Later on I am going to marry God, then I can go and live in
heaven and then I will have a fine view.
Girl aged six

Who do you like best, Aunt M. or God? – Aunt M. – Then you
will never go to heaven.
Boy aged seven

She wrote on a piece of paper whom she loved best: God, father,
mother. Really, she loved mother best.
Girl aged seven

I have so many friends, Mummy, the shopkeeper and God and Daddy.
Boy aged eight

I don't know whether I like God.
Girl aged eight

Is God really alive? I don't see him, I don't hear him, I would like him to come and live with us. But he is the funniest fellow, I talk to him, but he doesn't answer. How can I talk to him, how can he hear me?
Girl aged eight

When you think of him, then he exists.

CONTACT WITH GOD

I dreamt that God was with me, not here beside my bed, but that he had made me happy. I was able to talk to God.
Girl aged six

Sometimes you have the feeling that God is with you. It makes you want to cry. In your body you have a strange feeling.
Girl aged ten

One evening I was saying my prayers. Then I thought of God. And it was as if I had seen God, standing by my bed and saying to me that he would protect me and go with me everywhere I would go, and would watch me to see that I would never lose the way if I went into the wood and went a long way, a long way from home. And then I went to sleep, very peaceful.
Girl aged ten

Once when I was in church, it was as if God was with me, and then I began to think about what God is.
Boy aged eleven

One evening when I was saying my prayers before going to sleep, the room became very light. I thought it was an angel, but then he disappeared.
Girl aged eleven

One evening when I was in bed and was praying it got very dark

in the room. Then I suddenly saw a light. I thought it was an angel, but I wasn't quite sure. Since that moment I have completely understood that God exists.
Girl aged eleven

CHILDREN'S UNDERSTANDING OF PRAYER

At evening prayers: Where is God? – God is everywhere, in church and here as well. – God's got to go away. *He looked round fearfully.* Please go away back to church, otherwise Johnny is frightened. – There, now God's gone away hasn't he? *he said, relieved.*
Boy aged three

His mother wanted to get him used to evening prayers and looked out all kinds of prayers to use. To her surprise he was frightened of speaking to the invisible God and began to cry. So she began to sing evening hymns.
Boy aged four.

Mummy, can you not ring God up sometime?
Boy aged four

Could you not send a postcard to God? – What would you want to write on it? – Well, that he has always been so kind to us.
Boy aged four

Stormy weather. A little boy is letting a paper blow away into the air. What are you doing with that rubbish? – It isn't rubbish, it's a letter to God. It's got to blow up above with the wind.
Boy aged four

He is frightened of frogs in the garden. I have just prayed, because I was frightened, and real men do that as well.
Boy aged five

When we pray, the Lord Jesus counts us.
Boy aged five

A little boy sees a picture of a child praying. What is that little girl doing? – She is praying and talking to God. – But God is in

heaven, how can he understand it? Oh, I know, by electricity just like the radio.
Boy aged five

I don't want to pray, God never says yes or no!
Girl aged five

Now pray aloud properly. – I'm not going to pray to you, I'm praying softly to God, he can hear all right.
Boy aged six

How can God understand all the people at the same time?
Six-year-old

Can't you pray for yourself? – No, I haven't so many thoughts.
Boy aged seven

Lord, help us to listen to your voice. – Mummy, I never hear his voice.
Girl aged seven

Me and God, we know everything.
Girl aged seven

Why does God not speak to people any more? – Perhaps we no longer listen enough. – I know why, before there were a lot less people and now there are so many that God has to talk very loud to be heard on earth, and lots of people hear it as well who haven't anything to do with it.
Boy aged seven

Mummy, is it silly to pray that I can become a prophet? I prayed for that, I so much want to belong to God.
Girl aged seven

You never get an answer when you pray and it says in the Bible that God does give answers.
Girl aged eight

There are times when I am much closer than other times to the Lord and have such a safe feeling. Once they were shooting an awful lot, and I was terribly frightened, and then I prayed and then it was just as if somebody laid his hand on my head, and

I went to sleep. I would like that to happen again sometime.
Girl aged eight

Is praying always just asking?
Boy aged eight

My mother doesn't believe in God. At night she puts me to bed and opens the window. When she has gone away, I get out of bed and say my prayers.

It is just as if my head was spinning when I say the Our Father. Perhaps other ideas have got into it then.
Girl aged eleven

PRAYERS OUTSIDE HOME

At nursery school: In the morning we close our eyes and then we all wake up again together.
Girl aged four

The children are having a meal at the house of an aunt who doesn't go to church, who suddenly says rather timidly, Oh well, you'll want to say grace first, won't you? *The boy looks angrily at his hostess and says,* We never pray in people's houses.
Boy aged four

A little boy was staying with his aunt because his little brother was being born, and he found it strange to be saying his prayers there. He did this at home every evening. His aunt encouraged him, whereupon he said: Are there two Jesuses then?
Boy aged five

A little boy lost his rosary. Now I don't need to pray at night. Jesus has lost himself.
Boy aged five

A boy has just started school. Do we pray the whole day long now, Mummy? Before and after meals at home, prayers in the evening and four times at school!
Boy aged six

God knows everything. So he knows that I'm not disobedient when I look towards the cathedral while teacher is praying because I

already know what she is going to pray. Because it's always the same.
Girl aged six

A boy who only knows a silent prayer starts going to Sunday School and says, The teacher keeps on talking all through the prayers.
Boy aged seven

A little girl is saying her prayers at Grandma and Grandpa's house: Hail Mary, full of grace. *She blushes and says,* Sorry, I forgot that Grandma and Grandpa are Protestants.
Girl aged nine

ANSWERS TO PRAYER

A little girl lost her slippers, prayed and gave her address as well.
Girl aged four

I have already prayed four times for you, for myself as well, but I'm still not better, but the Lord Jesus has probably too much to do with all the sick children.
Girl aged four

A little boy prayed every evening for a sister. When it was a brother, he said, Well, of course the Lord hadn't any more little girls left and so he could only send a little boy.
Boy aged four

I got a little brother. If you want one as well, then you have to pray for one. I asked for a sister, but they hadn't any more, they had used them all up with Auntie.
Boy aged four

We have been asking ever so long for a little brother or a little sister. – Well, stop now, we have enough children. *A few days later,* An angel stood in my bedroom and he promised that it would really happen.
Five-year-old

Mummy, I prayed for you, and your pain is not so bad. – Yes, but it can come back, and then I shall have to go to the hospital. – Yes, but the Lord Jesus can do it himself through the air.
Girl aged five

I'm going to get to school in time, because last night I prayed to God for him to look after me.
Boy aged six

I pray all the time for a brother, do you? – No, for a brother or a sister. *Contemptuously:* Well, that's terribly stupid, because that way God will never know what you want.
Girl aged six

Will you make the sick children better, Lord Jesus? I will make a nice box for the birds, Lord Jesus. *Timidly he says,* The Lord Jesus says nothing back.
Boy aged seven

Why don't you say your daily evening prayers any more? All you say is: Thank you for this and thank you for that, have you nothing to ask our Lord? – Yes, but you hardly ever get anything you ask for. I asked about six times for something I didn't get. I think you do better not to ask for anything and only say thank you for what you do get. Then at least you are pleased, aren't you, Mummy? And you aren't sorry because it didn't happen.
Girl aged seven

Do you know, Mummy, what I meant in my prayers by 'the children a long way away'? – In other countries? – No, all children are just as close to God, but those ones have heard about God, but then they think, 'It's probably not true at all.'
Girl aged seven

Praying and holiness seem to me to be something worth while. – Grandma, I can't pray like you can. – You don't have to pray, I'll do that for you.

Can I pray to God for long hair if Mummy won't let me?
Girl aged eight

I think it's mean of the Lord Jesus, I've prayed to him every evening to win a prize, but he didn't listen to me.
After grace at table: If you only knew, I like Santa Claus better than the Lord Jesus. I get what I ask Santa Claus for, but not the Lord Jesus.
Girl aged eight

After a bus accident, in which some children were killed: The

fathers must have prayed in the morning that they would be kept safe but now they are dead.
Girl aged eight

CHILDREN'S PRAYERS

How do you do, Jesus, Amen.

Father in heaven, take care of us and all children, stay close to us, Amen.
Girl aged four

Thank you for the Christmas tree. Have you got one in heaven?
Girl aged five

May I never be in a war and later on have children.
Girl aged seven

I thank you because the snowdrops have come up, I thank you because the birds have started to sing again and because the trees are going to grow green again, I thank you because I have a father and a mother, who love me so much and also for my little brother and sister. I thank you dear God the Father, because I have so many nice books and because it is Book Week twice a year. Amen.
Girl aged eight

Dear Lord, you know about Grandma. What exactly is wrong with her I don't know, but you must see about it.
Girl aged six

AT INFANT SCHOOL

God, our Father, when will you send the sun through the clouds? I do so want to play outside.
Girl aged five

God, our Father, you made the stick insects grow, but I daren't let them run about on my hand, but Peter does.
Girl aged five

God, our Father, this morning I got a puppy. I don't know what he is called, I haven't asked him yet.
Boy aged five

God, our Father, do you know that there have been men on your moon?
Boy aged five

God, our Father, do you ever look for the people who are by themselves? Near us on the seventh floor a lady lives by herself.
Girl aged six

O God, I know how big your heaven is, it is all round the world.
Boy aged six

O God, my tooth has to come out and now I am getting a grown up tooth. I can feel the point already.
Girl aged six

O God, when I was very little and growing inside my Mummy, she always took me everywhere with her, but of course she doesn't any more.
Girl aged six

During prayers a marble rolls away. You are much more important than marbles.

You are much cleverer than the teacher, because you can hear us all at the same time and teacher always says, 'One at a time, otherwise I can't understand you.'

Thank you for the pears which you make grow, because I think they are delicious.

Will you take good care of the baby in John's mother's tummy?

Dear Lord, let my little brother grow fast, because when he is big, we'll both sleep in a bunk bed.

Will you please help my father, because he is so busy. He says he never gets finished.

Dear Lord, my father doesn't live with us any more. Now my mother has to go and work.

A little boy's mother is incurably ill. During prayers he said nothing. Have you nothing to say to God the Father? – Yes, I have, but I listened to what you said, but you didn't say anything either.

After the Easter holidays: Thank you very much for making Jesus alive, otherwise we couldn't pray to you.

CHILDREN'S PRAYERS FROM OTHER LANDS

O God, Creator of Light: at the rising of your sun this morning, let the greatest of all lights, your love, rise like the sun within our hearts.
Armenian Apostolic Church[1]

O God, who sends the light to shine upon this earth; God, who makes the sun shine upon those who are good and those who do wrong; God, who created the light that lights the whole world, shine your light into our minds and our hearts. Guard us from all that is harmful to ourselves or to others.
Coptic Church[2]

Thank you for the flowers that bloom by the road,
For birds that sing in the trees;
For clear waters that gush from the springs;
For the bread we are about to eat.[3]

Mountains, rivers and fields,
Clearly show God's love to us.
All things created by him dance with joy.
We children, also, will sing of his love.[4]

O God, who makes a thousand flowers to blow,
Who makes both grains and fruits to grow,
Hear our prayer:
Bless this food
And bring us peace.[5]

AN EVENING PRAYER FROM GERMANY

The day draws in; most lovely treasure,
Lord Jesus Christ, stay with me.
The evening darkens,
But let your light not fade
Over all of us here on earth.

The evening star already shines.

Good night, you dear ones, near and far; sleep in the peace of God.
The flowers close their tiny eyes, the little birds go to rest.
All the weary folk quickly fall asleep. But you do not sleep or slumber.
With you, O God, the night is not dark.
I put myself in your hands.
Take care of me, your child.
After a peaceful night, let the sun shine joyfully upon me.

Night comes over city and field,
God, bless the earth,
Guard the world.

AN ANCIENT PRAYER REVIVED

Just as the bread which we break
Was scattered over the earth, was gathered in and became one,
Bring us together from everywhere
Into the kingdom of your peace.
Huub Oosterhuis[6]

CHILDHOOD PRAYERS REMEMBERED

But, Lord, we found that men called upon Thee, and we learnt from them to think of Thee (according to our powers) as of some great One, who, though hidden from our senses, couldst hear and help us. For so I began, as a boy, to pray to Thee, my aid and refuge; and broke the fetters of my tongue to call on Thee, praying Thee, though small, yet with no small earnestness, that I might not be beaten at school.
Augustine[7]

'Take care of my parents and my friends this night ...'
The influence of that prayer was altogether a calming one. The main point was that we submitted ourselves to the protection of God which we had prayed for and we were aware that this was the main thing. Criticism came later. Why had God to protect me against the evil that threatened me? Would it not be better if God the Almighty should instantly destroy the evil or not even let it come into being? And why should just my parents and friends be protected and not those of a boy who had not learnt to pray?
Jan Ligthart

Like many children I had unfortunate experiences with the
efficacy of prayer. One day when there was to be an examination
in geography I prayed that our master would choose as subject
the tributaries of the Seine, which I knew, rather than those of the
Loire which I could never remember. He gave us the Loire and
my faith was shaken.
André Maurois[8]

'I say, do you believe that God loved Grandfather because he had
read the Bible through fifty times?'

'Yes, Selma, I suppose so.'

When I heard this answer, something remarkable happened to
me. I didn't work it out for myself, it was as if someone whispered
to me what God wanted me to do, so that my father might get
better.

I was afraid at the idea. Just think, such a terribly thick book.
And if there was nothing in it except sermons and exhortations!
But this didn't matter if only father were to stay alive.

I put my hands together and promised God that I would read
through the whole Bible if my father were only to get well again.
Yes, I would read it through from beginning to end, without
missing a single word.
Selma Lagerlöf

It may be some comfort to all those who in their childhood and
later have believed themselves to be dominated by the powers of
darkness, if I recall that as a child I was unable for many
years to take any decision and sometimes give any answer before
I had counted quickly and silently up to sixteen or had inaudibly
uttered the name of God six times.
Ernst Wiechert

My mother's death was the occasion of what some (but not I)
might regard as my first religious experience.

When her case was pronounced hopeless I remembered what I
had been taught: that prayers offered in faith would be granted.
I accordingly set myself to produce by will power a firm belief
that my prayers for her recovery would be successful; and, as I
thought, I achieved it. When nevertheless she died I shifted my
ground and worked myself into a belief that there was to be a
miracle. The interesting thing is that my disappointment produced no results beyond itself. The thing hadn't worked, but I
was used to things not working, and I thought no more about it.
I think the truth is that the belief into which I had hypnotized

myself was itself too irreligious for its failure to cause any religious revolution. I had approached God, or my idea of God, without love, without awe, even without fear. He was, in my mental picture of this miracle, to appear neither as Saviour nor as Judge, but merely as a Magician; and when He had done what was required of Him I supposed He would simply – well, go away. It never crossed my mind that the tremendous contact which I solicited should have any consequences beyond restoring the *status quo*. I imagine that a 'faith' of this kind is often generated in children and that its disappointment is of no religious importance.
C. S. Lewis[9]

RITUAL

A child learns quickly through impressions, images, and symbols, through the sensible and concrete, in movement, gestures and through his environment.
J. van Haaren

After the evening prayers and singing (which was always shared by our mother when she was at home), we lay awake a long time and tried to imagine what eternal life and being dead were like. We endeavoured every evening to get a little nearer to eternity by concentrating on the word 'eternity' and excluding every other thought. It seemed very long and gruesome, and, after some time of intense concentration, we often felt dizzy. I believed this ritual saved Dietrich from being 'devoured' by Satan.
Sabine Leibholz[10]

The young child is very conservative, a fact which represents the other side of his fear of what is unknown and therefore unreliable. The ordered path of life still floats against a dark shapeless background of what is undetermined. Every attempt to give form to ideas can destroy genuineness, in that a child becomes too attached to the form, so that it loses its character of an expression. The church and the mass become the faith.
M. J. Langeveld

GUIDING CHILDREN'S PRAYERS

The important thing is that he talks to God and that he knows God is listening, not how he talks, what he says or where he says it.
Frances Wilkinson[11]

Children will only pray when they see that to pray is holy, that it is aimed above and that it is different from our many everyday concerns. To be holy means to be attractive, to be great and so mysterious that it enthrals.

A child believes in a primitive fashion and experiences the relationship with God in direct association with his environment. Consequently there is no hurry about children's prayers, and it is better that we should not experiment too much with children's prayers, but rather leave the experiment to children themselves.
J. van Haaren

With regard to prayers, the danger of infantilism is considerable, when we see and hear the number of childish prayers that are current. We begin, therefore, with a plea to bring children aged from eight to ten years in contact with set prayers which have not been produced with one eye always on the child.

A child will notice that one cannot ask God for everything, something which a child is often inclined to do. He will learn to disregard himself, to look up towards God and to look around himself towards others.

Because children easily fall into routine, it is necessary to introduce variations into the prayers, and above all they must be short.
L. Kuylman-Hoekendijk

Schoolchildren ought not to have to pray so much. There should be more awe for him who is worshipped, more reverence for the earth itself on the part of the child, and less zeal for prayer as an achievement.
J. H. Huijts

PRAYER AS MAGICAL

Prayer is effective when there is belief in him who is worshipped and not in the power of the prayer.
Karl Rahner

There can be no doubt that prayer is often misused in a magical sense by adults.
Theophil Thun

You can no longer ask anything of God with a sense of decency if you know that the cause, circumstances and consequences of it lie in human hands, as would be the case if, for example, you asked: 'Let me pass this exam.' This is associated with the whole role which was previously attributed to God. If a great disaster took place somewhere, this was seen as the punishment of God.

The only thing that you can really say to God is: 'Let it be according to your word.'
Michel van der Plas

One can lean on God as a father-figure to gratify the needs of one's emotions or one's life, where there are open wounds. But God is then imprisoned in egocentricism.
Antoine Vergote

PRAYER: SOME DEFINITIONS

To adore ... That means to lose oneself in the unfathomable, to plunge into the inexhaustible, to find peace in the incorruptible, to be absorbed in defined immensity, ... to give of one's deepest to that whose depth has no end.
Pierre Teilhard de Chardin[10]

To pray is to live, really to live in the sight of God.

The content of the prayer of petition is the Kingdom. The creation is the horizon of the prayer of thanksgiving, and the *eschaton* the horizon of the prayer of petition.
K. H. Miskotte

To pray is to experience the resurrection. Every prayer in the Bible, however crushed and despairing its beginning, turns after a pause for breath to: 'Thou art the preserver of my life, thou art my God.'
Huub Oosterhuis

Many people cannot pray, I sometimes think, because they cannot talk, because they have never been able to have a conversation with their fellow men or to find someone who was paying attention to them and ready to be with them and listen.

Man becomes human very slowly, and most do so after a great deal of toil. But to collide is often also to pray, to sigh, to be struck dumb, not to know what to say. To be unable to pray any longer is to pray, because it can all be a very clear reaction on the part of human reality to the reality which is God. In these tensions, in this wrestling with God, in the darkness of God's apparent absence, many people grow mature, and become people who pray and who are able to do everything to bring their heart to God, because they have become wise through much experience and have discovered God to be what is closest to them in their life.
J. van Haaren

Just as faith resolves nothing, so prayer brings nothing of itself, but the act of praying is a liberating one, giving new freedom to live and die, to trust and love, to endure and submit. The more we depend upon the Father as the ground of our being, the more we shall ask him for things which are really decisive for that existence.
J. H. Huijts

God does not despise small things, because if he did, he would not have created them.
Augustine

A vast multitude of things which in Calvin's time could only be brought before God in prayer are now recognized without question as falling within the sphere of our own responsibility.
H. M. Kuitert

The man who really prays comes to God and approaches and speaks to Him because he seeks something of God, because he hopes to receive something which he needs, something which he does not hope to receive from anyone else, but does definitely hope to receive from God.
K. Barth[11]

PETITION AND ANSWER

Those who would remove supplicatory prayer for temporal things from our personal relationship with God are really acting as though he had not created the world; or, to put it differently: as if the world as it actually is no longer interested him.
E. Schillebeeckx[12]

What do we expect? An increase of our knowledge of God in prayers which are answered or not answered. This knowledge, this good is something added, an extra blessing.

In prayer we face up to 'it had to be', to the chain of circumstances, to arbitrariness, to fate.

In prayer we constantly renew our link with God in the face of fate.
K. H. Miskotte

The Christian is able to ask. The Christian is able to take, because God gives him Himself and all that He possesses. To all the true and legitimate requests that are directed necessarily to God, there is one great answer. This one divine gift and answer is Jesus Christ.
K. Barth[13]

The dedication of our heart which is then restored to us, makes us realize that we are really taking part in the history of God's world.
K. H. Miskotte

Somebody prays to be cured. He calls on God, his faithfulness, his friendship. In that prayer there is a change in the meaning of his illness, and his outlook; he changes himself and becomes greater than fear and pain. He dies, but he dies differently.

The petitions in the liturgy should intensify and purify the questions and desires with which we live ... In petitions the church questions itself and arouses its own conscience: the world is our horizon, Vietnam and Biafra are part of me; or we are war ourselves. And the request which lies behind all set formulas and remains when all words are spoken is this: whether we too will do what we see and be what we say. We pray for peace, exhort each other to show humanity, and the question is whether we ourselves are going to be men at peace. We pray for those who rule us and we thereby call each other to political commitment. We pray for the poor and the dying, and thereby point away from ourselves, outside the church, and tell each other who matters in this world. We pray for other people: we recognize our union with them, and desire to support and serve them and give directly to them. And busy as we are with this world, almost lost in the immensity of the present moment and time and again rephrasing our requests, we remain ready to accept that there is a different and greater answer than what we suppose; there is a meaning in our existence.

... Therefore those who believe dare to say, in the face of everything that happens: and yet ... Perhaps, if they no longer did this, they would be choked up to bursting point ... and would become war.
Huub Oosterhuis

11 The Black Side

It repeatedly happens that in the early years children are told by a neighbour's child something about 'hell and the devil'. Where did they pick this up? The source of most of this has been the infant school. It used to be a favourite theme of religious instruction to young children.

'Oh,' people will say, 'all that went out long ago and belongs to the past!'

Perhaps the past is not as far away as we think. Those who are now instructing children were probably themselves educated in the period this expression refers to. However complete an about-turn has been made in religious instruction, for example in Roman Catholic infant schools, there still remains deep in the heart of those who are teaching the children an ineradicable memory of the 'old days'. The principal recollection is one of fear. Who can determine how far resistance or rancour against the church and Christian faith on the part of many adults is derived in fact from this indoctrination in their early years at school? It must go very deep.

This is 'the black side' of religious instruction to children.

What severe moral and religious pressure has been imposed on defenceless, sensitive infants and growing children! What absurd demands have been made upon them! With what intensity and frequency children have had to take part in worship; how they have been glutted and worked upon with fierce zeal! It was dinned into them, the more the better; and the more often, the more chance that they would never break away from it. Missionary zeal was often stronger than psychological or educational insight.

On the Roman Catholic side, this was already admitted years ago. J. van Haaren tells of a sister who confessed to him that she had burnt the picture of purgatory, the picture which was supposed to be used in the infant class.

And how cautiously religious education is now undertaken in Catholic infant schools, so cautiously that many teachers no longer know what they are supposed to teach.

In Protestant infant schools, the occasional question is actually beginning to be raised as to whether it is right to teach children at such an early age the whole of biblical history, and to do so several times a week. But this question has only recently come to the fore. The missionary urge 'that you should not keep the Bible stories back from the children' is still dominant. 'At home the parents do nothing or almost nothing about it', and 'They will have heard it at least once in their lives', and 'The kids take in everything you say'.

There are children who panic when it rains at night after they have heard the story of the Flood, or become nervous towards Easter time because then – in great detail – the passion of Jesus is told. And what five-year-old child would not be worried to hear that you do not go to heaven if you do not love the Lord and do not pray at home and do not go to church?

Young children perhaps mislead the missionary zeal of adults by their receptiveness to worship and their immediate readiness to accept anything. But is it to be taken for granted that with their brief experience of life they should be confronted with the impressive drama of biblical history, with wars and disasters, marriage and adultery, Pharisees and publicans, the Holy Ghost and the doctrine of the atonement? That children can repeat all this is no indication that they can digest it!

And then there is hell and the devil. These seem to have been standard themes in all parts of the church, particularly for infants. How can this be explained? Undoubtedly a need has been felt from the earliest times to get children young and to admonish them as forcefully as possible at the beginning of their lives. The threat of divine justice came in very handy. The parents' own inability to lead a good life no doubt explains the exaggerated emphasis that has been laid on the demands of virtue and piety. It is tragic to realize how young children have been sacrificed to the ill-digested inner conflicts of adults. A psychological explanation could be found in the needs of adults to project their own suppressed fears and guilt feelings on to children. The effect of this on children is particularly powerful. They are very sensitive to fears and threats. Just listen to the stories they make up themselves! Here we are perhaps faced with an emotional transference which is closer to primitive religion than to the gospel. One might even speak of an unchristian demonism and spiritual sadism which seizes hold of children and as a result of which they are terrified to death of God throughout their lives. In human terms, this is one of the most puzzling aspects of children's religious instruction.

One element in the missionary zeal of teachers has certainly been the great need to bear testimony before the children to the overflowing love of God, but it is clear that a dark background was necessary if this was to be expressed to the full. Naturally, one cannot proclaim the message of the divine light without mentioning the darkness. In a certain sense one can appeal to the Bible itself in justification for this. In the Bible the light of God constantly breaks through into a profound and often hopeless human darkness. Anyone who thoughtlessly repeats Bible stories can easily overlook the dark depths in these narratives. And no one who has understood anything about the faith of the Bible can escape the fact that the righteousness of God has awe-inspiring consequences for human history on earth.

But why make these stories even harder for children, impose on them more and more and expose children in their earliest years to the full blast of the terrors of man's world, and even open perspectives of the eternal terrors of the righteousness of God? Whereas in the Bible hell and the devil are very rarely mentioned, they have clearly become central themes of the religious instruction of children. 'But look at the television,' one might reply, 'The kids only need to sit a few minutes longer after the end of the children's programme and they will see plenty of the horrors of this world of men.' There are even parents who say that they must get used to it early, as part of a realistic modern education. And what do they see? Hell on earth. Fons Jansen tells a story of St Peter talking to a new arrival at the gates of heaven: 'Hell? My dear fellow, that's where I have just come from!'

But the dark side of children's religious instruction is not simply a matter of the merciless portrayal of the world of darkness. What matters is that all this is related to morality, that a child is told all about it as if it were true. And that the terrors of the world are related to a God who punishes. The impression which a young child gets of God in this way is dangerous.

How many people are going about nowadays with this legacy from their religious instruction and can never shake it off? In their earliest years a religion of fear was firmly impressed upon them and many of them no longer seem receptive to the true gospel.

I can imagine that infant teachers will be reading these pages with profound indignation. As if this was still so nowadays! But as long as children still come home saying that teacher told them that heaven is made of gold and that you don't go there if you don't say your prayers and don't go to church, and as long as tens of thousands of people are going about with primitive conflicts of faith, it still has to be repeated. In this respect, the religious education of liberal Christianity has remained outside this tradition, but it too has not avoided moralism.

Because children have had no full place and function in the church, there has arisen alongside the church's tradition a separate tradition within the 'reserves' set aside in the churches for children. And this second tradition – or should it be called the first? – has been able to maintain itself for centuries in spite of developments in the church, biblical knowledge and theology. Even now, in the twentieth century, the religious instruction of children displays typical mediaeval features. The same ideas are clearly being taught from one century to the next. It is perhaps in those special reserves for children within the churches, where no church preaching or Reformation insights have had any influence, that conservative forces have been formed.

That the Roman Catholic catechism was able to maintain itself far into the twentieth century is a sign of this. There has of course been contact between religious instruction to children and the church, because initiation into the liturgy took place at school. Nevertheless, the children were kept as a firmly separate group: they went to confession with the class, to the school mass every morning – 'and Daddy only has to go once a week!' – while for the renewal of baptismal promises the creed was – and is – recited with the teacher leading it.

In the case of Protestants, the continuing tradition of religious education for children has grown even more remote from the rest of church life. For a century Sunday school associations have interested themselves in children, while more often than not the same biblical religious instruction is also given in Protestant church schools, where there is virtually no contact with the church congregation. In this special reserve for children within Protestant Christianity a distinct theology has been developed which differs profoundly from what is preached to congregations. This separate theology maintains a hidden and obstinate existence, especially in so far as it is still linked to certain systems of bible-reading for children.

In the past there was a clear difference between Protestant and Catholic instruction. The latter used the catechism while Protestantism used the biblical narrative. But the fact was overlooked that this very biblical narrative was reproduced amongst Protestants in a particularly Roman Catholic and even mediaeval pattern of thought. One has only to read the classic 'orthodox Protestant' children's Bibles to see this.

The devil sneaks through paradise – it is the fallen angel himself. What matters is the hereafter, getting to heaven. This depends upon man, his actions and his religious devotion. Consequently a clear distinction can be made between the devout and 'bad people'.

And all this is still associated with a fundamentalist understanding of the Bible from previous centuries, as though the biblical narrative was meant to be an accurate account of historical facts, even including the day the sun stood still. A human being's faith made the sun stand still!

Hardly any of those who hold responsible theological positions in the Protestant church have concerned themselves with this. They 'didn't know about it', even though people were actually teaching it to their own children. It was 'only just for children'. It has been too little realized that in this very area set apart for children the foundation was laid of the understanding of faith of those who now form the congregations, and that countless numbers amongst them were indoctrinated in this way for the rest of their lives.

In Protestant religious instruction for children, then, there has also been a separate dark side here, and it is still in operation. The intention was to teach the Bible, but unfortunately according to a very unbiblical pattern of thought. 'Who sows the wind, shall reap the whirlwind', and this is true here. The whirlwind of doubt, uncertainty and the rejection of the faith has not been caused solely by the modern age, but certainly also by the influences people have been subjected to in their youth. And we even have the feeling that we can no longer avert this storm by human means, through changes in instruction, a more psychological and less dogmatic approach and cheerful family services.

Let us in any case hope that 'the dark side' has gradually disappeared. There is much evidence to show that those who belong to the Reformation churches are less reforming in this respect than the Catholics. In any case something is happening. Questions are being asked which in the past were never raised. People are looking for new ways and a better approach to the child.

In all this, there is one thing that we must not forget. While the official church ignores it, innumerable lay people have done something about teaching children the faith. It is perhaps the most rewarding but also the most difficult task of the church. And how often have they been let down by those who should know better. But it is they who have built the bridges to the future for the new generation. And how could the church still have existed after twenty centuries if, in spite of misleading indoctrination, there had not also been from generation to generation, teaching that was closer to the original gospel?

SUNDAY SCHOOL AND CATECHISM

Just started school. The teacher knows nothing, she asks us everything.
Boy aged five

At school the boys know nothing about God. – How do you know that, don't you talk about him there?
Boy aged five and his sister

A little boy no longer goes to the church school. I couldn't get on with Jesus.

The curate tells you one thing, the teacher at school something else, only one of them can be true.
Boy aged six

He took part very seriously in preparation for first communion. You go to hell if you are bad.
Boy aged six

Preparation for first communion: I'm not a little lamb!
Boy aged seven

First communion: What do you all want to ask Jesus? – Help us to do my best, but can I be naughty just once a day?
Boy aged seven

A little girl cried in bed when preparing for communion, because she thought she was no longer God's friend.
Girl aged seven

With God it is just like at the grocer's, you pay with faith and you get heaven in exchange.
Boy aged eight

Mummy, what are sins against nature? *I paused for a moment because it is something a little bit difficult to explain to an eight-year-old boy and I don't want to fob him off.* Oh, I already know, it's when people pull the leaves off the trees and break the flowers.
Boy aged eight

A boy was taken away from Sunday school after the second year.

He often used to come back agitated and sullen, closer to weeping than to laughing. They are always punching each other during the prayers.

For a year he read the same story every morning: the twelve-year-old Jesus in the Temple. When he was ten, he said: I would really like to sing the Sunday school songs again.

HELL AND THE DEVIL

Teacher says that there is a hell and that you will burn in it eternally. What is eternally? – Always. – That can't be so because everything that burns turns to ashes.
Girl aged five

Questions put by children at infant school:
How big is the devil's chain? Why is hell not in heaven? Where was hell when the earth wasn't made yet? Where is purgatory, in heaven or on earth? Is it warm in limbo? Can no water get in to limbo? Are there devils in purgatory as well? I don't believe that there is a hell and that there's a fire in it and that people go there, God is much too good for that.

The devil can sometimes actually be in somebody. – You mustn't say that, I find it so horrid. Is it true that when you're ill it's the devil doing it?
Boy aged six

When I'm naughty, God sends me an illness. When children are naughty, he makes them die and they go to hell.
Seven-year-old

When I go to bed at night, I always get quickly into bed, then the devil can't get at me.
Girl aged eight

Crying: The devil always says to me that I am not a child of the Lord Jesus.
Boy aged eight

I believe that hell is when you are not in heaven.
Girl aged nine

What I think about heaven is, I imagine a great white palace of

marble or something, yards and yards wide and then there is a
very dark corner with a trap door and if you lift it up, you hear
a terrible crying and then you have to go down the stairs and then
you are in hell!
Girl aged eleven

CATECHETICAL REMINISCENCES

At 2.30 in the afternoon there were lessons in religion in the
dining room.

The three adults sat round the dining table while the minister
put a kind of top hat made of black straw on the sideboard.
Mamma, who once walked through the room, saw the hat in
dangerous proximity to her magnificent Sèvres vases, lifted it carefully with both hands and laid it on a chair.

In a subdued voice the children were asked why they were on
earth. Christiane knew that this certainly could not be in order
to keep animals, read enjoyable books, to save a favourite person's
life and do everything else that she wanted to do so much: ride
horses, drive, paint, play the violin and the piano ... no, that was
not why she was on earth, and certainly not to hunt a mustang
across the prairie ... but she repeated her verse: 'To serve God,
to love him and thereby to go to heaven.' This 'thereby' did not
suit her at all. No hour of sixty minutes lasted as long as the
religious lesson.
Mechtilde Lichnowski

My other painful memories of that school-time are the Catechism
and the hours we had to spend on it. A small book full of wooden,
bloodless questions and answers, wrested from the living Biblical
text, and only fit to occupy the arid minds of the aged and callous
had, during these useful years that seem so infinitely long, to be
chewed over endlessly and learnt by heart. Hard words and hard
penalties were all the instruction we got in this religious life;
anxious fear of forgetting a single one of the obscure words was
the incentive to it.

From my private and public life of play and pleasure the
Almighty was driven out.
Godfried Keller[1]

We have a teacher to teach religion, but we learn maxims, hymns
and psalms and when someone hesitates, our ears are boxed.
Where are the touching figures of my childhood, Ruth, Joseph

and the Christ Child? Before my very eyes they are dying the death of the spirit, and not until much later, far from school and church, will they undergo a tardy resurrection.

At this period I am going to an ageing minister whose voice takes on a weeping note when he wishes to ingratiate himself. The cast iron stove glows, the smell in the room is indescribable, and we sleep or read or get up to mischief. The minister is there, but God is far away. We learn verses from the Bible and a watered down extract of bourgeois morality is imparted to us. Everything is strange, unfeeling, and unreal, nothing makes any contact with us, nothing inspires us.
Ernst Wiechert

Even before any questions occurred to me I had to learn the answers from a book. Even before I could learn about life and the world, everything was already in its place from beginning to end. Long before I could know what evil is, they had already catechized me about all possible sorts of sins. Long before I could regard myself as lost, I was already offered salvation.
Rogier van Aerde

Sundays were conducted very strictly. Apart from the obligatory walk we could not go outside. We could not do any work with our hands. All we could do was play quietly, read and always be bored. Once, much later, I asked a friend who visited us how she had passed Sundays. 'Oh,' she said, 'I would have liked to play outside sometimes, just like the others, but then I thought "Well, we will go to heaven later for it".'
Childhood reminiscence

Brought up in the Catholic faith, I learnt that the Almighty had made me to his greater glory: it was more than I dared to dream. But as a result, I did not recognize in the fashionable God that was taught me Him who was waiting for my soul. I needed a Creator – I was given a Big Businessman. The two were one, but I did not realize it; I served the pharisaic Idol unenthusiastically and the official doctrine disgusted me with the idea of seeking my own faith. What luck! Trust and desolation made my soul a chosen soil in which to sow heaven; without this misunderstanding, I should have been a monk. But my family had been affected by the slow dechristianization which was born in the Voltaire-influenced *haute bourgeoisie* and took a century to spread to every stratum of Society ... An atheist was an eccentric, a hot-head whom you did not invite to dinner lest he 'create a scandal', a fanatic burdened with taboos who denied himself the right to kneel in church, to marry his daughters or indulge in tears there, who took it on himself to prove the truth of his doctrine by the purity of his conduct, who injured himself and his happiness to the extent of robbing himself of his means of dying comforted, a man with a phobia about God who saw his absence everywhere and who could not open his mouth without saying His name: in short, a Gentleman with religious convictions. The believer had none: for two thousand years the Christian certainties had had time to prove themselves, they belonged to everyone, and they were required to shine in a priest's glance, in the half-light of a church, and to illumine souls, but no one needed to appropriate them to himself: they were the common patrimony. Polite Society believed in God so that it need not talk of Him. How tolerant religion seemed! How convenient it was. In our circle, in my family, faith was nothing but an official name for sweet French liberty; I had been baptized, like so many others, to preserve my independence: in refusing me baptism, they would have been afraid of doing harm to my soul; as a registered Catholic, I was free, I was normal. 'Later on,' they said, 'he can do as he pleases.' It was reckoned, at the time, far harder to acquire faith than to lose it.

My mother had 'her private God' and asked little more of Him than to comfort her in secret. The debate continued, more feebly in my brain: another self, my dark brother, languidly challenged every one of the articles of faith: I was both Catholic and Pro-testant and I united the spirit of criticism with that of submission. Deep down, it all bored me to death; I was led to unbelief not through conflicting dogma but through my grandparents' in-difference.

Yet I believed: in my nightshirt, kneeling on my bed, hands folded, I said my daily prayer but thought less and less often about the good God...

Once only I had the feeling that He existed. I had been playing with matches and had burnt a mat; I was busy covering up my crime when suddenly God saw me. I felt His gaze inside my head and on my hands; I turned round and round in the bathroom, horribly visible, a living target. I was saved by indignation: I grew angry at such a crude lack of tact, and blasphemed, mutter-ing like my grandfather: 'Sacre nom de Dieu de nom de Dieu de nom de Dieu'. He never looked at me again.

I have just told the story of a missed vocation; I needed God, he was given to me, and I received him without understanding what I was looking for. Unable to take root in my heart, he vege-tated in me for a while and then died. Today when He is mentioned, I say with the amusement and lack of regret of some age-ing beau who meets an old flame: 'Fifty years ago, without that misunderstanding, without that mistake, without the accident which separated us, there might have been something between us.'

Nothing happened between us.

Jean-Paul Sartre²

THE CATECHESIS OF FEAR

A sermon for children from the last century:

Little children, let no one lead you astray.

I will tell you something more about the abyss of sin, the wicked seducers are already hard on your heels, the false path which temptation will lead you to. You lose your footing and can no longer stand up, you fall over the edge and ... Oh! how terrible it must be, falling down from rock to rock, faster and harder every time, your head covered with blood, your arms and legs shattered, until at last you crash down, as deep as the steeple is high, into the abyss, dead and shapeless, so that one can scarcely tell that this was a human being.

You commit sin when you are disobedient or lazy, if you steal or lie or swear, if you hate or envy anyone else, if you do not listen when God and Jesus are being spoken of and do not pray reverently. And you sin against God. When we forbid you some-thing wrong, this is because God forbade us first and we know that he, the Almighty, will certainly punish it. There is the cheat, the thief, the mocker, the godless: Oh, you could find so many of them in the house of correction or in great misery – and he dies. He dies and comes before God. How shall he stand there? How deep down he will sink, far from heaven and from God, from the Lord Jesus, his angels and the blessed, because he no longer has anything left to hold on to or to lift himself up by ... and all this for the brief enjoyment of a few sins, flowers and fruits picked from above the abyss. And God comes with death and destruction to the sinner...

C. E. van Koetsveld

Yes, if you behave as diligent, obedient, hard working and good children, then you can say to yourself with assurance: my dili-gence and obedience is known to God who knows all things. In this way you will gradually become a completely good child, an example to all your playmates, and how much the Heavenly Father, the all-knowing God, will love you! Then your life will be

so calm and happy, then you will have the greatest satisfaction from everything, and you may depend upon it that God, who knows all you do and all that happens to you, will keep watch over you and guard you when you are in danger of being tempted by bad children and wicked people. So flee the path of evil more and more and take pleasure only in walking in the path of righteousness. So God's providence will nourish you up for heaven.
J. van Balen Blanken

One misery, however, oppressed me greatly, and that was because my imagination made it worse. Someone must have told me about hell. I suffered terribly from this. I knew only too well that I sinned every day. Thus I was going to burn eternally, eternally. Just imagine that. No end to the torture, to the pain, never, never. The thought itself was as bad as the pains of hell. Oh, the terrible certainty of the inevitable. If I could only go back to not being born. But that was impossible. Once I had lived, it could never be undone. And nothing was to be gained by dying. Death was the passage to endless tortures in flames that never died down.

I knew quite positively that I envied the plants and animals, and that I looked jealously at the trees and cows, because they had no immortal soul. I knew that sometimes, suddenly, in the middle of my game, the fear of hell took hold of me like a poison beginning to take effect. But I also knew that fear would never preserve me from evil. It spoilt much, but made nothing good.

Should not religious education, or what is so called, renounce this un-Christian torturing of children?
Jan Ligthart

A child was pulled along by the arm. His infant school teacher held his finger in a candle flame to teach him a lesson. 'That is what it will be like for ever in hell,' she explained to the screaming child, 'and then for all your life.'

I had always been particularly impressed by purgatory. I hung up a picture of it in class, a picture of purgatory, just imagine, and had the children pray in front of it, 'Dear Jesus, help the poor souls. They suffer so much, they long for you so.'
A nun, teaching in infant school

At preparation for first communion the sister spoke about the consequences of sin. There was a picture of a throne in heaven, and then all the letters of the alphabet scattered round it at random. Where would we be in heaven? My name was Lena. The worst thing was that L was at the very edge, so that I was so to speak at the very gate of hell. For years I prayed to be forgiven for all my sins.

I remember in the second class that the curate, who gave the religion lessons, hung a large wall picture on the board. The whole picture represented the pains of hell. All I remember about it was that at the end the curate showed a clock which hung in hell and which showed twelve o'clock, because there was never any end to the pains of hell, so he explained. How overburdened we were at that time by stories of sin, death and hell.

My little five-year-old son plays outside with a friend who is at the Protestant infant school. There the children are menaced with guilt, sin and Satan. The child is terrified by it and has nightmares about it: 'There is Satan, he's coming through the wall.'

At school religion was taken for granted, you had set periods for it, there was a special tone of voice reserved for religion, that you met everywhere. Only in later life did I ever start to think about the punishment for sin, that is about hell, because I wasn't sure about it, and quickly dismissed the idea, because nothing could be done about the situation of guilt and sin.

In my youth the main idea was: 'God rewards good and punishes evil.' Even in this life, but especially in paradise or hell. This idea was given to me at school especially, by way of Bible stories.
A fifty-five-year-old

By and large, in an orthodox Roman Catholic milieu, to believe meant principally 'in the unlucky'; fear of God, who saw everything, was extremely righteous, more righteous than merciful; this certainly gave me no desire to make the acquaintance of God the Father. Indeed, one might rather ask whether you could make his acquaintance at all, since purgatory was the last evil you could look forward to and was something that practically everyone had to face, because no human being was perfect.
A forty-nine-year-old

Forty years ago: from the theological point of view the negative experiences are entirely an extension of morality. In theological terms this means eschatology, and in particular hell. Hell was the punishment for sin. And sin was unchastity. And that was ... nobody told you, except by allusions.

We learnt about the martyrs of Gorkum. I put up my hand and asked why the other group weren't martyrs, because they too had died for their faith. I was told that I would go to hell, I was bad. A letter on the subject was sent straight away to my home. I got a good thrashing from my mother and the catechism lessons became abominable to me.

God was everywhere on the watch to see if you did what was good, a kind of police, though one which was still good. Times have changed, thank goodness!

The infant school teacher made the children count off the days to the resurrection. Many children had fears as the result of these stories.

It would be fine if children were not so frightened and fearful of God and the devil and if there wasn't always so much talk about sin, when the love of God is so much to be desired.

Our personal reminiscences: imprisoned in the morality of what you can and can't do, characterized by fear of punishment. For a long time we thought of Christ as the judge, the punisher. We were made terrified of stealing: a boy who began by stealing an apple ended as a murderer. We hadn't to look at our bodies when we took a bath on Saturday on pain of sin.

What made the greatest impression on me was that God saw, knew and could do everything. Falling through the ice after being forbidden to go on it: God had seen it and given me just the punishment I deserved. I believed that God regarded stealing as very wicked. I regarded taking and eating a turnip from a field as stealing. My friends often did this, but I never dared. When they once said: 'Look, he still doesn't dare!', I didn't want to let myself down and jumped shivering over the drainage ditch to get into the turnip field. I got one of my feet wet and thought at once: God saw it again and you got your punishment. I quickly got a turnip, but when I ate it, I found it very bitter, so that I grew afraid and threw it away. I have never tasted such a bitter turnip. Naturally this was imagination, but I can still taste it.
A sixty-four-year-old

All my childhood memories about religion really revolve round the God who 'avenges' and 'rewards'.

    A boy was being teased. I wanted to join in. At once I began to taunt him violently in my own way. Suddenly I was overcome with fear that something would happen to me before I came home. It was a great relief that this did not happen.

A family got into difficulties. Through his recklessness the father was disabled. The punishment of God! It was questioned whether the Parish Relief Board was doing any good by going on helping the family. They did not once go to church twice on Sunday. The fearful mercilessness of this attitude never dawned on me. Now my ideas and feelings are quite different.

Between my fifth and seventh year there was a servant girl who was in the Salvation Army and told me stories from the Bible. The one thing I can remember was that when it rained I was in panic, especially at night. 'Imagine if the Flood should come again!' Obviously the promise that was made to Noah had been left out. I remember very clearly my terrible fears, lasting for years, which I did not dare to discuss with my parents. Even now, as the mother of grown-up children, I still feel miserable when it is raining hard. Thus it seems to have been a real trauma, caused by something as silly as a servant girl's chattering.

Another experience relating to her, when I was five. Every evening she lay very restless in bed, and constantly cried out, every single night, and asked strange questions, all relating to death. 'How do you die and does it hurt and why do you die?' I talked to her and said that when you are dead, you no longer breathe. The following night she called out and was very scared: 'I daren't go to sleep, because I am so frightened that I will stop breathing.' Then I began to worm out of her how her distress had started. It seemed that at school they had learnt about the Passion. At home we had always skipped the story of Good Friday and stuck down that page of the Children's Bible with sticky tape. I think it's wrong that the Children's Bible should contain a picture of the crucifixion.

I believe that there are lots of cripples walking about whose growth has been distorted because for years they have lived in panic. Do you know some as well? But did you yourself sometimes think as a child in bed: To burn for always, and the two thousand years which have passed since Christ, don't signify even a single second in eternity?

We constantly lived on the edge of eternal damnation, you were always peeping into the glowing furnace. And for this the

church has an immense burden of guilt, which it is only now paying for.
Godfried Bomans

We grew up with it; it was indeed quite clear to us how long eternity is and how long to burn for ever is. I lay awake in panic thinking about it.

By contrast, far too rarely, and in fact virtually never, was anything ever said about the good God and his infinite mercy . . .
Michel van der Plas

Going back for the commencement of my religious history which had made some steps before my twelfth year, I can remember my occasional fits of anguish from the fear of hell, and the possibility of being cut off before making my peace with the Almighty. My father gave us seasonably his strong religious views in very imperious fashion. There never was anything kindly or attractive about those religious lectures and inculcations; on the contrary, his style of lecturing was most forbidding. His most iterated theme was a denunciation of one and all of us, as in a headlong career to hell, without any reservation . . . The enormous amount of self-humiliation and self-denial at almost every turn gave me a sickening impression on the whole.

The minister used to put it direct in this form. 'If you will only now accept Christ, you will be happy for ever.' He even gave us the exact words that we were to employ in order to attain this magical result. I was very early impressed with this prodigious disproportion between the means and the end, and could not enter seriously into the attempt.
Alexander Bain[3]

I endured a great deal of religious conflict. The doctrine of eternal punishments and rewards occupied and frightened my childish imagination and in my eleventh year cost me numerous sleepless nights, when I thought that the calculation of the relationship between the suffering of Christ and the punishment which he had to take on himself could not result in a satisfactory answer.
Friedrich Schleiermacher

My religious training developed in me a great capacity for fear – I was perpetually tortured by the fear of hell – a superstitious conscience and a sexual embarrassment from which I have found it very difficult to free myself.
Robert Graves[4]

In reference to God's omnipresence he always dwelt on its punitive aspect. 'Man sinned, and flood overwhelmed him; again he sinned and fire consumed his cities; with famines and plagues God repaid the sinning people; and right now His sword hangs over the world, ready to cut down sinners. Misfortune and ruin will befall everyone who knowingly breaks His commandments.' And for emphasis, he rapped his knuckles on the edge of the table.

Such vindictiveness on the part of God was hard for me to believe, and I had a suspicion that grandpa was inventing it to make me fear him, rather than God. I was frank with him and asked, 'Aren't you saying all this to frighten me and make me obey you?'

Equally frank, he acknowledged: 'Maybe I am. Are you plotting new disobedience?'

'How about what grandma says?'

'Don't listen to the old fool!'

Maxim Gorky[5]

If I had the whole gang here, the whining, unctuous, cowardly, false crew, the parsons, the hot gospellers, the preachers of cant, I would kick them to death one by one. And now I will maintain to anyone that the God of the Jews in the Old Testament is a barbaric deity, without goodness, trust or love. An impossible immanent monster. I wouldn't want the privilege of worshipping such a god. The Bible stands like a dividing wall between me and my happiness. I shall declare war on it, it has a bitter enemy, a mortal enemy.

Frederik van Eeden

The teacher had been talking about hell and had given some description of it. 'Do you know what hell is like? A fair with roundabouts. So never go there.' I, in my stupidity, said that I had been to the Westermarkt and had sat on the roundabouts, on a horse, a wooden horse of course. And all the lights were on and the steam organ played and everybody joined in the singing. 'I suppose you think that's good fun, do you?' said the teacher. I admitted, 'Yes, great fun.' She knew exactly what the Lord permitted and what he did not and gave me an immense conviction that my whole life and the life of my whole family was a continual transgression. Only the teacher did not live in a godless fashion. But at the same time she taught us of the Lord God. He was so good, better than anyone. I thought of my grandmother Fiegen and I grew dizzy when I thought of it: someone even better than her.

Theo Thijssen

I was baptized a Roman Catholic at the wish of my mother. I gave little evidence of religion. I said my prayers faithfully because my mother had once told me that God saw everything and if I did not he would be angry.
E. du Perron

A system that seemed to have been invented only in order to catch you out in a weakness and cultivate a bad conscience. All that has remained is a memory of real panic.
Georges Bernanos

The outrageous education that people think necessary to force upon a child from eighteen months old until his eleventh year, just in the formative years in which a person is most impressionable and vulnerable. Such an education is full of things that you do not like, but the reason why you do not like them completely escapes you.

I have a son five years old. All I can say about it at the moment is that I will not force anything upon him without explaining to him why.
Hugo Claus

THE DARK SIDE OF RELIGIOUS EDUCATION

In religious education people often forget the way Christ himself taught.
Antoine Vergote

There is a kind of education which is capable of taking away from the child at a very early age his trust in the infinite goodness of the world. In fact it can also be found in the guise of religious education.
M. J. Langeveld

The most essential part of education is to convince a child as soon as possible of his wretchedness, weakness, dependence, and of the heavy burden of want. This is not only to teach him to appreciate that those who are educating him can help him to bear this misery, but above all to teach him at an early age to know his place and to prevent him ever being able to take any pleasure in resisting Providence.
Jean-Jacques Rousseau

To arouse fear and anxiety is nowhere as dangerous as in the

religious sphere. To threaten a child with hell can set his religious life on a false course for ever, and indeed, stifle its living power at the source.
P. Kohnstamm

The pleasure which certain women take, and the less enlightened they are the more is this the case, in frightening children with all manner of fantastic notions about a man who will steal them away, (thus today, May 5, out at Hirschholm I heard a girl tell a child that it must not go too near the water, that there was a man there who would come and take it away and that – after all a profound remark – it was enough to look down into the water for him to come and take it away) apart from being a way of keeping children quiet, it is intimately connected with egoism: it pleases or excites them to see the child frightened at something... woman has a mysterious relation to fear, and it excites her to see the child's real fear.
Søren Kierkegaard[6]

INFANTILE CONCEPTIONS

The religion of adults has much more to do with the religion of children than people have hitherto been prepared to admit, and notably with the decisive impressions made in childhood years. The roots of later religious development, the conditions for later religious decisions, lie in childhood religion itself. In the religious life of adults many significant features of childhood religion are retained.
Theophil Thun

Has sentimentality, which in the religion of adults so rarely dares to manifest itself, perhaps fled to the place where children gather?

No one can grow up to God if God is the little man with whom we play and walk hand in hand as a child.
J. van Haaren

In many circles educational practice was infantilized, and this was so even though it is bound to be pre-eminently a concern of adults. We were setting up playrooms and playgrounds, and setting streets and squares aside for them. We were making a religious 'toy town'. And accordingly the development of religion

in Christians largely came to a full stop towards the end of primary school. Had the child so little to learn, out of the whole of
life? Or perhaps the child's approach to things through play had
become alien to us?

Unconsciously, infantilizations have served as a camouflage for
the inadequacy of our own faith.

Religious conceptions must not become sweet and sentimental.
Do children like it this way? Perhaps they have a feeling that it
is a good thing to satisfy the expectations of adults. They like
sweets, but they can't live on them.
J. H. Huijts

We are in a Protestant church on Sunday morning, somewhere in the Netherlands. The church members, so far as they are present, are sitting in the pews and paying attention to the Word. They sit motionless while the singing and the prayers go up to heaven. They stay seated for an hour. You can see many elderly people and empty pews, and only here and there, tucked away behind your back, a few children who have been taken to church by their parents or their grandmothers. They sit there somewhat forlornly, and they look as if they are lost. In any case, no attention is paid to them, neither in the singing, nor in the prayers, nor in the sermon. It is as though they were not there. They fidget about, fiddle with things and are given sweets to keep them still.

Perhaps these children are there every Sunday. 'They must get used to it early,' say their parents. 'It's no problem for them at all, they know that it is right.'

Most Protestant services take no account of children. And if on any occasion there are more children present on some special occasion, not a few people are irritated. They are noisy, they disturb one's own devotion, 'it is just like a Sunday school...' There are even people who stay away from church when baptism is being celebrated.

In the Christian congregation there seems to be a resistance to children. The other extreme exists as well: the sentimentality with which children are regarded in church as though they were a special phenomenon, 'all the darling sweet children standing round the font!'

In principle, there is not yet any place for a child when the congregation meets to praise God and to celebrate their salvation. They may perhaps have been baptized and solemnly accepted into covenant with the Eternal, but expression is given to this for no more than a moment. Liturgically it lasts only ten minutes, and then the child disappears once again behind a door which officially is not supposed to be opened again until the age of eighteen has been reached. Not until then, apparently, can a person be fully recognized as a member of the church of Christ and take part in his Supper. The church is for 'over eighteens'.

'And yet so much is done for children in the church!'

There is a Sunday school, they have their own children's services and they can also go to confirmation classes until they are confirmed. To belong officially to the church, one has first to complete a long curriculum of twelve, or even fourteen years. During one of the most important periods of human life, one is officially excluded from participation in the fellowship of faith and may not even come with the others to the Lord's Table to celebrate the love of God.

In the Roman Catholic Church, since 1911, children have once again been admitted to communion in their seventh year. But there too, no special notice is taken of children at mass, neither in the liturgy nor in the sermon. And there too, there is a separate liturgical area set apart for children in the form of children's classes, for which the school forms the background.

The monopoly of adults in the congregation and, in addition, the monopoly of men, is still generally taken for granted.

The church which bears the name of Christ must alter its practice, to the end that man in all his forms can be accepted into its fellowship: as a child, as a youth, as an adult, as an old person, as man or woman, father or mother, as a single person, not to speak of race or nationality.

We lament the fact that so few young people come to church. It is evident that altogether sensational things would be necessary to draw them in. But if a human child cannot grow up from the very first in this fellowship, how is he ever to feel at home there?

Has a child not yet any right there? Has a child, then, not yet any faith, any relationship to God, to Christ? For what reason are children excluded – and when they happen to be there, why is no attention ever paid to them?

There is a passage in the gospels of which for twenty centuries we have apparently taken no notice, even though there are pretty Sunday school pictures and prayer cards made of it (Mark 10.13-16).

The superior and defensive attitude of adults towards children was expressed in a small incident in which followers of Jesus indignantly turned children away. Jesus resented this very strongly and in holy indignation said, 'Let the children come to me, do not hinder them; for to such belongs the kingdom of God. Truly, I say to you, whoever does not receive the kingdom of God like a child shall not enter it.' And on another occasion he called a child to him, set it 'in the midst of them' and said: 'Unless you turn and become like children, you will never enter the kingdom of heaven. Whoever receives one such child in my name receives me' (Matt. 18.2-5).

If we do not accept the child, access to the world of God is barred to us. The acceptance of the child is therefore a condition for a real Christian fellowship in faith. 'Must we then sit in church every Sunday with all the children? Poor lambs, how bored they will get, for they don't understand a word of the sermon.'

Why must we immediately side-track this matter of principle, which evidently concerns the heart of the gospel, into a matter of practice? Who is to tell us that if we change in this respect, sermons must remain incomprehensible, services too long, and the fellowship of faith inaccessible to children?

What is needed in the first place is a conversion, nothing less than that.

Jesus himself took the side of the child: the new, primitive, innocent, trusting being. The child has to be recognized as a human being in the full sense, and indeed as a beginning and growing human being, who like 'grown up people' can have a relationship to God, and can be transparent to his purposes.

As a result of this conversion, the form and experience of fellowship in the Christian church will change, and far from becoming childish or turning into a Sunday school, will grow towards fullness.

It may well appear that one does not always have to be together in order to form a fellowship, and that there can be different forms of celebrating and learning about the faith for each different group of persons. But when we turn to the central issue, the celebration of salvation and the common meal of the communion, then no one may be excluded, least of all those who by human standards are 'not yet up to it'. We should notice that we need the children in order really to learn what it is to celebrate salvation. What an unemotional, starchy, gloomy and dull business we make of it! How little rhythm and movement there is in our services, how little enthusiasm and joy. How rational it is, with ponderous arguments about God and life. A fresh wind has to blow through Christendom with its teaching, dogmatizing and moralizing.

A Protestant might well be jealous of the way in which a child is introduced into the Roman Catholic community of faith by way of baptism, first communion, confirmation, and renewal of baptismal promises. For the seven, nine, and twelve-year-old there is on every occasion a door which is open and a new step to be taken into this fellowship.

The Roman Catholic, on the other hand, would regret in his turn that except in the nuptial mass there is no opportunity of professing one's faith as an adult officially and personally, and one is not yet ready for this at twelve years old. For doubt and the conflict of faith do not begin until after this age, while the desire to involve oneself in the service of this fellowship comes even later.

The church ought to accompany a person throughout his life. On every occasion it ought to open a new door: to parents with their new-born child, to the child, who should take part in Christ's supper, to the twelve-year-old who is leaving childhood behind him and to the adult who wishes to commit himself in the congregation of Christ. For there is no fixed time of life at which a single entry into this remarkable fellowship can be realized. When is one really ready when it is a matter of faith?

However, we do not belong to this fellowship solely on the basis of our profession of faith, but above all by virtue of the love of God, which takes us up and acknowledges us, even though we scarcely believe it. We already belong to him before we believe it.

All these arguments probably seem somewhat unreal against the background of dechristianization, and perhaps even of the collapse of the church as an institution. When one thinks of all the cynicism with regard to the church, the rancour, the indifference, how can one still call for a place for children in the church!

And yet the fellowship of Christ has always been mysterious. It has survived in times of persecution, flourished in the face of oppression or moved to fresh ground.

A great deal is happening to the church at the moment, but is it nothing more than deterioration? Has there ever been so much concern for the church's problems? Is so lively an interest in theology and its changes not a sign of life? Perhaps it is just in these turbulent times that a new fellowship of Christ is being born, which will no longer bear any other name than that of Christ.

And even if we come to the point where more and more churches are closed, perhaps a father with his child will be walking past such a closed church. The child asks a question. The father has not gone to church for a long time, but now he is startled and thinks, 'I must not fail my child; for you must not send your child into the world without faith; we are still living on the strength of a spiritual inheritance, but is there no longer to be one for the children?'

The church of Christ is not dead, it is still alive – perhaps imperceptibly so in all sorts of forms. Its concern for the whole world, the impulse to give aid, the impatient demand for a renewal of society, may all be associated with this mysterious movement of Christ in the world. But the church must always continue to seek for what is more than common humanity and the love of one's neighbour, for what is more than world history, for that which ultimately defines this history.

One of the future forms of fellowship in Christ will be reborn in the contact between parents and children, between parents and the new generation. It is born of the disturbing sensation that we cannot leave children out in the cold, that we owe them responsibility, that we must devote everything to being able to give them a faith, even if we ourselves have to begin again at the very beginning with faith. Only faith in God, the God of Jesus Christ, and in the resurrection from the dead and from destruction can help them to come through the terrors of this world and enable them to realize that their lives have a meaning, whatever they make of them themselves.

The day may come when the celebration of this strange salvation will once again become more meaningful than ever before, when there will have to be somewhere a place where parents and children can sing in spite of fate, in spite of war, and in spite of chaos, and pray together for a liberation which cannot be found anywhere else in the world.

The church's time is not up yet.

And perhaps it will be the children who take us by the hand to find a new church.

THE CHURCH

A little boy absolutely insisted on taking his teddy bear with him to church, and showed the bear to God in the tabernacle.
Boy aged three

'Mummy, where is heaven? Oh, but I know, in church. Look, Mummy, there Jesus is and it's always his party and there is a roundabout.' *He points to a drawing of the Last Supper, and to the great chandelier.*

At church for the first time. What are the people doing there? – They're praying. – How can they be, they haven't got undressed.

The bells sound. You've got to go to Jesus' Church.
Boy aged three

What do people do in church? – Listen to the preacher. – What does he tell them? – About God. – Do they still not know about that?
Boy aged four

Why do we sing in church? – Because you're happy, you sing to God. – Why have you got to be on your knees and why can't you dance if you are happy?
Boy aged five

When Mummy's very busy, she can't go to church on Sundays, but God doesn't mind, though the pastor says that you have to. When you are looking after us, that's praying as well.
Boy aged five

Going past a church. Oh, look, he's at home. – Who's at home? – God, of course, there's his car outside.
Boy aged five

On the way to church with her parents. Most people are still asleep, aren't they, Mummy, they don't want to go and talk to God.
Girl aged six

Why do all the people look so sad, I thought New Year's Eve was a holiday.
Girl aged seven

Somebody goes out of Mass half way through. Huh, some people have had enough.
Boy aged seven

Do drunk people go to church as well? – No. *One of his aunts does not go to church.* Is she drunk too?
Boy aged eight

Who discovered the church?
Girl aged nine

Somebody went with me into church, where high mass was taking place. I was spellbound and remember the mysterious golden

movement and the shining in the distance. They had walked the whole length of the street before they noticed that I wasn't with them and they had to go back to get me, to where I stood completely absorbed by the magnificence. 'Auntie, it can't really be true what nurse says, that all Catholics are bad people?'
Girl aged ten

Mummy, the new master at school says that if I don't go to church I am not a child of God either. Is that true?
Girl aged eleven

THE CLERGY

A priest is a man who dresses up and prays.
Girl aged four

A little boy was playing at preaching a sermon. And God said, you mustn't be bad. And Jesus was born.
Boy aged four

A friar with a beard entered the pulpit. 'It's one of the Seven Dwarfs,' *cried a little boy at the top of his voice through the church.*
Boy aged four

Just ask the church man.
Girl aged five

Why is that man so stern? *Looking round:* Was Jesus born in this church?
Boy aged five

The minister has just gone into the pulpit. Where has Jesus gone now?

Do you know who lives the longest? The ministers at church, because they have to help everybody else to get to heaven first and they can only go after that.
Boy aged five

The minister's daughter comes on a visit. She is given a little apple, because she's so small. She asks: Does God see everything? – Of course. – Well, he must be thinking, why are they giving that minister's daughter a little apple!

A little girl is playing at being a priest and is giving a sermon:
People, you must be nice to each other. Anyone who believes in
people believes in God. Anyone who doesn't believe in people,
doesn't believe in God. That's the end of the sermon.
Girl aged six

When the pastor preaches, God is preaching. Everybody says that
because he's in church. When the pastor isn't in church and is
talking on the street, he isn't God, but an ordinary man.
Girl aged six

Who's the boss of the church? – The minister. – Yes, but God is
as well, God is the boss of all the churches in the whole world.
Boy aged six

BAPTISM

What is required of persons to be baptized? – A baby.

Mummy, his head wasn't clean and it was washed with holy water
and then dried with a tea towel.
Girl aged four

He was baptized because he is a child of God, God made him. –
Before he was baptized, who made him then?
Boy aged four

I think it's queer that you're not baptized, that's an insult to
God.
Girl aged five

At a baptism. Now there are two of the Lord Jesus.
Boy aged five

I have seen a baby baptized at church twice and then I just think
again and again that God made it and how good that is.
Girl aged eleven

Renewal of baptismal promises: It doesn't make much sense, tomorrow I have to choose my own faith, and I only know one faith,
and you can't choose out of one. But anyway it doesn't make any
difference to me, I might as well do it.
Boy aged twelve

HOLY COMMUNION

At Holy Communion for the first time. Was there really blood in the cup?
Girl aged five

He wants to know all about everything and can't understand why children can't go to Holy Communion.
Boy aged nine

Mother is kneeling at the communion rail. I want a peppermint as well!
Boy aged three

Mother prays: Lord, I am not worthy ... but only say the word and I shall be healed. *Her little son gives a worried tug at her sleeve:* Don't you feel very well?
Boy aged three

She drew a monstrance with a little figure in it and insisted that she had seen Christ.
Girl aged four

We get a piece of bread with Jesus in it and we eat it up. – Oh, then you've got lots and lots of Jesus's in your tummy, haven't you? – No, there's only one. – Yes, but he's in heaven. – No, he can be in lots of places at the same time. *He didn't believe this at all, thought about it for a minute and then said:* Oh, when the bell goes, Jesus comes back out of your mouth again.
Boy aged four

What do we do in church? – We have a meal with God.

Mother came back from the communion rail. What have you got?
Boy aged four

What is Holy Communion? – I know, it's when you're talking to God.
Girls aged six and four

Mother went to the communion rail. I'm going to receive our Lord. – Where have you got him, in your handbag or in your hand? I can't see any our Lord.
Girl aged five

Can I have sixpence? I would like to go and buy a newspaper
for God. He sits the whole day long behind that little golden door
and then he would have something to do.
Boy aged six

I have seen God. – Where? – In church, of course, in that golden
thing on the altar, only he looks all white.
Boy aged six

What have I to say when Jesus is here? *He points to his stomach.*
Boy aged six

God can do everything, even make my scooter, and if he doesn't,
I'm not ever going to my first communion.
Boy aged six

Who lives in the church? – Our Lord. – What does he say to
you? – Nothing. – Have you seen him, then? – Yes. – What does
he look like? – Red with white. *Five days later:* There was a little
boy who went round with a dish collecting pennies and then he
went to the pastor to change it into something else and then all
the people went to the front to eat out of the dish.

*Watching at the church door, where a number of people were
already on their way out:* Have they eaten up everything that was
cooked?
Girl aged six

A little girl doesn't want to go to mass any more on Sundays:
I'm only going to sit tight, I don't like communion.
Girl aged seven

I won't listen to all about the church till I've had a piece of bread
from the church.
Boy aged seven

How can Jesus get right into that piece of bread?
Girl aged seven

A little girl is slicing bread. When I go to communion, I eat Jesus,
a piece of his arm, a piece of his leg, but that can't really happen. –
We told her that going to communion is thinking about what
Jesus did, about how he gave himself for men, and that we try to
do good ourselves when we remember that.
Girl aged seven

Communion is a piece of white bread which they bless and so it becomes the body and the soul of Jesus and they give us it.

I have never eaten a man yet, and I've been in the world nine years already.

We eat the body of God and the next time we do it again and we go on and on doing it.

We eat the sacred Host to do a good work and so we can do other good works you never become a burglar or anything. The bread we get in church is holy and that is the Father and we don't see him and we only see a round white piece but that piece is the holy Father is in that piece that's all people see but in that piece there's the holy Father who is in heaven and everywhere with all people and he is with everybody and how can he be everywhere, and sometimes divide himself up into little pieces?

Fourth class in a Roman Catholic primary school

WHAT ARE PROTESTANTS?

Protestants are people who do not believe in God and are disobedient towards God. They do not listen to Jesus when he tells them.

They believe in many false gods. They don't go to church.

Protestants are almost the same as us but much worse. Protestants are people who protest, who do not believe in Mary and who in the past were wicked men, sort of thieves and murderers, villains and other evil-doers, they murdered and strangled lots of people the robbers.

Protestants are human beings too, but I know that in the past they took the churches away from the Catholics, but fortunately that's all over, we can go to church any time. Really it should be so that Catholics are with Catholics and Protestants with Protestants and then they wouldn't fight with each other any more and the Protestants could do what they wanted and the Catholics could do what they wanted and then there would be no more rows between them, but I hope that will never happen again.

Protestants are people who believe in God they go to church as well like we go to church and Protestants can do this for God as well they can also go to heaven they also eat the body of God in the past it wasn't so nice with the Protestants but they also go to church and when they come out of church they go to a café and drink a glass of beer and talk a bit and then they drink another glass of beer and they go home after that.

Fourth class, Roman Catholic primary school

OTHER CHRISTIANS

I'm not a Roman Catholic, I'm a little girl.

Grandma, were Adam and Eve Catholics or Protestants?
Girl aged four

Were Mary and Joseph Roman Catholic or Reformed Church?
Boy aged five

Was Jesus Catholic or Protestant?

What are you, Roman Catholic or Protestant? Oh, what does it
matter, God loves everybody.
Girl aged six

Mother, has the Reformed Church got a Reformed our Lord?
Boy aged five

Grandpa, the people at the big church and the Catholics, do they
belong to the Lord Jesus as well?
Boy aged eight

There are in the world Catholic school people, Protestant school
people and ordinary school people. We ordinary school people
don't have much to do with the church. When there are ill
people, they pray to God and then they quickly get better. We
ordinary people who are nothing, we eat and go and play again.
Ten-year-old

ECUMENICAL DIALOGUES

We have Mary. – We have the Lord. – We have God, that's worst
of all.

Are you not Catholic? – No. – It doesn't matter, you can still go
to heaven all right, or did you think that the Lord Jesus only
died for Catholics? Come on, let's play.

But it's really true. He comes himself into the church every time.
Yesterday I went and I saw it myself. – My mother goes every

Sunday to church and she never ever said that he comes there, I don't believe it. He's in heaven. – Well, can he ever come out of heaven? – No, he can't. – Yes, he can. – Then he isn't going to go into your church, but he will go into mine, every Sunday and more often, my father says so. And I'll tell you something else, that's why you have to kneel down and pray and so on, and there's a nice little bell! But you have to close your eyes, because you mustn't see him. The priest doesn't want you to. – Our Lord on an ordinary bicycle! That's all lies, he would be mad, surely he would come on a motor bike, no, a motor bike is much too ordinary. He could only come in an aeroplane, but he would rather stay up above! – How do you know that? – Well, it's like this, it's much nicer there than here and he must have the nicest of all, he can't just walk about amongst ordinary people. – No, that's true, but what about the Queen? – Our Lord is much higher than the Queen. And cleverer too? – Oh yes, much cleverer. – And nicer too. *After a pause:* I don't know.

Do you like Catholics? They get lots of nice pictures, but Johnny talks all the time as if our Lord is his; I can't stand that! – He's ours as well, isn't he, Mummy says so. – No, Mummy says that we are his, see!
Four- and five-year olds

CHILDHOOD REMINISCENCES OF CHURCHGOING

However thoroughly mother impressed upon us in our earliest childhood what we had to expect if we did wrong, I believe I loved God, but it was all so vague, and so lifeless; I associated it with stuffy parish rooms and gloomy pews, where I had to spend eternities with no other pleasure than the peppermint my mother gave me during the hymns.

My mother's family belonged to the Reformed Church, but except that she sang beautiful metrical psalms, I have never heard her talk about her belief. My father also sang a lot, but talked more about it. I don't mean about his personal experiences, but his criticism of sermons. At the end of a service he would go calmly up to the minister and pounce on the poor fellow, if there had been something in the sermon which he did not agree with.

Then Grandma, with her white starched cap, would come for lunch with another friend of the family and the whole thing was raked over, chewed over and dissected until there was nothing left of its religious message. And the children were there all the time, because games or cycling were not allowed on Sundays. We went to church twice every Sunday, with hymns in between!

Later on we went to regular liturgical children's services, and there I first felt that I really believed.

The great churches were constantly the house of God to me, the majesty of God. Later I read Rudolf Otto's *The Holy*. There was an unconscious connection.

My despairing anger, when, as a child of less than three years old, I was not allowed to go to my sister's baptism.

What did the church mean for me on Sunday? I was taken to church, and sat there, and that was all, and I have no idea of what was going on in the church right up at the front, sitting there far from the altar and behind the backs of all the grown ups as well. And anyway I was too young to understand what was going on.

As children we thought it stupid that father alone was obliged to go to mass on Sundays. When we were older, we protested against this obligation. A beating usually helped to reconcile us to it. Once I was married, I no longer believed. It had nothing to do with the world. Until I had children ...

Going to mass every Sunday meant boredom for me. I often sat playing with my hair to the annoyance of my parents, and later, when I was in the fifth and sixth class at primary school, showing off new frocks. Besides this, we went to low mass for half an hour every day in the week, that was extra, it didn't mean anything to you but it went down in your weekly report from school. I have a powerful and shameful memory of once being put out of church by the Sister for wearing a skirt that didn't come down as far as the knee. Ugh!

I understood nothing of the sermon, but from my seventh year on I dutifully and 'devoutly' heard mass every Sunday. But I was fascinated by the colour, light, organ music and the mystery of the liturgical actions. It was as dependable as the warm pressure of your parent's hand during the sermon.

My grandfather took me with him to church. I did not understand much about it, but I was very impressed, I know. The whole atmosphere of rich vestments, incense and the strange language.

The processions were glorious, a pleasure for eye and ear, and so was the high mass on Sundays, and yet it was also a sort of mystical experience. I felt myself completely sublimated into an unearthly (un)reality.

Father's excessive religion provoked resistance. We went to church twice every Sunday (without any choice) and occupied ourselves there counting the window panes and multiplying the numbers on the hymn boards.

Going to confession was a nerve-racking business, the same list every week. Once I got a huge penance because I simply named all the sins for a change. In all those years, I personally and alone prayed my whole family into heaven a good three times.

I can remember little about my first communion except that I was given six holy water stoups and three rosaries. It was different with the renewal of baptismal promises at the age of about twelve. I found that terrifying: to swear a dreadful oath on the Bible never to abandon the faith. I felt then all the heavy burden of that kind of spiritual blackmail. I sat on the second row and hesitantly held up two fingers. The alternative of abandoning the faith was a mortal sin!

In fact as a little girl I did not know very much about what went on at mass when the priest's back was turned. Boys were servers, but girls were passive members of the church and they were kept strictly away from the altar.

We were little concerned with religion. Even earlier than 1847 I saw at the house of a boy whom I was visiting a book with a picture of the crucifixion. I asked what it was. He shook his head in reply. A servant girl once took me to church. She was from Mainz and as a girl she had seen the Emperor Napoleon at the theatre. She was a Catholic and took me with her to the little Catholic church on the Seltersberg. The priest stood with his back turned to us, moved in a ceremonious way and wore a special garment. When he came out, I asked her, 'Was that God?'
C. F. Knapp

I sat watching on a pew without a backrest and watched for what was going to happen. A man in a black robe went up on to the pulpit and began to talk, things which I didn't understand, in a monotonous and strangely elevated voice. I grew tired and dozy

and mother had great difficulty in keeping me on the pew.
Friedrich Paulsen

Even in the church, when I was taken to be baptized, I cried so
loudly that the parson, who my mother always said was an irritable
man, exclaimed, 'That child sounds like a cat squealing,' – words
which my mother never forgave him.

An old seamstress altered my late father's overcoat into a confirmation coat for me; I thought I had never before worn such a
fine coat, and for the first time in my life I was given a pair of
boots. My joy at having these was extreme, and the only thing I
was afraid of was that everybody would not be able to see that
they were boots, and so I drew them up outside my trousers and
thus went to church. The boots squeaked, and this gave me
profound delight, for the congregation would now be able to
hear that they were new. But my devotion was spoiled. I was aware
of this and at the same time had a dreadful conscience because
my thoughts were just as much centred on my boots as on God. I
prayed to him from the bottom of my heart to forgive me, and
then thought of my new boots again.
Hans Christian Andersen[1]

There were always difficulties about going to church, because it
was such a supreme bore. Boredom to me was an active torment,
not a passive one, and I just raged and seethed with impatience
all the way through the service. I remember once how the congregation stared at me when I leapt enthusiastically to my feet at the
sound of a premature 'And now' from the parson; and how
miserably I sank back into my place as he went droning on
again. I believe my poor mother felt that if only she could get us
to church, some of the meaning of it might sink into us unconsciously; but I don't see how it could with anyone in my usual
church-going mood of white-hot indignation.
Gwen Raverat[2]

When we had looked to see that everything was in order and each
thing in its proper place, we had nothing more to do with the
rest of the service. When the organ sounded, there was no sheer
pleasure in listening to it, because in the church of East Arnstervik
no one dared to sing. We sat with the service book in our hands
and followed the hymn, but none of us ever once dared to join in
the singing. Once, when I was still small, I did not understand
how you had to behave and I sang a hymn as loud as I could.
I used to like singing at home all day long. When we came to the

second verse, Anna bent over towards me and told me that I had
to stop. But the fact that I could never understand the sermon –
our pew was too far away to hear it – I found very annoying,
because we were close friends of the minister. He was very friendly
to us children and he was also very handsome – always, but never
as much as when he stood in the pulpit and preached. He spoke
vehemently and waved the large handkerchief which he held in
his hand, and the longer he preached, the more handsome he
grew. And at almost every sermon he preached, he became so
moved that he wept. And then I wondered whether he was weeping because he could not make us better or convert us, whatever
he said. But for us, sitting on the back pew, it wasn't so easy to do
what he wanted, because we never understood a word he was
saying. The adults were used to being bored – they didn't mind –
but it was difficult for us children to bear it for so long. Emilie W.
told me that she counted the heads of the nails in the church
roof. Ingrid N. told me how she watched the farm people in
the church giving each other pinches of snuff. Emilie added up
the numbers on the hymn board and then subtracted, multiplied
and divided them. She said that at least she was not having any
sinful thoughts as long as she did that. It would have been worse
if she had looked at Hilda's hat and wished that she could have
had one like that. I didn't do arithmetic and I didn't look to see
people taking snuff. No, I imagined what it would be like if
lightning struck the church tower and the whole church caught
fire. Then all the people would be terribly afraid, they would
rush out and almost trample each other to death. I would stand
up on my pew and raise my voice and ask them to remain calm.
Then I would organize them into a long line, just as we read in
Triljof's Saga: 'From the temple to the beach there stretched a
chain of hands.' And through my level-headedness the fire would
be extinguished and people would write about me in the Wärm-
land Journal.
Selma Lagerlöf

If I would promise to sit quietly and not say a word, except very
quietly, then I could go with her to church, said Agatha. I had
of course no idea what to expect. Hitherto I had thought that the
church was for storks to build their nests on. And the very tone
in which they said I could go sounded as though something
enjoyable were to be expected. In general I always liked to experience something new. And therefore I promised to be quiet and
devout all through the service. When I first went into the church,
I was greatly surprised at the unbelievably high and broad room,

which did not look like a living room nor like a restaurant, but looked most like Götti's brewery, and yet not even like that, because there it was dark and here it was light, there there were vats and here there were pews. When my eyes had gradually got used to it, I suddenly saw on the side wall something marvellous, glittering windows, tall and narrow, with beautiful coloured panes in them as in a fairy tale. My gaze remained fixed in wonder on the windows. If I had not known that Agatha was next to me and had not known that outside the door there was the town of Liestal, I would have thought I was in heaven. And listen, suddenly the heavenly windows began to make music, and such beautiful sounding music, making you so happy, that it made me feel utterly blissful. There was an unbelievable mass of sound at once, and every note was beautiful, and all the beautiful notes were friends with each other. Were the musical windows secretly alive? Or were there angels hovering behind them, who, invisibly sang through the church windows? Agatha turned my head and pointed to a vast shining instrument set up high in the church. 'Organ,' she said, and now I understood that the music did not come from the windows, but from the organ.
Carl Spitteler

From F.'s eighth birthday, we were taken to church when they went on Sundays. Well prepared by the priest, we took part in the mass with fervent devotion. The sight of many people at prayer, the expression on their faces, and the singing moved me and took hold of me. I loved them, I felt an affinity with them, because I was born on the same patch of earth as they. The sound of the organ exalted me and with an inexpressible delight my heart rose to meet the appearance of the Lord, and I was filled with joyful humility when the bell proclaimed his coming, and the Lord came from heaven to us on earth in our shabbily decorated church; my sweet and holy trembling was filled with his divine presence. When I got home, I took out a box which contained a complete set of vessels for mass made of tin and tried to say mass myself.
Maria von Ebner Eschenbach

Once we had realized that it was very boring in church, we always tried to come late. The only time my father went with us, we naturally had to be there for the whole sermon. But we didn't listen. However, I did not sit there feeling bored. There were gas lamps on the end of long tubes and in my imagination I climbed round the whole building. I climbed on to a tall pillar, caught

hold of a gas pipe that lay along it, fastened my fingers round it, swung along the ceiling, climbed down by another gas pipe, and made my way to the pulpit and the organ. These were dangerous journeys, but my imagination stopped at nothing. If necessary, I leapt through the air and always reached the desired point. No ledge was so narrow that I could not go along it.
Jan Ligthart

And now every Sunday I noticed in a bright frame by the side of the organ a shaggy face which was continually turning about and looking down into the church. So long as the organ was playing and the singing going on it was visible, but as soon as my father was praying at the altar it disappeared. When the playing and singing began again it reappeared, but as soon as my father began his sermon it was again lost to sight, to show itself once more for the closing hymn and voluntary. 'This is the devil that is looking down into the church,' I said to myself, 'but as soon as father begins with God's Word, he has to make himself scarce!' This weekly dose of visible theology gave quite a distinctive tone to my childish piety ...

From the services in which I joined as a child I have taken with me into life a feeling for what is solemn, and a need for quiet and self-recollection, without which I cannot realize the meaning of my life. I cannot, therefore, support the opinion of those who would not let children take part in grown-up people's services till they to some extent understand them. The important thing is not that they shall understand, but that they shall feel something of what is serious and solemn. The fact that the child sees his elders full of devotion, and has to feel something of their devotion himself, that is what gives the service its meaning for him.

During the last weeks of the preparation period Pastor Wennagel used to keep a few of us back after each lesson in order to speak to us individually about confirmation. When my turn came, and he tried with affectionate questioning to learn with what thoughts and resolves I was going through the holy time, I began to hesitate, and to answer evasively. It was impossible for me, much as I liked him, to let him look right into my heart. The conversation had a sad ending; I was dismissed with coolness. Deeply troubled about me, Pastor Wennagel afterwards told my aunt that I was going through confirmation as one of the indifferent ones. In reality, however, I was during those weeks so moved by the holiness of the time that I felt almost ill.
Albert Schweitzer[3]

Now I believe that the child felt more assured and correct than all those who were supposed to give guidance to the children. They were not wicked and were full of good will and had good intentions for us like all those who took us by the hand to guide us towards life, but their ways and purposes had gradually ossified; we still stuck on the threshold and what was unique to us had for them been so often repeated that it had lost its pristine brightness. Thus they looked unmoved at what was sacred to us and they spoke as though from the safe and ordered world, while we demanded and expected the silence of the sacred.
Ernst Weichert

He is in church with his grandfather. He is bored. He is not very comfortable. He is forbidden to stir, and all the people are saying all together words that he does not understand. They all look solemn and gloomy. It is not their usual way of looking. He looks at them, half frightened. There are moments when he does not recognize even his grandfather. He is afraid a little. Then he grows used to it, and tries to find relief from boredom by every means at his disposal. He balances on one leg, twists his neck to look at the ceiling, makes faces, pulls his grandfather's coat, investigates the straws in his chair, tries to make a hole in them with his finger, listens to the singing of birds, and yawns so that he is likely to dislocate his jaw. Suddenly there is a deluge of sound: the organ is played. A thrill goes down his spine. He turns and stands with his chin resting on the back of his chair, and he looks very wise. He does not understand this noise; he does not know the meaning of it; it is dazzling, bewildering, and he can hear nothing clearly. But it is good. It is as though he were no longer sitting there on an uncomfortable chair in a tiresome old house. He is suspended in mid-air, like a bird; and when the flood of sound rushes from one end of the church to the other, filling the arches, reverberating from wall to wall, he is carried with it, flying and skimming hither and thither, with nothing to do but to abandon himself to it. He is free; he is happy. The sun shines . . . He falls asleep. His grandfather is displeased with him. He behaves ill at Mass.
Romain Rolland[4]

My first day at the Rouen Lycée. At that time it was the custom to begin the academic year with a mass. The purpose of this mass was to invoke the benediction of the Holy Spirit upon the labours of the students. A few minutes before the ceremony the Head

Usher called us together in the great courtyard and said:
'Dissenters, withdraw!'

The dissenters were the Protestants and the Israelites. About twenty Protestants and three or four Jews stepped out of the ranks.

'The others,' the Head Usher went on, 'will form in a column of twos and follow me into the chapel.'

There was the prolonged sound of tramping feet and the student body disappeared into a vaulted passage. Our little group remained alone beneath the trees, disconsolate and with nothing to say. From the nearby chapel rose the music of the organ magnificently played by my master Dupré, and the murmured responses. We strolled sadly beneath the chestnut trees of the courtyard. We felt no shame at being Protestants or Israelites, but we felt ourselves separated for an hour's time, on a solemn occasion, from a community which was, after all, our community, and we were unhappy, very unhappy, without knowing why.
André Maurois[5]

In my childhood I was sent every Sunday to a Sunday-school where genteel little children repeated texts, and were rewarded with cards inscribed with them. After an hour of this we were marched into the adjoining church, to sit round the altar rails and fidget there until our neighbours must have wished the service over as heartily as we did. I suffered this, not for my salvation, but because my father's respectability demanded it.
Bernard Shaw[6]

I had none of the feelings I should have had at the American church in the Avenue de l'Alma. To speak plainly. I was bored there, save when sun, moon, rain, snow, and man were asked to magnify the Almighty. I sometimes plucked my mother's sleeves, whispering that one of the stained glass windows had been put in upside down, and she ordered me to hush. I examined the window with all the attention lent by boredom, and that is all I remember of the church, except my admiration for the red velvet cushions on which we knelt; I would have liked to take mine home with me.

Sometimes we ventured as far as Notre-Dame de Grâce de Passy and went in for a moment. Dark and a little mysterious, I thought of it as an enchanted spot, for no sooner did you go into the church than you left behind you everything that is commonplace, everything you saw daily.
Julien Green[7]

When my father took me to the synagogue for the first time, he
explained to me the confession of the great Day of Atonement: no
one can take away from me the sins which we young people have,
but everyone can try to control them and to make his life better
so that – as the devout teach us – his name is ultimately written
in the book of life. I can still feel the warmth of my father's hand
when he led me into the synagogue. The men bowed to him,
happy that I was in good health. I heard the organ playing the
prelude and the singing of the boys in Hebrew sounded like a
choir of angels. I perceived in the songs the note of lamentation
and melancholy, but also felt myself uplifted and strengthened by
them. I shall never forget the moment when everyone stood up
and the chief rabbi stretched out his hand and spoke the blessing:
'The Lord bless and keep you.'
Max Tau

My aunt told me that when you were saved you saw a light, and
something happened to you inside! And Jesus came into your
life!

The whole congregation prayed for me alone, in a mighty wail
of moans and voices. And I kept waiting for Jesus, waiting, waiting, but he didn't come. I wanted to see him, but nothing happened to me.

I heard the songs and the minister saying: Why don't you
come to Jesus? Sister Reed, what is this child's name?

'Langston,' my aunt sobbed.

'Langston, why don't you come? Why don't you come and be
saved? O lamb of God! Why don't you come?'

Now it was really getting late. I began to be ashamed of myself,
holding everything up so long. I decided that maybe, to save
further trouble, I'd better lie, too, and say that Jesus had come,
and get up and be saved.

So I got up.

Suddenly the whole room broke into a sea of shouting, as they
saw me rise. My aunt threw her arms round me. The minister took
me by the hand and led me to the platform.

When things quietened down, in a hushed silence, punctuated
by a few ecstatic 'Amens', all the new young lambs were blessed
in the name of God.

That night, for the last time in my life but one – for I was a big
boy twelve years old – I cried. I cried, in bed alone and couldn't
stop. I buried my head under the quilts, but my aunt heard me.
She woke up and told my uncle I was crying because the Holy
Ghost had come into my life, and because I had seen Jesus. But I

was really crying because I couldn't bear to tell her that I had
lied, that I had deceived everybody in the church, that I hadn't
seen Jesus, and that I didn't believe there was a Jesus any more,
since he didn't come to help me.
Langston Hughes[8]

I was an extremely devout child until my eighth or ninth year. I
melted when I saw the sacred host, until one particular moment
I realized that there was absolutely no one inside. For a child this
is a ghastly moment, because from then on you are all alone,
you can never let anyone see it, certainly not at a boarding school
like that. And then all the time I was haunted by the fear that at
any moment, as the Sisters explained, God's thunderbolt can strike
you: in bed, on the playground. At that point my religious feeling
was turned completely upside down: first into unwillingness, and
then into a completely unreasonable form of aggressiveness.
Hugo Claus

THE CHILD IN THE CHURCH

It is important that we should come together in a human, living
and purposeful encounter, in which the child is accepted together
with us. To meet together brings us completely into the full
reality of what faith means to us. Religious education is not a
matter of talking, but of making the truth live.
M. J. Langeveld

We cannot be with God if we cannot come together with each
other, because human community is always a sign that God is
amongst us.
J. van Haaren

Everything about adults – everything, as we tend to forget –
derives its attraction and its significance from the child who is
present in some way or another.
J. H. van den Berg

It is not possible to conduct the holy mass with children alone.
Children do not form a community, they belong to the community, the must be able to watch their parents.
 Children can quite happily sing mature hymns, they are mirrors
into which they can always look; they grow into the sacred action
in the church. We sit there full of formulas, but we cannot pray

and sing, and perhaps we are at present too poor in spirit to celebrate.
J. van Haaren

When children take their first steps in the life of the church they receive their most powerful impressions from the outward actions, for the outward always precedes the inward. What takes place within is given its only expression and form in what is visible and audible, and it is this expression and form which influences the inward events of religious growth.
Theophil Thun

A child has a right to belong to this community. It is his rightful inheritance. But a child cannot be brought to it. He has to be accepted into it.
Herman J. Sweet

In public worship the threat of the infantilization of the life of faith and therefore the isolation of children's religion from that of adults is still a real one. The symbolism of the church must still be allowed to speak for itself and its demonstrative character must not be overshadowed by comments addressed to the children.
J. H. Huijts

Public worship in which children take part must above all contain two invariable elements: solemnity and joyfulness. One can imagine an atmosphere of life and movement, full of happening, where there is always something to look at, to do, to answer or to sing, or of an atmosphere of a more strictly liturgical kind.
L. Kuylman-Hoekendijk

13 Religious Education

What is to be done? In what way can you pass on to your children something of your own faith, or bring them into contact with Christian faith? This has always been known as religious education. But this task has been handed over all too eagerly to other bodies, and particularly to the school and church. At the present day, we are more inclined to say: Is it not in the first place the concern of parents themselves? You can send your children wherever you please, but what really matters happens at home. There the concern is for life rather than for religious rites; how to speak at table, how conflicts are resolved and strangers received. What matters is that children should notice that their parents still recognize 'a higher calling' and believe in something that is more than life itself. What matters above all, is whether they believe in God, whatever happens.

Inwardly and perhaps unconsciously to notice, sense and eventually share a feeling is more important than any Sunday school. Children may have heard the whole of the biblical narrative until they are weary of it, but what use is it to them if they do not realize that it finds an echo in the most intimate sphere of their lives?

From the religious point of view, many parents have an inferiority complex. There still persists the old belief that one is 'only a layman', that one does not know enough about it, one cannot give any answer to questions and that it is of little use to daily life.

This view has perhaps also played into the hand of the church, as though you had to be half a theologian before you could be recognized as a believer, and as if those who know the answers are really the clergy.

Now that the full rights of the laity are under constant discussion, parents must set aside the layman's feeling of inferiority. Whether they wish or not, they are in the first instance the right people to introduce the child to the world of faith. They are equipped to do so by being his father and mother. In that respect they have everything.

Unfortunately fathers all too frequently leave it to their wives to talk to the children about God or to pray. This has more negative influence than they perhaps realize, especially for a boy, who, as he grows older, gets the feeling that religion is more of a woman's affair.

It is naturally sometimes not possible for parents to share this role, for the simple reason that the father belongs to no church or still rejects a youth which was overburdened with religion; he is not against his wife going to church, but ... Other parents prefer to 'leave their children free': 'they can chose for themselves later'. This seems to be the dogma of those who stand aside, and it is still widespread. But how impossible it is to carry out in practice. Leaving children free is an illusion, even if it is only by way of the unconscious passing on of the views the parents hold. A plea must be made for a sense of reality and veracity. Parents who cannot provide an answer or an example should not force themselves. False holiness is odious. It is better for a child to be aware that its parents do not know the answers themselves or have difficulty with it than that religious ceremonies should be practised in a false way.

It may perhaps be a matter of very simple things. What was it that was of decisive importance in your own youth? It could have been some small thing, something fortuitous, an incidental remark which made a profound impression, or a particular area at home, without anything ever being said about faith.

It may even be that the children themselves break down their parents' paralysing feeling of inability by their interest, their questions, and their demand to be brought into contact with the mysterious world of God. And why should not parents who are half unbelievers allow themselves to be carried along by their children and come to think clearly about the matter once again, or even for the first time? For the reason for half belief is that a person has not gone into it deeply enough, and every other interest in his life takes precedence. The more a person hears and reads about it, the more interesting it becomes, the more we are seized hold of and can no longer let go. This can also be a good remedy against ill-feeling towards the church, which frequently is very emotional. If the church has disappointed you, why not seek for the origin of Christian faith, or the source itself?

It is more important for children to see that their parents are concerned about the matter than that they get a satisfactory answer to all their questions.

What does religious education in the family consist of if not in living together and looking at the world together, and explaining to each other what it is all about? The celebration of faith and the telling of the Story then take their natural course.

Is it still possible to celebrate faith as a family in a little ceremony at meals or on special occasions? With growing children the chance can be lost, for life is often too busy and too disordered. Where it is possible, a degree of creative imagination is necessary. Consequently this element in religious education should probably concentrate in particular on the youngest children; those to whom ritual play still appeals and who are fascinated by stories. It is in the family that the recounting of the ancient narrative of faith from Christian tradition is most appropriate. What a pity that children are so overburdened with biblical history at school, at Sunday school and all sorts of other places. The 'priesthood' of the parents should have been trusted, the unique sphere of life represented by the family. Things have been taken out of the hands of parents, and the stories are dinned into children, time and time again, until by their tenth or eleventh year they are sick of them.

In practice the form of celebration and the telling of the stories becomes more difficult the greater the differences between the ages of the children, especially when an argumentative adolescent sits next to an infant at table. With older children religious education is more a matter of answering questions, talking about everyday things, and discussing problems. They are confronted with so many things, especially on television, that it is of the utmost importance that they can take them up at home and do not have to work out on their own the oppressing problems of the present age. The older children grow, the less directly they are likely to be affected by explicitly religious ceremonies. And certainly a fifteen-year-old must be given the freedom to disagree with them and be against them. Ought they to be allowed to miss church or confirmation classes instead of being forced to go reluctantly? Parents are often rather afraid of letting adolescents 'please themselves'; they are afraid that the link will be broken altogether, and that all their activities in this direction in the course of the years now seem suddenly to have been for nothing. A child who is trying to achieve his own individuality and to re-orientate himself must be left alone and certainly not forced to go to church or confirmation classes. The only effect of the latter is to make things worse. In fact the pressure in this direction is quite possibly in inverse proportion to the degree to which the parents' faith is a reality! The influence of the home can seem apparently in vain, but who can say whether the son may not

show considerable interest in these matters through contact with
a girl-friend, or once he has started his own family and is faced
with bringing up his own children? Old memories then return
to the surface, and earlier influences seem indelible.

But it would be wrong to place the whole responsibility for
religious education on the shoulders of the parents. The older
children become, the more this responsibility is shared with others.
But the younger the children, the more the parents have to accept
this responsibility – or rather, this opportunity.

But they too need the inspiration of a larger community, even
if this is nothing more than a discussion group of young parents.
'The church' is often too big, and 'the parish' not a clearly defined
community. Those who are faced with the same task and have
common problems, should seek each other out and form a 'little
church'.

It is naturally also of extreme importance to make contact
with the teachers whose task it is to guide one's children in
the same direction. And is it even always the same direction?
There are often complaints about parents' lack of interest in
what their children hear at school and what happens to them at
Sunday school. Are not both sides afraid to talk about these
problems?

We might at this point ask the general question whether the
time is not past for such distinctly separate bodies to share responsibility for the religious education of children. What school and
Sunday school have done in the past could only happen by virtue
of the renunciation of one of the essential functions of the believing community itself.

Christian faith can live only in a larger community than the
family, in which the faith is celebrated together and the old story
continues to be told century after century. And when the wind of
the present age almost blows shut the door to the larger community that can provide this inspiration, then let parents and
their children once again force their way inside through the door
– or look for a back door! – and bring into it the lively activity
which they previously so much missed in the church. However
enthusiastic one is for activities aimed at a better society, we cannot do without the source of inspiration. And if the door to the
source of inspiration is still blocked up in the official congregations and churches, why should not small communities be formed
with the general purpose of handing the faith on to the new
generation? These would be groups of parents who are making a
deeper study of the questions of faith and are then looking for

forms in which they can hand it on to their children, and celebrate in common with them the fact that there is still hope for
this world. Might this not be a liberation for many weary Sunday
school teachers to see help being offered from this side? For what
is at issue is the setting up in this way of a community of faith
of the future, where Catholic or Protestant, orthodox or liberal
no longer matter. And in so far as such a community comes into
being, it will be able to exercise a lively pressure on the existing
congregations, which – inevitably – find themselves in difficulties
and in their isolation are becoming lifeless.

There is every chance that such a fellowship would be viable
if it left behind it all ill-feeling against the church and resistance
to the past, and concentrated on what matters: the one thing that
is needful.

This does not just concern parents and their faith. Anyone who
realizes what is at issue knows that what matters is not just ourselves and our faith, nor even what we make of them in our lives.
As we tell our children the old story, we can point to the faith of
Abraham, Isaac and Jacob – not the faith of wise men and philosophers. And if it is the one thing that is needful which is at issue,
then religious education is pointing towards Jesus Christ. Thereby you will have given your child the most important thing, re-
gardless of your own weak faith and questionable life. For he made
it a reality: God with us and human existence for others. He is
still our most fundamental inspiration. After twenty centuries,
we have not yet said all there is to be said about him. It is the
children who are bringing us back to this. They have something
to say about it!

CHILDHOOD REMINISCENCES

One other thing stirs me when I look back at my youthful days,
viz. the fact that so many people gave me something or were
something to me without knowing it. Such people, with whom
I have, perhaps, never exchanged a word, yes, and others about
whom I have merely heard things by report, have had a decisive
influence upon me; they entered into my life and became powers
within me. Much that I should otherwise not have felt so clearly
or done so effectively was felt or done as it was, because I stand,
as it were, under the sway of these people. Hence I always think
we all live, spiritually, by what others have given us in the significant hours of our life. These significant hours do not announce
themselves as coming, but arrive unexpected. Nor do they make a

great show of themselves; they pass almost unperceived. Often, indeed, their significance comes home to us first as we look back, just as the beauty of a piece of music or of landscape often strikes us first in our recollection of it.

Albert Schweitzer[1]

In her youth Mamma had suffered much from religious doubt, and in particular had undergone a severe struggle with regard to her confirmation and first communion.

In order to spare us similar difficulties at that age, the solution she had found was to cut us off from religious concepts, just as she had done with death. But the experience of the divine is present in the soul from the first, at least in my soul.

I believed in the Greek gods. In the quiet of the early morning I crept out to a stone altar to make sacrifices in the form of flowers and ears of corn and to indulge in the contemplation of a great exalted being. I must have had great reverence for the chief of the gods. A World Father, Creator and Maintainer of all that existed was a natural and necessary idea. My religious adoration was paid to him. I did not bring my personal concerns to him, he was too exalted for that. I did not even bring them to my earthly father, for to have anything to do with him was just as exalted and more spiritual. They were taken to mother alone.

These quiet, holy hours were my closest secret.

But the word got round in the village that idolatry was practised behind our walls. An eleven-year-old village girl, the child of a neighbour, who brought our milk, asked me one day if I had ever heard of the Lord Christ. I said that I had not, full of curiosity. She invited me to climb on to the wall which separated our gardens. She would bring a basket of the best pears on the condition that we would listen carefully to what she was going to tell us. We weren't to tell this to our nurse Josephine, because she was a heathen as we were. Full of expectation we went to the place that had been arranged, where our apostle, full of moving zeal, with inadequate powers, introduced us to the story of the creation. This approximately coincided with our Greek conception. But when she tried to explain the mystery of the incarnation and the redemption, her intellectual equipment failed her. We could imagine the divine only in the greatest splendour. Why, why did he permit all that to be done to him? Blows, floggings? A god? Why did he not let lightning fall from heaven? No, we resisted this with a feeling of indignation.

She became abusive, we were abusive in our turn, and a dispute broke out. Horrified, she took hold of her empty basket and slipped down from the wall, while we, exhausted, dropped down into the grass on the other side.

What I had learned had its effect on me and as usual I went to my mother and asked for an account of the god who was crucified. She replied that I was still too young for such matters and that I had to go on playing without worrying. When I was older, she would talk to me about all that.

I cannot approve this on the part of my mother. For this reason, if for no other, that one does not make life easier for a child by isolating him so strictly from the outside world that he is not even aware of the religious ideas of his contemporaries. But there was one good consequence of this: that I later encountered the unimaginable figure of the Son of Man fresh and direct in the gospels, untainted by rhetoric and tradition, as the early centuries of Christianity had known him. The girl had complained in the village and one day the village boys marched up with sticks and stones to our garden gate and called us out to fight.
Isolde Kurz

In the difficult times of persecution my friends never understood why often, with a matchbox in my hand, I watched attentively to see if the match would burn right down. When the war was finally over and I sat peacefully in my room in Norway and lit a match, I recalled an image from my youth.

As a child I once met a miner who, before he went down the pit, lit his carbide lamp. He set the match on the hook of the lamp and said, 'Look, if it burns right down, I have the feeling that I will come back to the light. You must realize' – I scarcely understood this at the time – 'that all those who can kindle light in others are rich. And to kindle light in others means above all to be able to listen to them.'
Max Tau

THE END OF CHILDHOOD

Once, on the threshold of adolescence, I was shaken to the depths by the thought that, even though there may be no such thing as a meaning in life, the very search for meaning would render life significant and meaningful. It is to this that I desired passionately to dedicate my life. This insight marked a true inner revolution which changed my whole outlook ... This was undoubtedly a kind of conversion – the most powerful and perhaps the only one in my life.
N. Berdyaev[2]

Around this time when I was about fourteen years of age, something happened to me – happened in me – which no words can ever tell. Whether I can tell it now, or ought to try to tell it, is doubtful.

To youth sorrow is new, strange, terrifying, all the more because it does not understand: it does not yet know the quiet joy of an outlived sorrow. I felt like a lost soul, baffled. It was a summer day, still lucid, gentle. Not knowing what to do, I went for a walk, climbed a hill near our town, and sat down. Before me lay the valley of Willa Walla creek, and beyond a woodland, and in the distance the prairie. Not far away a lone cottonwood tree stood stately against a violet sky. Suddenly all my trouble, all my fear, left me. Life itself seemed to speak to my spirit. God became very near, very real, not awful but gentle as a Friend. Jesus infinitely enlarged in every way – but something more. My whole being was aware of Him, with an intense stillness. There was no voice, no vision, but old Bible words came into my mind, almost as if someone had spoken them into my ear: 'Fear not; underneath are the everlasting arms.' It was not merely an idea of God needed to explain life – I was not thinking of Him. No, it was God Himself, He without whom we cannot live, He upon whom we rely, unconsciously, when all else fails. Since that hour I have never been lonely, never afraid of death. Here is the one certainty of my life in the midst of many uncertainties – the center of all my habits, memories, purposes, hopes and efforts.
J. F. Newton[3]

When I was thirteen years old I had a period of great devoutness. I read Thomas à Kempis and a devotional book on the Passion. I prayed prayers from it on my knees and lived in a glorious and cheerful obedience and loneliness of heart.
Albert Verwey

When I was about twelve years old I began to ask myself: God, yes, but how, who, where, what? God, who are you, where are you? One fine day the answer suddenly came as though a screen had fallen away and revealed an enormous room. I still recall it, I was in a meadow, stood still and knew: great, great God, our Father. Later, when I learnt to know and pray the Te Deum I knew that the words: *Pater immensae majestatis*, the Father of an infinite majesty, expressed what I felt that day. I know that for years and years it has been a joy to me.
A nun

Near a draw-bridge in a street that was still quiet on the edge of the town I had a kind of blinding vision, a feeling of joy which united me to God. Everything became utterly beautiful, I was alone, walked along and thought, 'Now I really know.' I still know exactly where that was.

I came early in the morning out of church, alone, and made a short detour over the top of a dune which lay behind our house which was a fine place for running down. Then I walked down the little path to the house. The sun was shining and it was quite still. And then it suddenly happened. I really do not know how to express it, but He *was* there. He touched me and overwhelmed me with his caresses. It was such an overpowering experience that I think it could only be explained to someone who had experienced such a thing himself. I stood stock still and the tears ran down my face. I felt a powerful urge to kneel down and at the same time a vague fear that someone would see me. I walked to a seat when the most violent emotion was over. While I was walking to the house, I constantly repeated to myself the same phrase: 'He kissed me.' After more than thirty years this experience is still so real that I know exactly where I stood and what the seat looked like which was opposite the bushes.

FAITH AND EDUCATION

Education is showing what life means.

A child can only live in a world which is secure and assumes a world which is good and therefore secure and fit to live in. The task is to make the child proof against the fact that good does not always triumph in the world.

There is no faith without education.

A child possesses the points on to which faith can be grafted, but if education does not carry out the task of grafting, everything is left to chance.

M. J. Langeveld

A child will believe anything, however improbable, from anyone he trusts. His universe at first is small but his trust is infinite. From the first he knows his dependence and acknowledges it in no uncertain voice.

Ruth Robinson[4]

The most important thing is to let God act, to put no obstacle in

the way of his mysterious action.
René Voeltzel

The educator should not attempt to present as obligatory something which he does *not* believe ... It is hopeless, in this domain
as in any other, to attempt to give others what you do not possess
yourself.
Pierre Bovet[5]

You cannot behave otherwise than you are with children.
Fons Jansen

In education, and especially in religious education, you have to
give more than you possess yourself.

I would rather do differently, and for some time tell a child only
the comprehensible things and teach practical Christianity, being
good to one's fellow men, helping others, but I find even this
difficult, because can we imitate everything Jesus did at the present day without being taken for an idiot? It often makes a conflict for us because they take everything seriously. Must I teach
children to let themselves be struck on the other cheek? I'm quite
happy when my daughter asserts herself, because she has a tendency to hold herself timidly back.

Once I was married I no longer believed until I had children. I
could bear no witness to them which sounded true and I simply
began the search again, because something which had lasted two
thousand years must have something interesting to offer me as
well. In this matter I have firmly resolved to bear witness, but
not on the basis of fear. And the thing is that to believe does not
seem so difficult, although I often have to look for simple language
which children understand. And it seems that simplicity of language increases faith. In this way I was once again able to take
part in organized religion, but with both feet in the world, and
so prayer once again came to have a meaning. But I found with
my family that when one does not have the courage to set out
once again on the path of discovery, one lets everything drift on,
finds no inspiration for life, and does not understand the message
of hope.
Parents

It is more important to speak to God about the child than to
speak to the child about God.
Augustine

FIRST IMPRESSIONS

Essentially I have never shaken off what I experienced as a child and what became the driving force of my life.

I have seen that children who, whatever their circumstances, have not received faith in their childhood are no longer receptive to it in later life, even if they wanted to be. On the other hand, many people return in later life to the religious education of their childhood, even if they have lost all faith in the course of life.
A fifty-year-old

Similar feelings still persist in my unconscious mind, half a century later. It is unimaginably difficult to shake off concepts and emotions from childhood or to control them. I still feel that they are alive and vocal in me when I think about who God really is and how he exists. By virtue of a young child's great suggestibility we can easily establish in him a conviction of which he cannot rid himself in later life.

There is only one way open to a child: to take on the colour of his surroundings. This defenceless openness to the world explains the decisive influence which the environment – parents, mothers – exercise on a child in the early stage of his development.
J. Kijm

The child is unable to discriminate between what is allegory and what is not; whatever he receives and believes at that early age is apt to become permanent and indelible.
Plato[6]

THE INFLUENCE OF PARENTS

Since parents have conferred life on their children, they have a most solemn obligation to educate their offspring. Hence, parents must be acknowledged as the first and foremost educators of their children. Their role as educators is so decisive that scarcely anything can compensate for their failure in it.
Second Vatican Council[7]

It is my conviction that the inward experience of the family is automatically handed down to children and grandchildren. What made the greatest impression on me as a child is the profound conviction of the faith of my parents, both father and mother, the atmosphere in which I experienced this and the conviction which they possessed and which they silently propagated amongst the congregation.
A seventy-two-year-old

My husband and I did not send our children to Sunday school, nor to church, nor for religious training. For there was so much missing, the reality of revelation. And yet it often follows invisible paths. Once a week we read aloud. I am so afraid of telling the child too many stories and ones he cannot understand.
A mother

My parents gave me such a magnificent example of life in communion with the Invisible that I began of myself to long for the beauty that gives you strength, for secret converse with God.

You feel yourself completely overwhelmed with thankfulness every time you look back: an atmosphere of love and living faith. My parents really did nothing about religious education, at least I don't think that they ever consciously saw themselves as concerned with it.

But I felt – unconsciously of course at first, but I felt it – that each in their own way, but each as sincerely as the other, they loved Jesus Christ very much and lived by his grace and for his kingdom.

As a child you want nothing better than to share in all these things; you see how fine it all is, how happy it makes you, how real it is. You begin then to hunger for the living Lord, whose presence is sometimes so really tangible, to know him for yourself, completely, to love him with everything in you, and to belong to him completely and utterly.

For me and all my brothers and sisters the living faith of our parents was decisive.
A reminiscence

Does not the child live the life which the parents create for him? In so far as the parents are concerned with God, they allow the child to live in a world of faith.

It is at home that a child participates most in life, at home where he can be more himself, and therefore it is there for the most part that he lives most intensely.

A child becomes a person at home, and also becomes a believer at home.

In the family the conversations at home, at bedtime, or on walks, are the opportunity to help the searching mind of the child on its way.

For a child God can only be experienced in the world of adults, of calm wise persons who have gradually come to God and who know on the basis of their own lives that God can usually only be found after a long time.

J. van Haaren

You must know that there is nothing higher and stronger and more wholesome and good for life in the future than some good memory, especially a memory of childhood, of home ... If a man carries many such memories with him into life, he is safe until the end of his days.

Feodor Dostoevsky[8]

Father told us the sacred stories with which my people grew up. In the evening hours, we as a family took our great decisions.

A Hindu

It has been in the attempt to share and communicate our deepest convictions about life with our children, on their wave-length, that we have been forced time and again to ask ourselves, 'Is this what I really believe?'

Ruth Robinson[9]

Perhaps your parents very rarely went to church, and you feel they did pretty well by you. There is undoubtedly a deposit of inherited faith 'in our bones', but in many families in this generation this inherited capital is getting very low. It takes two generations to breed Christianity out of a family. Does that matter to you? Does it make you feel sorry for your son?

Frances Wilkinson[10]

We cannot say that the child's religion stands or falls with that of his parents.

M. J. Langeveld

Education in the faith is so hazardous in the family because it is

so far-reaching and so dependent on emotional relationships and the example of the parents.
M. W. Steenmeyer van Rij

Religious ideas and statements cannot simply be brought to light out of the vague memories of our childhood and handed on to children.
Herman Sweet

We have to give an example to our children. Not to be untrue ourselves, to keep our promises. And to dare to say that there are many things that you do not know or that you have failed to trust in God.

I actually joined the church when I was married and had children and suddenly had a feeling of responsibility about the future. I did not want to send my children into the world without faith in Christ.
Parents

I still have the feeling that as a child I learnt more from my father than from dozens of books which I have read since. And with the people I have come to know and the things that have happened to me, I have often remembered what he told me long ago.
Rogier van Aerde

The child's faith is dependent upon the way in which his father and mother live, not on the way in which they speak. Their words, their punishments, and even their anger are only a performance to the child, mere thunder and lightning. He feels instinctively what they really value. A child sees what we are through what we want to be. He goes as far as he can with us, he is a real diplomat. Without knowing it he is subject to the influence of each one of us and reflects it, adapting it to his own level. A child is a distorting mirror.
Frédéric Amiel

THROUGH HUMAN CONTACT

Life itself is the most authentic lesson. Genuine, simple humanity is often the way to faith.
J. van Haaren

It is our own reality which is always and ultimately the test of the value of our contacts with the child; and it is this which is recognized by his unconscious. It is the sum total of our personality which we give to the child.

Children gather from us the atmosphere of all that we most carefully ignore ourselves.

Many of us are so practically minded that we realize the importance of the objective experience, but are quite blind to the intensity and forces of those intuitive experiences, which come when the child feels all that lies below the surface, though he is unable consciously to formulate these feelings even to himself.

Children pay little attention to what we say to them, they intuit what we are.
Frances Wickes[11]

Human language is not confined to the spoken word, though this is a large part of it. We communicate with each other at a much deeper level. Our actions and attitudes, our choices and responses, what we don't say as much as what we do – all that we are speaks the living word between man and man in terms of flesh and blood.

Jesus ... in terms of flesh and blood spelt out for us the meaning of our life, not only by what he said but by what he was. Our task as parents is to help our children to 'hear' this living Word for themselves and to hear it as naturally as breathing or sleeping, below the conscious level. And we must make sure that our spoken language, our explanations and definitions, make it easier, not harder for them to hear with the inner ear this Word of life.
Ruth Robinson[12]

TOO MUCH OF A GOOD THING

I believe that many children are brought up in too religious a way, to the extent that with most children God gets little or no chance.

When we teach a child about God, we must not overwhelm or frighten him. We must be able to give the feeling of a security which man has in God.
J. van Haaren

We should be aware of robbing a child of a spiritual reality already within the scope of his experience by putting too great a value on the religious categories in which we dress it up.
Ruth Robinson[13]

The view which so many people hold, that the essential require-
ment of religious life should be that a child should spend his day
in an element which even in its outward forms is recognizably
Christian, is due to a confusion of quantity and quality, of the
forming of habits and training with the formation of conscience
and education.

Length of time is not decisive. Experiences, short but overpowering, can set their seal upon the whole period of development.

We cannot bring the child frequently and for a long time into
the sphere of the experience of the presence of God. He cannot
bear the pressure for so long or so often. The effect of this is not
educational, but deadening and destructive. A school where there
are prayers with the children four times a day I would regard as a
danger to religious education rather than a blessing. If one tries
to give the whole of the teaching a Christian stamp, then the
danger of familiarity with the Holy is almost inevitable.
P. Kohnstamm

If the teacher, in the name of God, makes demands that are too
great, the child will not be able to match up to them and will take
a dislike to God. And this is wrong in its turn because you have
to love God. No wonder that people reject a God like this when
they grow up. Just think of Christian books for children, which
go on about being naughty, being sorry and being forgiven. As
adults we should give a firm no to such a theology.
L. Kuylman-Hoekendijk

We do such an enormous amount for children and for their religious education, but sometimes I think that I am doing children
a great favour when I plead for much less activity on the part of
adults.
J. van Haaren

We did too much to make children believe. There was too little
connection between what had to be learnt and what was experienced. This way a great deal of the faith remained outside the
reality of a child's existence. This is the beginning of the breach
between faith and life. The child is open to these values in so far
as we experience them ourselves.

The patience that is able to wait for their own assent to faith is
swallowed up in an anxious zeal to establish firmly in the mean-
while, albeit undigested, the truths of faith which are necessary
for salvation. This has very little to do with the patience with

which Christ himself proclaimed his gospel of redemption in such a fragmentary way.
J. H. Huijts

Religious instruction between the age of seven and the beginning of puberty is of value only in so far as words are learnt. One may well laugh. A child learns stories and hymns of which he understands nothing. The significance is that the child learns the words. The words remain and are filled with meaning in the course of life. All these uncomprehended words are points of crystallization for thought.

Children become too easily tired of words and lose interest. The atmosphere of religion then becomes one of immense boredom.
H. C. Rümke

I SEND MY CHILDREN...

Finally, parents are beginning to realize that they must draw together the threads of all these forms of education, even in the religious sphere. These institutions have taken over with too much self-assurance the task of what they think of as ignorant parents. Parents have too easily allowed themselves to be pushed aside from the apex of education.
J. H. Huijts

I went to a State school, but was sent to Sunday school. I also learnt as a small child to say prayers at night and for years my mother said grace. But religion and faith were never spoken about. And this was something I usually longed for. On the quiet I tried to find out about it all. I was always slipping into churches in the holidays.

When education came to be my daily work, I came to the firm conviction that religious education must take place in the first instance at home. In any case we hold the view that certainly in the primary school period the influence of the home is greater than that of the school and that every child at this age has an enormous respect and admiration for his parents.
A childhood reminiscence

Most parents leave religious education to the school.

At Sunday school I often noticed the indifferent attitude of parents, they don't care whether they go or not. In this respect it is still a very responsible task for us teachers. One of the chil-

dren stayed away and when we enquired it appeared that she used to get nervous and found it hard to make sense of the stories. The parents took no interest at all, and therefore there was no reaction to the child's feeling in the family.
A teacher

Because his parents refuse him religious instruction, he will receive it from educators, not chosen for him but encountered by chance.
Pierre Bovet[14]

The very fact that they receive Christian education from so many different people who often hold different views about it, makes it so difficult to answer their questions.

Many people lay emphasis on the fact that stories and events at school and Sunday school have been of permanent and of great influence upon their belief.

The children sometimes repeat verses which they have learnt at Sunday school. When a mother, in a Japanese prison camp, was weeping about someone's death, her nine-year-old daughter said, 'What God does is well done.' She had just learnt it at Sunday school. The child also applied it to herself when she heard the Japanese shouting and was afraid about her father.

Apart from this I myself read aloud for years from various Children's Bibles and sent her to Sunday school. The result is that once she was eighteen she no longer went to church and certainly not to any classes. Somehow you feel your inability to pass it on as a heavy burden.

To our horror our daughter began to grow weary of the Bible stories. In our view it is the fault of the church school. Why should there always be nothing but Bible stories every day? This means that as parents you have nothing new to offer. We ourselves read aloud two or three times a week out of the Children's Bible.
Parents

The renewal of religious education must begin with a renewal of the personal preparation of teachers. For they will never be able

to give good guidance to children if their own religious life is immature, or worse, deformed.
Nijmegen Catechetical Institute

Not so long ago, religion – just like sexuality – was too frequently seen and dealt with as a kind of separate nature reserve within or rather above the ordinary affairs of life. Religious education too was a sphere apart, largely conducted by separate recognizable functionaries in separate set periods put aside for the purpose. In addition, it consisted principally of the inculcation of knowledge, the learning of a kindergarten theology and an early familiarity with essentially adult religious acts.
J. Nieuwenhuis

The business of bringing up children is like a pyramid. At the base it is broad, and the influence of the parents and the home is everything. Slowly it narrows, as the child becomes more independent, and the parents' sphere of influence less. It consists very largely of just being there, being interested and standing by.
Frances Wilkinson[15]

In practice there seems to exist with most children two worlds: one, the world of everyday reality, and the other of religion and the Bible, the latter sometimes with a marvellous content of things not understood and not apprehended, lying far beyond their field of vision.
M. W. Steenmeyer van Rij

NOT TOO SOON

The guiding principle of instruction must not be to teach everything now which the lack of later teaching may prevent from being learnt then. The view, 'at least they've heard about that', is a fact the source of later difficulties.
J. H. Huijts

Theories introduced too early remain alien to the child. The danger that these theories may permanently replace a genuine and personal faith is not hypothetical.
M. J. Langeveld

It is not important for a child to know much in the religious sphere before he goes to primary school. All that is important is

that his mind should remain open to a reality which goes beyond everyday experience and which will gradually be more revealed to him in the course of the years.
N. Snijders-Oomen

We must be thrifty with faith, we must not give everything at once. We must wait for questions. And it is not just a question of giving a little less, but very much less.

Concepts only have any meaning if they can be digested.

A child may well be brought to grief by our zeal and our haste.

We have no right to lay burdens on the faith of a child, it is still an untested faith. Like very brittle ice, formed only last night, which cannot yet take much weight, which has not known any heavy frost and not borne any heavy burden.
J. van Haaren

Religious concepts introduced too soon may lead to regressive thinking in religion.
Ronald Goldman[16]

STARTING WITH THE CHILD

The child develops through what he discovers himself.
M. J. Langeveld

If the teacher does not respect the child's world and imposes his own adult patterns upon it, it is not possible for them to constitute symbols which can be means of contact with the living God.

The adult looks on the child either as his equal or as of less value than himself.
Antoine Vergote

To allow the child's personal faith to develop always supposes that one calls upon what the child himself has to offer.
M. J. Langeveld

The problem to which we should address ourselves is how to promote this growth from within. Unless that is effected, religious instruction will impose only a superficial layer upon the personality of the child, and his religion will be a veneer, without any depth ... a false, arrested religion, a pseudo-religion ... His

religion must grow up within him as an integral part of him. It must be his own, not something lived by him second-hand.
R. S. Lee[17]

The child learns to know God as Creator when he has taken a part, however small and insignificant, in the process of creation. For the development of religion, the teaching of visible phenomena must come before the teaching of words; the Creator must first reveal Himself in His visible works, before He can be apprehended as the invisible God of our spirits.
E. Read Mumford[18]

The most valuable work of infant teachers is to stimulate them to inquire, explore and examine all aspects of the world about which they are so naturally curious. Spontaneous questions about people, events, things, problems and many other experiences form the basis of a great deal of educational activity.

In religious education at this stage, to begin by talking in 'religious language' is as inappropriate as using advanced mathematical symbols with children. There must first be accumulated many and varied experiences of life of which religious language speaks.
R. Goldman[19]

Every piece of knowledge which is introduced from outside the world of experience is worthless from the religious point of view.
J. H. Huijts

I want as a parent to provide the soil of experience in which these spiritual seeds can germinate, so that later – much later, and without forcing – they may blossom into conscious commitment and response.
Ruth Robinson[20]

A child must first be able to love God before he can be taught about God in any extended fashion. Faith begins to live only through love.
J. van Haaren

A primary school teacher once said, 'We must love the Lord Jesus and follow him.' I wanted nothing better, but how to do it? And I did not dare to ask. You must always make yourself clear to children, because what is logical to us can be a problem for children.
A childhood reminiscence

The time of quiet little listeners who pass no comment is over in good educational practice. Children like to listen, they like to join in and talk about things if they affect them.
M. W. Steenmeyer van Rij

DOUBT

The uncertainty about faith which can nowadays be observed in many teachers is largely due to the rigid way in which religious education was undertaken in the past.
J. H. Huijts

A child must be allowed adequate breathing space to make his own choice and take his own decisions, and also must be given an opportunity to choose by not being left in a vacuum or in a place where only one trumpet sounds.
   What can a child do if he has not experienced that there are such things as problems? A child who has had the experience of being allowed to look for himself and being able to find for himself is much more firmly set on the way to a faith of his own.
M. J. Langeveld

With regard to the equipment which we provide for our children as parents, they must be ready and able to endure tension. They must find uncertainty, lack of clarity, change and conflict quite normal.
L. Kuylman-Hoekendijk

The religion of childhood and the faith of a child collapses, once the child, as his intellect matures, asks new questions and has to go without an answer.
J. van Haaren

We must leave room for doubt, and must make room for the impulses towards doubt to develop, for doubt has a function of its own. I regard it as of great importance within religious education. Doubt should not bring with it a burden of guilt. The consequence of that is that doubt does not develop with the personality, but is born as a secret guilt. My own personal experience is that doubt itself is not a factor in the origin of unbelief. In the great crises of life we constantly see doubt recurring. Doubt about everything, about ourselves, about our neighbour. Every growth is preceded by doubt. Can the growth of our religious life be possible without doubt?

I am convinced that if we do not make room for doubt, then our faith becomes inexorably ossified and the words we use are gradually deprived of their significance and of their power to move us. It seems paradoxical, but to be unable to sustain positive doubt is a hindrance in the development of the life of faith. It is certain that doubt which can be evaluated positively is closely linked to all experiences which have inspired us at the high points of our life.
H. C. Rümke

It is obvious that the way in which you believe and the content of your belief change as you grow older, just like the way you love or your feeling of responsibility. This is also most desirable, because an adult has not much use for an infantile faith. And it seems to me that doubt is an indispensable pacemaker in the process of growing into an adult faith.

But in the period during which I grew up doubt was regarded as the worst thing that could happen to you: it was clearly the beginning of the end. Anyone who ever admitted a doubt would see it gradually penetrating his whole faith and then he would have nothing left. The whole system, which you now abuse so much, was constructed with the aim of excluding any doubt, even over the very least point. Everything had to be established beyond doubt; and for centuries a mad zeal had been devoted to this. In general they were completely impervious to the idea that faith and doubt belonged together. They had no idea that the doubt which – as they had accurately observed – was penetrating everything could work as a leaven to make the dough rise and that this is indispensable. They preferred to offer bread like a stone rather than allow the process of fermentation, with the risk that it would get out of hand. As a child my questions were often answered by, 'You mustn't think so much, you will begin to doubt.' Faith was a fragile vessel, we were taught; it could obviously not stand much.
Rogier van Aerde

I WILL LET MY CHILDREN DECIDE FOR THEMSELVES

The opposite of force is not freedom, but union. To be in a state of union, one must first be independent.
Martin Buber

If a child comes from a non-religious environment, then until

adolescence there will probably be no signs of religious life. I
say probably nothing, because just as parents who diligently try
to make sure that their child hears nothing of the misery of the
world suddenly notice that the child has picked up all kinds of
things from servants or friends, so there is no child who has not
heard of God or the devil, heaven or hell, and even a child from
an extremely 'enlightened' scientific family possesses these words
as points of crystallization for the marvellous emotions and
images within him.

H. C. Rümke

On the one hand they realize that they are believers, because
their father and mother are, while on the other side they also
begin to sense that it must become a personal matter of their own
and that they are being required consciously to accept or reject the
offer of faith at some time.

For many parents and teachers there is a difficult dilemma
here: how far can the child, as he grows older, be left to himself
in the religious field? They feel that an unconditional obligation
is not in accord with faith itself; but on the other hand there is a
real concern that the child will be wholly alienated from faith if
there is not some pressure in the background.

In general one can say that the dangers of an unconditional
obligation, imposed at any cost, are greater than those of an
understanding flexibility and a calm patience, in particular because the latter have a connection with true faith and trust.

As a child grows older it can be allowed to realize that believing is not a certainty like twice one are two, but a gift which
must repeatedly be defended.

J. Nieuwenhuis

HARDLY A CHILD ANY LONGER

In most cases a child undergoes fairly profound changes in the
course of the eleventh and twelfth years. Something mysterious
enters the child, something which sometimes silences parents and
seems like the first movements of approaching spring.

At the age of eleven and twelve many children become outward
looking to an intense degree.

The whole world comes into the living-room. He does not
simply hear of wars, he sees them. He does not simply listen to
race riots, he is present at them. And this means that at a much
younger age than we ourselves and in a much more intense way,

he is affected by the world events of the present day.

To him the world is smaller than it has ever been for adults or ever will be. And this very smallness, this very closeness, provokes questions and confusions which can sometimes profoundly oppress a child.

A twelve-year-old child begins to look and ask for what is genuine, authentic, and really true. He is no longer content with a mere story or a mere formula, he also wants to look behind the story and behind the formula.
J. Nieuwenhuis

There are many children who during their twelfth year or thereabouts undergo an experience of faith which is decisive for their further development.

The experience of being meaningfully related to the whole of existence is almost always first recognized in the condition of being cast loose. It is no accident that it occurs at the age at which a more or less stable period of life is passing into another. Adolescence is such a period to the utmost degree. At this stage a person looks for new landmarks, suppressed urges come to the surface, and former certainties disappear. The contemplation of nature is often the first and most powerful impulse to this religious experience.
H. C. Rümke

14   Postscript

We pray to you for our children and descendants,
for all who are born after us,
that we may give them bread and not stones,
and not leave them an inheritance of war, but of
   freedom, prosperity and peace.
Huub Oosterhuis

For the moment, we bring to an end this discussion of 'the theology of children'.

But the last word on the subject has not yet been spoken. The purpose of this book has been to draw attention to the importance of taking children seriously in this respect, and of not brushing aside their 'theology' too hastily on the grounds 'that it is not their own' and that 'they only repeat what their parents say'.

Perhaps this book may also be a challenge to psychologists and educationalists to address themselves more than hitherto, from their own point of view, to the theme of 'the child and faith'. This dimension in the life of children is rarely touched by research or included in developmental psychology.

You may have received the impression that what has been presented is largely a picture of the past. This is due to the numerous childhood reminiscences of persons of previous generations, but some of the statements of children too were taken from books yellow with age. Yet this very past can be important for a better understanding of the reactions and movements of the present day. When young parents no longer recognize the same situation or have quite different experiences with their children at home, they have only to recount these experiences. These people who are in the midst of things, indeed, and not just grandmothers who now have time to write, could give something of value.

For we are not yet finished with 'the theology of children'. The subjects: creation, birth, good and evil, death, heaven, the future, Jesus Christ, his birth, life, death and resurrection, and above all the question of the Bible for children still remain incomplete.

Although we have not brought the matter to a conclusion, and in these pages perhaps may seem to have presented you with more questions than answers, what matters is the children, and how they can find and maintain faith in this world.

Look at a small child, being carried in a pram through the black clouds and the uproar of the traffic in our crazy world. How can we be other than horrified if we think of the future? Will he have freedom, prosperity and peace on this earth? There is no answer.

But a Chinese prayer reads: 'When there is a great drought, we long for rain clouds. When we are prisoners we yearn for peace. When we are slaves we pray for release. When we have God, we have hope.'

Notes

Chapter 1

1. Ruth Robinson, 'Spiritual Education in a World without Religion', in J. A. T. Robinson, *The New Reformation?*, p. 140.
2. Heinz Zahrnt, *What Kind of God?*, p. 4.
3. Pierre Teilhard de Chardin, *The Future of Man*, p. 260.

Chapter 2

1. Frances Wickes, *The Inner World of Childhood*, p. 83.

Chapter 3

1. Leo Tolstoy, *Recollections and Essays*, p. 23.
2. W. B. Yeats, *Reveries over Childhood and Youth*, p. 20.
3. Julien Green, *To Leave before Dawn*, p. 8.
4. Selma Fraiberg, *The Magic Years*, p. ix.
5. C. G. Jung, *Memories, Dreams and Reflections*, p. 95.
6. R. S. Lee, *Your Growing Child and Religion*, p. 13.
7. Ronald Goldman, *Religious Thinking in Childhood and Adolescence*, pp. 14, 25.
8. Frances Wilkinson, *Growing Up in Christ*, p. 28.
9. Pierre Bovet, *The Child's Religion*, pp. 9, 102.

Chapter 4

1. John Ruskin, *Praeterita* I, p. 62.
2. Pierre Loti, *A Child's Romance*, pp. 21f.
3. Quoted in Pierre Bovet, *The Child's Religion*, p. 31.
4. Pierre Teilhard de Chardin, quoted in the Introduction to *Le Milieu Divin* (Fontana edition), p. 17.
5. Gwendolen Freeman, *Children Never Tell*, pp. 50f.
6. Edmund Gosse, *Father and Son*, pp. 30ff.
7. F. Hebbel, *My Childhood*, quoted by P. Bovet, *op. cit.*, p. 35.
8. Dorothy F. Wilson, *Child Psychology and Religious Education*, p. 31.
9. Ronald Goldman, *Readiness for Religion*, p. 79.
10. Ruth Robinson, 'Honest to Children', in *The Honest to God Debate*, pp. 283f.
11. Pierre Bovet, *op. cit.*, p. 43.
12. R. S. Lee, *Your Growing Child and Religion*, pp. 67f.

Chapter 5

1. Selma Fraiberg, *The Magic Years*, p. ix.
2. William James, *The Varieties of Religious Experience*, p. 27.

3. Roy Campbell, *Light on a Dark Horse*, pp. 27f.
4. Leo Tolstoy, *Recollections and Essays*, p. 23.
5. Albert Schweitzer, *My Childhood and Youth*, pp. 37f., 65f.
6. Helen Parkhurst, *Exploring the Child's World*, pp. 1f., 4f., 11.
7. Edmund Gosse, *Father and Son*, p. 22.
8. Nathan Isaacs, *The Growth of Understanding in Young Children*, p. 7.
9. E. Read Mumford, *The Dawn of Religion in the Life of the Child*, pp. 14, 28, 49f.
10. Dorothy F. Wilson, *Child Psychology and Religious Education*, p. 38.
11. Frances Wickes, *The Inner World of Childhood*, in part from pp. 20f.
12. Francis Thompson, quoted by E. Read Mumford, *op. cit.*, p. 49.
13. E. Schillebeeckx, *God and Men*, p. 147.
14. Ruth Robinson, 'Honest to Children', in *The Honest to God Debate*, p. 282.
15. Marjorie Hourd, *The Education of the Poetic Spirit*, p. 25.
16. Violet Madge, *Children in Search of Meaning*, p. 30.

Chapter 6

1. Violet Madge, *Children in Search of Meaning*, pp. 13, 19.
2. W. Stern, *Psychology of Early Childhood*, pp. 171f.
3. Ronald Goldman, *Readiness for Religion*, p. 88.
4. Pierre Bovet, *The Child's Religion*, p. 14.
5. Romain Rolland, *Dawn and Morning*, p. 30.

Chapter 7

1. J. A. T. Robinson, *Exploration into God*, pp. 98f.
2. Violet Madge, *Children in Search of Meaning*, pp. 128f.
3. Eadmer, *Life of Saint Anselm*, ch. 1.2, pp. 4f.
4. Godfried Keller, *Green Henry*, pp. 20f.
5. C. G. Jung, *Memories, Dreams and Reflections*, pp. 28, 39f.
6. Ronald Goldman, *Religious Thinking in Childhood and Adolescence*, p. 87.
7. L. Köhler, *Old Testament Theology*, pp. 22ff.
8. F. Nietzsche, *The Joyful Wisdom*, pp. 167ff.
9. J. A. T. Robinson, *Exploration into God*, pp. 38f., 52.
10. Martin Buber, *The Eclipse of God*, pp. 17f.
11. Harvey Cox, *The Secular City*, pp. 244f.
12. J. A. T. Robinson, *Exploration into God*, p. 31.
13. Paul Tillich, *The Shaking of the Foundations*, p. 57.
14. Rudolf Bultmann, 'The New Testament and Mythology', in *Kerygma and Myth*, I, p. 4.
15. J. A. T. Robinson, *Exploration into God*, pp. 66ff., 71.

Chapter 8

1. Ronald Goldman, *Religious Thinking*, p. 88.
2. J. A. T. Robinson, *Honest to God*, pp. 13f., 59f.
3. Karl Barth, *Church Dogmatics*, II/1, p. 461.
4. Dietrich Bonhoeffer, *Letters and Papers from Prison*, pp. 155, 207.

Chapter 9

1. Hans Christian Andersen, *The Fairy Tale of my Life*, p. 25.
2. Charles Darwin, Letter to Dr Asa Gray, 22 May 1860, in F. Darwin, *Life and Letters of Charles Darwin*, Vol. II, p. 312.

3. Feodor Dostoevsky, *The Brothers Karamazov*, pp. 243ff.
4. Ludwig Feuerbach, *The Essence of Christianity*, p. 174.
5. E. Schillebeeckx, *God and Man*, pp. 234f.
6. Paul Tillich, *Systematic Theology*, Vol. I, p. 296.
7. Emil Brunner, *Dogmatics*, Vol. I, pp. 253f.
8. J. A. T. Robinson, *Exploration into God*, pp. 108ff.

Chapter 10

1. D. Spicer, *Children's Prayers from Other Lands*, p. 49.
2. *Ibid.*, p. 53.
3. From France. *Ibid.*, p. 69.
4. From Japan. *Ibid.*, p. 36.
5. From Holland. *Ibid.*, p. 65.
6. Cf. the *Epistle to Diognetus*, 9.4.
7. Augustine, *Confessions* I.9.
8. André Maurois, *Memoirs*, p. 24.
9. C. S. Lewis, *Surprised by Joy*, p. 26.
10. Sabine Leibholz, in *I Knew Dietrich Bonhoeffer*, ed. W. D. Zimmermann and R. Gregor Smith, p. 25.
11. Frances Wilkinson, *Growing Up in Christ*, p. 29.
12. Pierre Teilhard de Chardin, *Le Milieu Divin*, pp. 127f.
13. Karl Barth, *Church Dogmatics*, III/3, p. 268.
14. E. Schillebeeckx, *God and Man*, p. 252.
15. Karl Barth, *op. cit.*, p. 269.

Chapter 11

1. Godfried Keller, *Green Henry*, pp. 66f.
2. Jean-Paul Sartre, *Words*, pp. 67-70.
3. Alexander Bain, *Autobiography*, pp. 10f., 34f.
4. Robert Graves, *Goodbye to All That*, p. 13.
5. Maxim Gorky, *Childhood*, pp. 81f.
6. Søren Kierkegaard, *Journals* § 1219 (pp. 441f.).

Chapter 12

1. Hans Christian Andersen, *The Fairy Tale of my Life*, pp. 1, 29.
2. Gwen Raverat, *Period Piece*, p. 223.
3. Albert Schweitzer, *My Childhood and Youth*, pp. 11, 57f., 55f.
4. Romain Rolland, *Dawn and Morning*, pp. 19f.
5. André Maurois, *Memoirs*, p. 26.
6. George Bernard Shaw, *Sixteen Self-Sketches*, p. 45.
7. Julien Green, *To Leave before Dawn*, pp. 40, 48.
8. Langston Hughes, *The Big Sea*, pp. 19f.

Chapter 13

1. Albert Schweitzer, *My Childhood and Youth*, p. 82.
2. Nicholas Berdyaev, *Dream and Reality*, pp. 78f.
3. J. F. Newton, *River of Years*, pp. 41f.
4. Ruth Robinson, 'Honest to Children', in *The Honest to God Debate*, p. 280.
5. Pierre Bovet, *The Child's Religion*, pp. 115f.
6. Plato, *Republic* II, 378D, trans. A. D. Lindsay.
7. Second Vatican Council, Declaration on Religious Education, 3.
8. Feodor Dostoevsky, *The Brothers Karamazov*, p. 819.

9. Ruth Robinson, 'Spiritual Education in a World without Religion', in *The New Reformation?*, p. 123.
10. Frances Wilkinson, *Growing Up in Christ*, p. 15.
11. Frances Wickes, *The Inner World of Childhood*, pp. 21, 38.
12. Ruth Robinson, 'Spiritual Education', *op. cit.*, pp. 124f.
13. Ruth Robinson, 'Honest to Children', *op. cit.*, p. 281.
14. Pierre Bovet, *op. cit.*, p. 113.
15. Frances Wilkinson, *Growing Up in Christ*, p. 119.
16. Ronald Goldman, *Religious Thinking*, p. 227.
17. R. S. Lee, *Your Growing Child and Religion*, pp. 13f.
18. E. Read Mumford, *The Dawn of Religion in the Mind of the Child*, pp. 51ff.
19. Ronald Goldman, *Readiness for Religion*, p. 88.
20. Ruth Robinson, 'Spiritual Education', *op. cit.*, p. 124.

Bibliography

J. van Balen Blanken, *Verzameling van kinderpreken*, 1848
Karl Barth, *Church Dogmatics*, T. & T. Clark, II/1, 1957; III/3, 1958
A. Becker, *Kinder fragen nach Gott*, 1963
J. H. van den Berg, *Metabletica*, 1957
'De "rêve éveillé" van Robert Desoille', in *Persoon en wereld*, 1953
H. Berkhof, *Spreken over een onvanzelfsprekende God* (Oecumenische III: I), 1965
D. Bonhoeffer, *Letters and Papers from Prison*, third edition, SCM Press, 1967
Pierre Bovet, *The Child's Religion*, Allen and Unwin, 1928
E. Brunner, *Dogmatics*, Vol. I: *The Christian Doctrine of God*, tr. O. Wyon, Lutterworth, 1949
M. Buber, *Reden über Erziehung*, 1953
— *The Eclipse of God*, Harper and Row, 1955, 1967
Charlotte Bühler, *Das Märchen und die Phantasie des Kindes*, 1918
R. Bultmann, 'The New Testament and Mythology', in *Kerygma and Myth* I, SPCK, 1953, pp. 1-44
Harvey Cox, *The Secular City*, SCM Press, 1965
Jean Pierre Deconchy, 'L'idée de Dieu entre 7 et 16 ans', in *Lumen Vitae*, 1964
Ruth Dirx, *Das Kind das unbekannte Wesen*, 1964
H. Faber, *De godsdienstigeontwikkeling van onze kinderen*, 1952
Sophia Fahs, *God en de kinderen van nu*, 1968
Ludwig Feuerbach, *The Essence of Christianity*, Harper and Row, 1957
Hans M. M. Fortmann, *Als ziende de onzienlijke* 3b, 1968
Selma Fraiberg, *The Magic Years*, Methuen, 1959
Ronald Goldman, *Religious Thinking in Childhood and Adolescence*, Routledge and Kegan Paul, 1964
— *Readiness for Religion*, Routledge and Kegan Paul, 1965
J. van Haaren, *Uit de mond der kleinen*, 1962
— *Voor hen is het koninkrijk*, 1963
— *De kleine gelovigen*, 1962
W. Hansen, *Die Entwicklung des kindlichen Weltbildes*, 1938
H. J. Heering, *Dogmatische verkenningen*, 1968
Erika Hoffmann, *Kindheitserinnerungen als Quelle pedagogischer Kinderkunde*, 1960
Marjorie Hourd, *The Education of the Poetic Spirit*, Heinemann, 1949
J. H. Huijts, *Godsdienstige opvoeding in overgangstjd*, 1961
W. G. van de Hulst, *Bijbelse vertellingen voor de kleintjes*, 1926
Nathan Isaacs, *The Growth of Understanding in Young Children*, ESA, 1961
W. James, *The Varieties of Religious Experience*, 1902 (Fontana Books, 1960)
F. Jansen, *Drie kleine kleutertjes*, 1967

Göte Klingenberg, 'Les "images perceptions" dans l'expérience religieuse de l'enfant', in *Lumen Vitae*, 1961

Odiseria Knechtle, *Glaubensvertiefung durch das Symbol*, 1963

L. Köhler, *Old Testament Theology*, Lutterworth, 1957

C. E. van Koetsveld, *Een tiental kinderpreken*, 1851

P. Kohnstamm, *Persoonlijkheid in wording*, 1929

P. W. Kors, 'Denken kleine kinderen?', in *De speeldoos*

O. Kroh, *Die Psychologie der frühen Kindheit*, 1931

H. M. Kuitert, *De mensvormigheid Gods*, 1962

L. Kuylman-Hoekendijk, *Geloven met kinderen*, 1969

J. Kijm, 'De godsdienstige ontwikkeling van kinderen', in *School en godsdienst*, February 1964

M. J. Langeveld, *Kind en religie*, 1956

— *Studien zur Anthropologie des Kindes*, 1964

R. S. Lee, *Your Growing Child and Religion*, Penguin Books, 1963

E. Lewis, *Children and their Religion*, Sheed and Ward, 1962

Violet Madge, *Children in Search of Meaning*, SCM Press, 1965

— *Introducing Young Children to Jesus*, SCM Press, 1971

Bernard Mailhiot, 'Et dieu se fit enfant', in *Lumen Vitae*, 1961

E. Michaud, *Action et pensée enfantine*, 1953

August Miehle, *Die kindliche Religiosität*, 1928

K. H. Miskotte, *De weg van het gebed*, 1968

H. J. W. Modderman, *Kinderen vragen naar God*, 1954

G. C. van Niftrik, *Kleine dogmatiek*, 1961

F. Nietzsche, *The Joyful Wisdom, Works*, Vol. 10, Allen and Unwin, 1910

J. Nieuwenhuis, *Van school af*, 1968

Nijmegen Catechetical Institute, *Godsdienstige opvoeding op de kleuterschool*, 1961

Huub Oosterhuis, *In het voorbijgaan*, 1969

P. Osterrieth, *Introduction à la psychologie de l'enfant*, 1964

Helen Parkhurst, *Exploring the Child's World*, Harper and Row, 1953

E. G. Pitcher and E. Prelinger, *Children Tell their Stories*, Harper and Row, 1963

W. Preyer, *Die Seele des Kindes*, 1908

Karl Rahner, 'Pour une théologie de l'enfance', in *L'anneau d'or*, 1964

E. Read Mumford, *The Dawn of Religion in the Mind of the Child*, Longmans, 1915

H. Renckens, SJ, *Israels visie op het verleden*, 1956

O. Rieder, *Die Entwicklung des kindlichen Fragens*, 1962

J. A. T. Robinson, *Honest to God*, SCM Press, 1963

— *Exploration into God*, SCM Press, 1967

R. Robinson, 'Honest to Children', in J. A. T. Robinson and D. L. Edwards, *The Honest to God Debate*, SCM Press, 1963

— 'Spiritual Education in a World without Religion', in J. A. T. Robinson, *The New Reformation?*, SCM Press, 1965

Jean-Jacques Rousseau, *Émile*

H. C. Rümke, *Karakter en aanleg in verband met het ongeloof*, 1939

E. Schillebeeckx, *God and Man*, Sheed and Ward, 1969

L. W. Sherrill, *The Rise of Christian Education*, The Macmillan Company, 1944

N. Snijders-Oomen, *Spelend voor Gods aangezicht*, 1966

D. Spicer, *Children's Prayers from Other Lands*, The World's Work, 1956

E. Spranger, *Psychologie des Jugendalters*, 1924

M. W. Steenmeyer-van Rij, *Godsdienstige opvoeding in deze tijd*, 1969

W. Stern, *Psychology of Early Childhood*, Allen and Unwin, 1928
J. Sperna Weiland, *Dogmatische verkenningen*, 1968
A. Stückelberger, *Die religiöse Entwicklung des Schulkindes*, 1958
Herman J. Sweet, *Führe dein Kind zu Gott*, 1966
Pierre Teilhard de Chardin, *The Future of Man*, Collins, 1964
— *Le Milieu Divin*, Fontana Books, 1969
Theophil Thun, *Die Religion des Kindes*, 1959
P. Tillich, *The Shaking of the Foundations*, SCM Press, 1949 (Penguin Books, 1963, to which references are given)
— *Systematic Theology*, Vol. I, Nisbet, 1953
J. W. van Ussel, *De geschiednis van de sexualiteit*, 1969
Second Vatican Council, 'Declaration on Christian Education', in *The Documents of Vatican II*, ed. W. M. Abbott and J. Gallagher, Collier-Macmillan, 1966
Antoine Vergote, *Godsdienstpsychologie*, 1967
René Voeltzel, *Petite pédagogie chrétienne*, 1960
Anne de Vries, *Groot vertelboek voor de bijbelse geschiedenis*, 1938
— *Kinderen in de bijbel*, 1964
O. Weber, *Grundlagen der Dogmatik*, 1955
Frances Wickes, *The Inner World of Childhood*, Appleton, 1927
Dorothy F. Wilson, *Child Psychology and Religious Education*, SCM Press, 1928
Heinz Zahrnt, *What Kind of God?*, SCM Press, 1971

AUTOBIOGRAPHICAL AND BIOGRAPHICAL WORKS

Rogier van Aerde, *Geloof je het zelf?*, 1969
Frédéric Amiel, *Amiel's Journal*
Hans Christian Andersen, *The Fairy Tale of my Life*, The Macmillan Company, 1954
Alexander Bain, *Autobiography*, Longmans, 1904
Augustine, *Confessions*
Simone de Beauvoir, *Memoirs of a Dutiful Daughter*, André Deutsch and Weidenfeld and Nicolson, 1959
Nicholas Berdyaev, *Dream and Reality*, Geoffrey Bles, 1950
Georges Bernanos, quoted from Yves Bridel, *L'esprit de l'enfance dans l'oeuvre romanesque de Bernanos*, 1966
Godfried Bomans-Michel van der Plas, *In de kou*, 1969
Roy Campbell, *Light on a Dark Horse*, Hollis, 1951
Hans Carossa, *Geschichte einer Jugend*, 1957
Moritz Carrière, *Lebenserinnerungen*, 1914
Hugo Claus, *40+, radioportretten*, 1969
F. Darwin, *The Life and Letters of Charles Darwin*, Vol. II, John Murray, 1887
F. Dostoevsky, *The Brothers Karamazov*, Penguin Books, 1959
Eadmer, *Life of St Anselm*, ed. and tr. R. W. Southern, Oxford University Press, 1963
M. von Ebner-Eschenbach, *Kindheitserinnerungen*, 1906
Frederik van Eeden, *Mijn dagboek, 1933/1941*
Gwendolen Freeman, *Children Never Tell*, Allen and Unwin, 1949
Bogumil Goltz, *Buch der Kindheit*, 1908
Edmond Gosse, *Father and Son*, Heinemann, 1907 (Penguin Books, 1970, to which references are given)

Maxim Gorky, *My Childhood*, Elek, 1960
Robert Graves, *Goodbye to All That*, Cassell (1929), 1957
Julien Green, *To Leave before Dawn*, Peter Owen, 1969
Marie Hamsun, *De Regenbogen*, 1954
Langston Hughes, *The Big Sea*, Allen and Unwin, 1940
C. G. Jung, *Memories, Dreams and Reflections*, Routledge and Collins, 1963
Godfried Keller, *Green Henry*, Calder and Boyars, 1960
C. F. Knapp, *Eine Jugend*, 1926
Søren Kierkegaard, *The Journals of Søren Kierkegaard*, tr. A. Dru, Oxford University Press, 1938
Wilhelm von Kügelchen, *Jugenderinnerungen eines alten Mannes*, 1870
Isolde Kurz, *Aus meinem Jugendland*, 1918
Selma Lagerlöf, *Aus meinen Kindertagen*, 1958
C. S. Lewis, *Surprised by Joy*, Geoffrey Bles (Fontana Books, 1959, to which references are given), 1955
Mechteld Lichnowski, *Kindheit*, 1934
Jan Ligthart, *Jeugdherinneringen*, 1962
Pierre Loti, *A Child's Romance*, T. W. Laurie, 1891
Jacques Lusseyran, *Et la lumière fut*, 1953
André Maurois, *Memoirs*, The Bodley Head, 1970
W. August Messer, *Die Philosophie der Gegenwart in Selbstdarstellungen*, 1922
M. K. P. Moritz, *Anton Reiser*, 1795
J. F. Newton, *River of Years*, Allen and Unwin, 1946
Jean Paul, *Wahrheit aus Jean Pauls Leben*, 1826
Friedrich Paulsen, *Aus meinem Leben*, 1849
E. du Perron, *Zijn leven en werk* by Ada Deprez, 1960
Gwen Raverat, *Period Piece*, Faber, 1952
Romain Rolland, *John Christopher*, Vol. I: *Dawn and Morning*, Heinemann (1910), 1960
J. Ruskin, *Praeterita*, Vol. I, Allen and Unwin, 1900
Jean-Paul Sartre, *Words*, Hamish Hamilton, 1964
Anna Scheiber, *Doch immer behalten die Quellen das Wort*, 1932
Friedrich Schleiermacher, *Aus Friedrich Schleiermachers Leben*, 1958
Albert Schweitzer, *My Childhood and Youth*, Allen and Unwin (1924), 1960
Bernard Shaw, *Sixteen Self-Sketches*, Constable, 1949
Archimandrite Spiridou, *Mes missions en Sibérie*, 1968
Carl Spitteler, *Meine frühesten Erlebnisse*, 1914
Max Tau, in: *Die Kraft zum Leben; Bekenntnisse unserer Zeit*, 1963
Theo Thijssen, *In de ochtend van het leven*, 1956
Leo Tolstoy, *Recollections and Essays*, Oxford University Press, 1937
Albert Verwey (M. Uyldert), *De jeugd van een dichter*, 1948
Simon Vestdijk, *Surrogaten voor Murk Tuinstra*, 1940
Maria Waser, *Sinnbild des Lebens*, 1930
Ernst Wiechert, *Wälder und Menschen*, 1948
W. B. Yeats, *Reveries over Childhood and Youth*, Macmillan, 1916
Wolf-Dieter Zimmermann and Ronald Gregor Smith (eds), *I knew Dietrich Bonhoeffer*, Collins, 1966

Acknowledgments

Permission to quote copyright material is gratefully acknowledged as follows: to the Bodley Head for André Maurois' *Memoirs 1885-1967*, translated from the French by Denver Lindley; to Calder and Boyars Ltd for permission to quote from *Green Henry*, by Godfried Keller; to Hamish Hamilton for permission to quote from *Words* by Jean-Paul Sartre, copyright © 1964 by Editions Gallimard; translation copyright © 1964 by Hamish Hamilton Ltd, London. Translated from the French by Irene Clephane; to George Allen and Unwin Ltd for permission to quote from Albert Schweitzer, *My Childhood and Youth*; to Oxford University Press for permission to quote from Eadmer, *Life of Anselm*, translated by R. W. Southern; and to Peter Owen for permission to quote from Julien Green, *To Leave Before Dawn*.